Japanese Economic Policy Reconsidered

Japanese Economic Policy Reconsidered

Edited by

Craig Freedman

Acting Director, Centre for Japanese Economic Studies, Macquarie University, Australia

In Association with the Centre for Japanese Economic Studies, Macquarie University, Australia

Edward Elgar
Cheltenham, UK • Northampton MA, USA

Published by
Edward Elgar Publishing Limited
8 Lansdown Place
Cheltenham
Glos GL50 2HU
UK

Edward Elgar Publishing, Inc.
6 Market Street
Northampton
Massachusetts 01060
USA

A catalogue record for this book
is available from the British Library

Library of Congress Cataloguing in Publication Data

Japanese economic policy reconsidered / edited by Craig Freedman.
"In association with the Centre for Japanese Economic Studies, Macquarie University 1."
Collection of papers from a conference held in August 1996 at Macquarie University.
1. Japan—Economic policy—1989– —Congresses. I. Freedman, Craig, 1950– . II. Macquarie University. Centre for Japanese Economic Studies.
HC462.95.J365 1998
338.952—dc21 97–51473
CIP

ISBN 1 85898 843 8

Printed and bound in Great Britain by Bookcraft (Bath) Limited.

Contents

PART THREE: THE FINANCIAL SECTOR

List of Figures

List of Tables

Preface

It often seems that, by definition, an edited collection of any sort should be an unwelcome visitor to any bookshop or bookshelf. 'Guilty until proven innocent' is how a discerning reader approaches such volumes, wrapped in the publisher's carefully solicited praise. This is all too true since most of these volumes seem to be one of two types, the unrelated odds and ends of a conference, or a chance for the friends and acquaintances of the editor to dive into the bottom left-hand drawer of their desks where they keep those orphan papers yet to find a home in any reputable journal.

This collection is of the former variety but I hope more than an ill-assorted bundling. The conference held in August 1996 at Macquarie University under the auspices of the Centre for Japanese Economic Studies had as its objective an attempt to take a fresh look at Japanese economic policy. To do so the Centre invited a limited number of noted scholars to approach the subject from several disparate directions.

Upon my appointment as acting director of the Centre it was one of my first duties to prepare these varied contributions for publication as part of our research paper series. But it seemed to me at the time that these papers deserved greater circulation than our mailing list could afford. This collection, instead of rooted in the past, as so many other books on Japanese economics seem to be, was clearly looking toward the future, willing to evaluate the problems facing Japan without applying the standard blinkers so commonly seen in much of what has previously been produced. I became convinced that it was worth taking time from my own research and from friends and family to put this collection on the market with all due speed.

Accomplishing what at times seemed an impossible task took the concerted effort of many individuals, some directly, some more obliquely, but not for that reason unappreciated. Above all I mus thank Debbie Jeffery for her tireless typing and layout skills. She managed to persevere through less than optimal conditions and still somehow maintain professional standards. Glennis Yee provided Debbie Jeffery with timely assistance when work seemed about to overwhelm all concerned. Phillipa Brennan rescued the project from fatally capsizing during the crucial final preparations. My publisher, Edward Elgar, has been a consistent gentleman throughout this whole marathon affair, thus dispelling some of my beliefs about people who take up his line of work.

Credit must of course be given to my predecessor, Associate Professor Leslie Stein, who organized the conference and had the good sense not only to select such an eminent group of contributors but to convince them to travel all the way to Australia in order to discuss Japan. His ability to coordinate the various aspects of a conference leaves me with a very high standard to maintain for the future. Only subsequent volumes will confirm whether I have achieved the standard set by this, the Centre's first effort for Edward Elgar.

Lastly, I have to thank my family for putting up with an ever increasing number of absences as deadlines drew near. Seen through the eyes of my two-year-old girls, my tapping away at a computer keyboard seemed the height of idiocy. Perhaps, as always, they were not far wrong.

List of Contributors

Menzie Chinn
Department of Economics, University of California, Santa Cruz

Michael Dooley
Department of Economics, University of California, Santa Cruz

Craig Freedman
School of Economic and Financial Studies, Macquarie University

Kazumasa Iwata
Institute of Social Science, University of Tokyo

Takafumi Kaneko
Japan Economic Planning Agency

Masahiro Kawai
Institute of Social Science, University of Tokyo

Akio Kuroda
School of Political Science and Economics, Meiji University

Colin R. McKenzie
Osaka School of International Public Policy, Osaka University

Daniel I. Okimoto
Asia Pacific Research Center, Stanford University

Gary R. Saxonhouse
Department of Economics, University of Michigan

Yoshio Suzuki
Member, House of Representatives, Japan

Shujiro Urata
Department of Social Sciences, Waseda University

Chapter Summaries

PART ONE: MAIN ISSUES FACING JAPAN'S ECONOMY

The Japanese Economy at a Historical Crossroads
Yoshio Suzuki

In 1991 the Japanese economy entered a severe recession brought about by a large fall in investment and by a contraction of the current account surplus. The government responded by raising expenditure and lowering interest rates. The stagnation persisted. This paper analyses the political and economic environment that continues to hold back Japan's future growth. Modifications in such characteristic institutions as lifetime employment, corporate governance and the banking system are necessary if Japan is to avoid economic stagnation.

JEL# O23, O40, O53
Keywords: Japanese Economic Policy, Microeconomic Reform

Structural Reforms Proposed in Japanese Government's Mid-term Economic Plan
Takafumi Kaneko

Japan is moving away from an industry policy characterized by guidance, to one where structural reforms will allow market forces to reign. The need for these reforms have been prompted by the rapid globalization of the world economy, technological breakthroughs in information systems and telecommunications, demographic changes in Japan and an increasing dissatisfaction among Japanese consumers with their style and standard of living. This paper looks at the ways in which the latest medium-term economic plan seeks to redress these problems.

JEL # H3, H5, H6, J1, J5
Keywords: Japanese Economic Planning, Japanese Market Reform

Theoretical Approaches to the Japan–America Security Alliance
Daniel I. Okimoto

Daniel Okimoto points out the basic incompatibility of Japanese and American security objectives in a changing economic as well as political context. Underlying frictions become explicit when external environmental shocks threaten the alliance's continued viability. The paper tries to understand the nature of those conflicting objectives and the future of the alliance.

JEL# H56
Keywords: Japan/US alliance, Security Pact

PART TWO: FOREIGN TRADE AND INVESTMENT

Japan and the 1994 *Economic Report of the President*
Gary R. Saxonhouse

Saxonhouse weighs the credibility of the Clinton Administration's attempt to define a new approach to US–Japan trade relations. The policy articulated by the Council of Economic Advisors in the 1994 edition of the *Economic Report of the President* is found to be wanting on the following fronts:

1. Ignores macroeconomic determinants of trade imbalance focusing instead on trade barriers
2. Employs irrelevant or incorrect data
3. Ignores overwhelming evidence provided by past studies
4. No sound basis for suggesting magnitude of US exports prohibited by Japanese trade barriers

JEL# F11, F12, F13, F14
Keywords: Managed trade, US/Japan trade relations, Economic Report of the President

Foreign Direct Investment in Japan: Empirical Analyses of Interactions between FDI Inflows and Trade
Masahiro Kawai and Shujiro Urata

Foreign direct investment into Japan has traditionally been lower than that occurring in most other developed economies. The cause has often been ascribed to uniquely Japanese characteristics; Government industry policy or the structure of Japanese industry. Many commentators have viewed such non-tariff barriers as an underlying strength of the Japanese economy. By using a traditional 'gravity model' of trade, this paper points out that foreign direct investment and the level of Japanese trade are mutually determined. Countries with large foreign direct investments tend to trade more with Japan and vice versa. By removing any disincentives to foreign investment, the Japanese government would be encouraging Japan's trade and its economic growth.

JEL # F13, F14, F15, F21
Keywords: Direct foreign investment, Japanese trade, Japanese trade policy

Japanese Foreign Direct Investment: The Role of Technology and *Keiretsu*
Colin R. McKenzie

This paper empirically analyses two decisions taken by the Japanese firm: whether to produce overseas or not; and if production overseas is undertaken, how much overseas labour to employ relative to domestic labour. Cross sectional firm level data is used based on a survey conducted by the Toyo Keizai Shinposha in October 1994. A firms's stock of technology is found to be positively related to the likelihood of producing overseas in both developing and developed countries. Membership in either a vertical or horizontal *keiretsu* does not appear to influence the initial decision to produce overseas. However membership in a vertical or horizontal *keiretsu* appears to reduce significantly the relative use of labour in developing but not in developed countries.

JEL# F2
Keywords: Overseas Investment, Japan, Keiretsu

PART THREE: THE FINANCIAL SECTOR

Monetary Policy in Japan, Germany and the United States: Does One Size Fit All?
Menzie Chinn and Michael Dooley

We present evidence that simple policy reaction functions fit apparently different central banks. What differs is the description of policy rules that these central banks feel obliged to present. Following the work by Clarida and Gertler (1996) we demonstrate that the policy reaction function followed by the Bank of Japan is not significantly different than that favoured by Germany or the US. Central banks adjust very short term interest rates in response to innovations in prices and output. Central banks are not assumed to react to the permanent component of the shock ('bygones are bygones') but to that part which is unexpected.

JEL# E42, E52, E58
Keywords: Monetary policy, Bank of Japan, Interest Rate Targets

Prudential Policy in Japan
Akio Kuroda

Japanese financial regulation is no longer adequate to respond to either the current or future financial environment. Reforming the current Japanese system will bring it more in line with those of other industrialized countries where markets are allowed to exert needed discipline on financial institutions. For such reforms to work, current financial accounting systems also need to be changed to allow for a greater and a more transparent flow of information to the relevant regulatory bodies.

JEL# G21, G28
Keywords: Banking Regulation, Bankruptcy Proceedings, Accounting Procedures

Asset Prices and Consumption: The Risk Premium Puzzle in Japan
Kazumasa Iwata

Lucas (1987) concluded that post-war cyclical fluctuations have resulted in only minor welfare losses for consumers. But this depends on the assumptions of time-separability and state-separability implicit in the standard von Neuman–Morgenstern expected utility function. By assuming, at least in Japan, a tendency for consumption habits to persist, we derive an Euler equation where economic fluctuations have a more serious impact on consumer welfare. Speculative swings in the price of risky assets seem to have a greater impact on consumption than previously imagined. This indicates that central bank policy might need to be directed toward asset price volatility as well as short term interest rates.

JEL# E21, G12
Keywords: risk premium, asset valuation, consumption volatility

1. The End of Economic Miracles

Craig Freedman

> ... we can again conclude that a miracle, whether in contravention to, or beyond, nature, is a mere absurdity; and, therefore, that what is meant in Scripture by a miracle can only be a work of nature, which surpasses, or is believed to surpass, human comprehension. (Spinoza 1951: 87)

If miracles fill us with wonder and awe they can also breed envy when their beneficial glow falls outside our own reach. Economic miracles are no exception. It should come as no surprise that a recent poll[1] reveals that the economic animosity that for over a decade characterized relations between Japan and the US seems to be on the wane. This is perhaps the most reliable signal that the era of invincible economic growth is past history for Japan.[2] Rather than proving an exception, Japan is following a path well trodden by a number of other developed countries.

This fall from grace, the realm of inexorable economic growth, into the ranks of dependable plodders, may only be a sign of economic maturity, but it has provided the impetus for many scholars to re-evaluate whether the Japanese approach to economic matters is really distinctive, or whether it has only followed standard economic practices all along. A more fundamental issue is at stake in questioning the received wisdom when attempting to understand the Japanese economy. Does one gain a better grasp of what drives the Japanese economy by focusing on the ways it differs from textbook economic approaches, or is it more important to find the common basis behind economic growth no matter in what country it may reside?

Unfortunately, research concerns are not unaffected by the perceived pressing issues of the day. The rising economic power of Japan, especially in the 1980s, encouraged investigation into that unanticipated and sustained period of growth. If Japan could somehow succeed against more established economic powers, they must almost by definition be doing something radically different from their Western competitors. By extension, the Japanese must be a special race, utilizing an alternative approach to economic problems, perhaps the sort of Asian brand of economics enunciated if not sufficiently specified by former Singapore Prime Minister Lee Kwan Yew and Malaysian Prime Minister Mahatir. In raising this issue, proponents of a distinctive Asian approach to economic growth seem sadly forgetful that Germany at the turn of the century was similarly regarded by the English.[3] Of course every nation's developmental path must be shaped by its historical and institutional evolution. This does not rule out the possibility that there are basic economic relationships driving each separate and different nation's growth.

A number of authors have tried to convince us that Japan has never warmed to the idea of market competition.[4] The top-down nature of the Meiji Reformation[5] ensured that much of the feudal structure that channelled and controlled economic activity would remain despite the development of a more westernized market organization. For supporters of industry policy,[6] Japan came to represent a prime counter-example where the visible hand of government was indispensable to Japanese economic success. Unfortunately, an unbiased reader, if such a creature exists, might, after careful reflection, decide that each side of the debate was overly adept at finding support for whatever pre-existing belief it held. In a country where the *tatamae* (appearance) is so hard to disentangle from the *hone* (reality), even the most unbiased investigator may find it especially difficult not to be misled by official statements of either government servants or business leaders.

Ideally we would not like to stray decidedly to either side of the balance, neither rejecting the importance of underlying similarities nor ignoring essential differences. But it would seem possible that while countries often differ in their development strategies and the role played by the government sector, mature industrial economies may operate under very similar constraints. This is especially true given the greater movement to a globalized economy which limits the ability to move along a too idiosyncratic growth path.

Our rule of thumb, then, should be that good policy analysis demands that we distinguish between dominating economic similarities and defining, if not decisive, economic differences. By this standard, the chapters in this volume make a concerted attempt to reconsider current Japanese economic policy in the light of recent events, a few even going so far as to peer into the future. What each does in its own way is to revisit some of the more comfortable economic facts that have become the commonplace assertion of policy discussions. None of the chapters of course can conclusively end this ongoing debate. But no matter what one's conception of Japanese economic policy might be, reading these contributions should make each of us re-examine our previously held convictions. Whatever in fact may be the case, only by re-evaluating deeply ingrained assumptions can we remove any lingering preconceptions that constrain our ability to understand the significant changes in the Japanese economy. By doing so, we may also gain some insight into what defines the transition from a developing to a developed industrial nation.

Our first three chapters take a broad view of Japan's past problems and its potential for needed restructuring. In doing so they provide a critical evaluation of Japanese economic policy. To a remarkable degree, both Yoshio Suzuki ('The Japanese Economy at a Historical Crossroads') and Takafumi Kaneko ('Structural Reforms Proposed in the Japanese Government's Mid-term Economic Plan') belong to that large group of economists of whom Tadahiro Sekimoto, vice-chairman of Keidanren, has said, 'Who needs these economists?'[7] The issues raised in both of these chapters, however, go far beyond being merely a regrettable nuisance. They agree that there is need for a fundamental change in the way the Japanese economy, and thus indirectly Japanese society, works. As Suzuki puts it:

> It would not be an overstatement to say that Japan is now at a historical crossroads comparable to the Meiji Restoration of 130 years ago and its defeat in World War II 51 years ago (page 20).

He is part of a growing consensus among economists that suggests Japan must now begin to look more like the rest of the industrialized world. Such a change would perhaps be an even greater transformation than that accomplished during the Meiji Restoration. It would certainly transcend the course of reconstruction and development pursued following the devastation of World War II. The Meiji Restoration forced Japan to look outwards, to follow a crash course in westernization. But in many ways, though to the casual onlooker it might seem that the Japanese were merely adept at copying the best practices and features of the ruling Western powers, they actually accomplished more than that. They infused those practices with the essentially feudal characteristics of Japanese society. In many ways the samurai code of bushido still survived in the humble *sarariiman* of postwar Japan. The warrior code was channelled into a business environment rather than extinguished by the loss of the war. Only the more overt military characteristics disappeared from everyday Japanese society. As previously noted, the initial Meiji Restoration was a top-down revolution maintaining much of the traditional hierarchy that defines Japan. The reconstruction of Japan following World War II not only allowed a perpetuation of many of the same prewar structures but sustained much the same cast of characters in an array of leading economic and political roles.[8] That the existing Japanese economy must undergo some process of change and reform is unquestioned by most commentators. This seems as certain today as when US warships patrolled Japanese coastal waters in the nineteenth century. But adjustment need not imply a major break with the past. The Japanese have always seemed to be able to turn the apparent weaknesses or rigidities inherent in their society into sources of strength.[9]

Both Kaneko and Suzuki indicate that the reformist view current in Japanese government circles is to some degree revolutionary in objective. This is perhaps most clearly distinguished in Kaneko's discussion of the 1995 Mid-term Economic Plan. As he points out, there is a certain malaise in the Japanese population, a feeling that their success has been a hollow one. Given the wealth generated by the Japanese economy, a proportionately small percentage of it has translated into a higher standard of living, a hallmark of a classic 'jam tomorrow', economy.[10] As a result, Japanese consumer demands are evolving concurrent with a significant change in the economic environment. These domestic objectives cannot be reconciled to this new global context without an appropriate transformation of the economic determinants that currently characterize Japan. For Kaneko, growth and efficiency are time- and place-dependent. The current institutional structure of Japan is out of sync with both the needs of its population and the constraints of global competition. As he points out:

> The group-centred and company-centred thought and behavior of many Japanese has provided a solid base for effective achievement in high-volume, production-driven, economic growth. Now, however, these characteristics are increasingly recognized as impeding the development of new industries by suppressing creativity (page 31).

Added to these hard-to-reconcile demands, demographics also define the necessity for such bold departures. The significantly changing composition of the Japanese population creates what both of these commentators see as a potentially long-run intractable problem. A rapidly ageing population undermines labour structures such as permanent employment policies bolstered by a strong seniority system. The subsequent repercussions on government spending are too well known to need any explication here, especially when these trends are combined with slower economic growth. Trusting market competition largely to sort out these fundamental problems would certainly mark a departure in Japanese policy. Simply curtailing the reach of entrenched ministries would reflect a combined economic and political reformation. What is surprising is that the Liberal Democratic Party under Prime Minister Hashimoto, an organization once described as being none of those three things, seems reluctantly to be embracing at least some elements of this transformational programme. But often that has been the case in Western economies as well. Significant reform can best be accomplished by the most conservative of political machines.

Economists, though, often forget the concomitant political and diplomatic aspects associated with any significant economic reform. Part of Japan's coming of economic age and subsequently facing the sobering reality of a slowdown in growth, is its need to reassess its security objectives and structures along with those which are usually classified as more purely economic in nature. The security imperatives of a nation can never rightly be isolated from a country's changing economic objectives and environment. The Japan–American Security Alliance has been a keystone in ensuring economic stability in the postwar Pacific Rim. Daniel Okimoto ('Theoretical Approaches to the Japan–America Security Alliance') notes that for the first time there is a serious possibility that the conflicting economic and political aims of these two long-term partners may create an irreparable rupture to this agreement. Professor Okimoto analyses why the alliance has remained a noticeable source of certainty despite a seemingly unequal division of benefits. He stresses that the underlying strengths of the agreement may be the very traits that now impede the flexibility necessary to adopt to a new post cold war political and economic environment.

The tension in the alliance manifests a basic inertia resulting from an institutional inclination toward the *status quo* compounded by a series of well-defined external shocks that describe the different stages of the treaty agreement. The alliance itself was born out of the economic and military shocks which occurred when mainland China fell to Mao Tse Tung's communist troops in 1949. Japan, which had been viewed as a country best kept economically and militarily weak until democratic structures were firmly in place, was suddenly viewed as the key strategic partner in the region. Many of the prewar ruling élite were rehabilitated and the Japanese economy itself given a deliberate boost by the US. The Korean conflict only confirmed the importance of the alliance. Japan, being both economically and militarily weak at the time, accepted its role as a US surrogate in exchange for the certainty of protection and the clear economic advantage the treaty provided. The price the US paid at this time seemed high, but given the circumstances, the relevant cost accounting was only an inconvenience. Japan for its part was able to concentrate on economic growth without needing to divert funds to military objectives.

As the economic divergence between the two countries narrowed, Japan became less willing to respond to US pressure. As part of its growing economic maturity Japan wanted more say in its security affairs, particularly when it crossed into the economic sphere. In a mirror-like stance, the US wanted a greater financial offset for its provision of security. But to gain these objectives neither side wished to compromise any existing advantages. Japan wanted to avoid large increases in its financial contributions while the US was loath to relinquish any decision-making authority. The loss of the Vietnam War was the next external shock which brought this underlying problem to the forefront. A realist, as Japan often appears to be, would at that time have needed to question both the intention and the ability of the US to sustain an adequate defence of the Pacific. The 1970s initiated a long struggle between the two countries with the US, made nervous by Japanese economic success, demanding larger contributions to fund future joint security, while Japan increasingly resisted overt US pressure to comply with its wishes.

The end of the cold war has called into question the need for the same sort of continuing alliance. While the US still sees Japan as not paying its fair share, Japan itself has begun to question whether it should depend on the US for its security. Again, external shocks caused by the rape of an Okinawan girl in 1995 and by the seeming disintegration of North Korea has highlighted the strain of being military allies while continuing to be fierce economic competitors. With China's military and economic might increasing, Japan has begun seriously to consider whether its constitution should be amended to allow for its own defence establishment. The external shocks may be great enough to break the institutional path-dependency previously keeping Japan tied to a very restrictive military spending policy. If in fact inertia has been the major force opposing the economic interests pulling the alliance apart, then the current period should provide a severe test of whether the needs of the two alliance partners are strong enough to allow them to adapt the terms of any such pact to the reality of the new political/economic environment.

The natural extension of the frictions felt between two competitive nations locked in the inertia of a continuing military alliance is reflected in the often acrimonious trade relations that have characterized the economic policies of the two countries. It was, after all, the original US security umbrella that provided the opportunity for Japanese economic growth. The very success of that arrangement eventually undercut its value for both parties. This duality is not a recent phenomenon. The interwar period was characterized by analogous clashes, perhaps having their seeds in the US-brokered peace of the Russo-Japanese War. The current trade frictions flow to a large extent from the mephistophelean arrangements previously described. Given the cold war realities, the US needed a surrogate Asian supporter. The Japanese needed an economic environment conducive to rapid growth. The subsequent tensions speak of the initial success of that arrangement. The unforeseen economic success meant that, more rapidly than could have been imagined, Japanese firms were competing for the same markets as those based in the US. As Japanese economic power grew, it was also inevitable that the subservient military status originally accepted by the Japanese would eventually be viewed as a constraint, one which provided the US with leverage in trade disputes. In a sense, the search for a workable defence alignment between the two countries is paralleled by a need to find an accord on the trade front. Just as it is imperative not to have policy dominated by myths and misinformation on the security front, it is equally vital where trade is concerned. The three middle chapters try to clear away some of the obfuscation surrounding Japanese trade policy. Again, the issue facing Japan and those who seek either to advise or analyse such policy matters is whether Japanese trade practices differ greatly from those of other industrialized nations. If, indeed, at this stage of economic development, the similarities have become more important than the way in which Japan differs, than the recommendations will be much the same for Japan as they are for other developed countries. The issues addressed to varying degrees by each of these authors are: first, whether Japanese trade policy is the chief engine driving Japanese trade patterns; second, whether in either case there is anything different about the institutional structure of Japan (possibly aided and abetted by government policy) that makes Japanese trade policy special. The consensus view offered here is that, at a minimum, recent trade patterns are best understood by the sort of economic fundamentals common to all industrialized countries.

Gary Saxonhouse does an excellent job in laying out the terms of this debate. In his chapter 'Japan and the 1994 *Economic Report of the President*' he takes on the idea of managed trade[11] via an analysis of the Report produced by the Council of Economic Advisers under the aegis of Laura Tyson. As he has done throughout his career, Saxonhouse here marshals his arguments against bilateral trade negotiations to force open the Japanese market to US exports. If, as Saxonhouse and others contend, the current trade patterns are due to economic fundamentals like resource endowments and subsequent development, there is in fact very little to negotiate. The empirical evidence provided seems to indicate that there is no significant protection of manufactured goods in the Japanese domestic market, nor any concerted government action to restrict foreign investment.[12]

> Just as the low level of Japan's intra-industry trade may reflect distinctive features of the Japanese economy that have nothing to do with the government policy, the same might be true of the extremely low levels of foreign investment in Japan (page 95).

This of course leaves open the role of government, either directly or indirectly, in fostering and supporting such distinctive features as permanent employment. However, it is difficult not to agree with Saxonhouse that such employment practices are not 'the proper object of international negotiation' (page 95).

Saxonhouse's treatment of the 1994 *Report* as an economic document[13] does raise some other questions. 'This *Report*'s Japan content might have been of largely academic interest save that its substance undoubtedly helped frame the Clinton Administration's bilateral trade policies with Japan' (page 102). This may be emphasizing the economic nature of this document to the exclusion of its more obvious political objectives. These yearly economic reports do reflect the political marching orders of the day.[14] To some extent they provide a rationale or best case that can be made for some policy goal.

This is not to impugn the integrity of the authors of the cited *Report*. But the president does tend to chose advisers who hold congenial policy views. It is far from clear that the Clinton Administration has ever been inhibited by strong economic views or that it has been unduly influenced by its economic advisers. It is likely that the Administration saw the report as a way to define the terms of debate in a manner which might gain the president credibility in domestic politics. Given the subsequent strength of the US economy, and the sustained slump in Japan after 1994, there was no longer any political advantage to be reaped by taking on the Japanese. That would at least in part explain why the '1997 *Economic Report of the President*, the final Report of the Clinton Administration's first term, devotes no more than one short paragraph to Japan' (page 102). Trade relations, especially with Japan, were simply not part of Clinton's campaign strategy.

In the next two chapters the authors (Kawai and Urata; and McKenzie) pick up strands of Saxonhouse's analysis and subject them to empirical testing. Once again we are forced to focus on whether Japan has pursued and is pursuing a distinctive trade and investment policy. For instance, Encarnation (1992) sees government regulations as explaining the low levels of foreign direct investment. Mason (1992) and Lawrence (1993b) look to that peculiar Japanese industry structure (the *keiretsu*) as providing sufficient discouragement for potential overseas investors. To understand the scope for change in current Japanese economic policy we need to reassess the basis of its former success. This means calling into question what has been taken for granted concerning Japanese trade priorities. Non-tariff barriers have been seen as the basis for export-led growth. Masahiro Kawai and Shujiro Urata ('Foreign Direct Investment in Japan: Empirical Analyses') examine the strength of this charge. These authors start by casting significant doubt that government policy was ever influential in deterring direct investment.

> A recent survey conducted by the Ministry of International Trade and Industry found that the high cost of operating business in Japan was an important factor discouraging FDI in Japan. The high cost is attributable largely to high land prices and office rental rates, high wages, high materials and transportation costs, and high tax rates. The survey also found that government regulations discouraged FDI inflows, but this factor was not as influential as those causing high operating costs (pages 118 and 123).

More importantly they argue, based on their empirical work, that at least in recent years (since 1991) discouragement of such investment leads to a lower rather than a higher rate of growth. Most significantly, 'FDI inflows in manufacturing stimulate Japan's exports while FDI inflows in commerce and trade do not' (page 133). In a parallel fashion, those countries more likely to trade with Japan are those more likely to invest directly. This conclusion moves beyond the one dimensional idea that trade is mutually beneficial. Trade encourages foreign direct investment which in turn generates greater trade. Direct investment does not simply concentrate on the domestic market (though in this case the added competition within the domestic market may well add to the efficiency and growth of the economy). At least given the current structure of the Japanese economy, any protection of the Japanese domestic market constrains rather than supports export-led growth. Japan is then no different from any other industrialized country. Unilateral policy initiatives that encourage a more open Japanese market can only assist economic growth.

The *keiretsu* organizational form is unarguably characteristic of Japanese industry. If such distinct structures have little or no influence on trade or direct overseas investments, it becomes harder to maintain the *Japan as a special case* approach. Rather, as Saxonhouse would have it, we need not abandon standard economic analysis when faced with Japan's international trade and investment practices. Colin McKenzie, in an arresting piece of empirical analysis ('Japanese Foreign Direct Investment: The Role of Technology and *Keiretsu*') provides convincing evidence that the reason for Japanese firms going overseas is no different from those of other developed countries. Certainly the *keiretsu* organizational form is less significant than has often been proposed. If the organizational structure yielded a clear competitive edge one would expect members of such groupings to be more likely to exploit overseas opportunities. Should McKenzie's work be largely correct, then much of the clamour indicating that *keiretsu* create anti-competitive barriers is misleading. The need for an anti-trust policy to break up these loosely defined organizations would be seriously misplaced.

The support for a market-based view of the current Japanese economy, where economic fundamentals define policy and analysis, is lastly extended to the sphere of finance. For decades commentators, especially those in the business press, believed that the Ministry of Finance, even more so than the Ministry of International Trade and Industry, provided the basic policy initiatives to ensure continuing economic growth. But even before the recent *sokaiya* scandals, the Ministry of Finance has seemed increasingly to be a bureaucratic impediment to the financial reforms needed to return Japan to a path of sustained economic growth. The current efforts by the Hashimoto government to deregulate that sector and to reign in the Ministry of Finance demonstrate that past analysis of the financial system needs to be rethought. At the very least, the current trend in Japanese financial markets, which parallels similar deregulatory moves in the US, England and Australia, indicates that increasingly what is most important about such markets is their underlying common principles rather than any regional variations.

The last three chapters all have the same comparable financial theme. The tradition that the Ministry of Finance afforded financial institutions the opportunity to serve the long-run interest of the Japanese economy rather than allowing them individually to pursue more narrowly defined paths of self-interest seemed to underwrite the financial stability of the country. But in the past few years, it has appeared that in a number of notorious instances, the Ministry of Finance has promoted the private concerns of the banks and other financial institutions without regard to any larger economic impact. The strength of the Japanese financial system was thought to be the Ministry of Finance's willingness directly to guide financial institutions which strayed from desired activity. The financial system was not left to the vagaries of the market but instead was buttressed by bureaucratic corrections. Now it appears that the decisions of the Ministry of Finance differed insignificantly from the disastrous US policy of keeping its thrift sector afloat well past its use-by date.

In the late 1980s the world's biggest banks were almost all Japanese.[15] The sheer bulk of their financial power was thought to assure them top place in the more cut-throat commodity business of bond trading. This was to be only the first step from which they would go on to dominate most financial sectors. Such forecasts now seem as much of an illusion as a belief in the guiding hand of the Ministry of Finance. The dangers of extrapolating into the future are always obvious after the fact.

As Chinn and Dooley ('Monetary Policy in Japan, Germany and the United States: Does One Size Fit All?') demonstrate, the Bank of Japan targets the short-run interest rate no matter what their pronouncements may be to the contrary. This policy may be insufficient to stem speculation in risky assets. The consequences for the Japanese economy may be greater than in the US since the Japanese seem quicker to turn speculative gains into durable consumption goods while maintaining consumption habits that persist in spite of income movements. A single-minded concentration on short-term interest rates, in common with other central banks, may be misplaced in Japan. Of course, as Chinn and Dooley's chapter implies, this may be the only thing that central banks can successfully target.

It does seem that Japanese monetary policy and bank regulation are far from unique to Japan. The current Japanese banking crisis finds echoes in the US nightmare with its thrifts. The only possible exception is that, perhaps as a result of continuing to operate in an overly cosseted sphere, Japanese financial institutions have lagged behind the West in developing and exploiting new financial instruments. Like much of the rest of the Japanese economy, the convoy system meant that the weakest bank had to be protected against failure, holding back those that were stronger. This was meant to reduce systemic risk but ultimately led to a classic case of moral hazard.

Japanese banks and other financial institutions were brought back to life when the more effective course of action would have been to flip the switch on the respirator. In a detailed analysis Akio Kuroda ('Prudential Policy in Japan') elucidates the causes and consequences of this approach. Carefully and painstakingly Kuroda lays out the recent history of the Ministry of Finance's vain attempts to maintain the convoy system of regulation in a piecemeal manner. Saving all ships in a single-minded fashion ultimately risks scuttling the entire financial system. Kuroda's methodical and incisive attack on the current inoperative financial policy clears the way for his subsequent proposed reforms. These are unsurprisingly similar to those that would apply to any country with a sophisticated financial system: clear accounting standards, better information, bankruptcy procedures that don't provide a refuge for delinquent institutions, a regulator that is truly independent and not an appendage of the Ministry of Finance. The message is once again clear: Japan is part of the rule rather than an economic exception.

Iwata ('Asset Prices and Consumption: The Risk Premium Puzzle in Japan') does signal something in the nature of an exception to the general comparability of the Japanese economy with those of its peers. If, as seems likely, there is a tendency in Japan for consumption habits to persist longer than in other similar countries, economic fluctuations have a more serious impact on consumer welfare. Speculative swings in the price of risky assets will have a greater effect on consumption than would normally be expected. This indicates that central bank policy might need to be directed toward asset-price volatility as well as short-term interest rates. Whether these peculiar consumption habits may be gradually fading is not clear. But if there has been a change in the consumption patterns in Japan, then this caveat to standard monetary policy need not play any significant role in the future. It is, however, an important factor for those who control Japanese policy to bear in mind.

On a number of levels the chapters included in this volume endorse a back-to-basics approach to economic policy, one that stresses the primacy of market forces and a limited role for government. They don't so much address past Japanese development as look squarely toward the coming century, based on current realities. These authors in no way settle the issues raised. But they do make a valuable contribution in shaping the terms of debate. Two of the most fundamental mistakes any economist can make is to think that similar things are actually different and, on the other hand, fail to see that differences are not similarities. Successful economic policy demands that we get these distinctions correct. This volume provides a solid contribution toward that process.

NOTES

1. As reported in *Business Week* (March 31 1997:29) a Yomiuri Shimbun-Gallup Organization poll of 3000 people in Japan and the US found that 46% thought that the relationship between the two countries was good. This is up from less than 30% in 1995 in a similar poll. An even greater contrast can be seen in a January 1990 NBC News/ Wall Street Journal poll of 1510 US residents which found that by a four to one margin Japan was thought to be the stronger economic power. A majority of the respondents favored some form of protectionist policy to redress this perceived imbalance (reported in Stokes 1990:19). What is unremarkable is how such polls mimic the US business cycle. During an economic downturn, US voters look for a foreign cause of their problems.
2. An equally reliable signal is the disappearance of Japanese villains from Hollywood films. American insecurities, economic and otherwise, are almost instantly reflected on screen. There is a long history of countries believing that any challenge to their economic supremacy must by definition be based on unfair practices. The vitriol aimed at the Japanese by the US in the eighties recapitulates the English reaction to the growing economic might of Germany at the turn of the century. Certainly the fear that the Japanese were intent on muscling into Western preserves harks back to the xenophobia of the thirties as accurately reflected by Ogden Nash:

   How courteous is the Japanese;
   He always says, 'Excuse it, please.'
   He climbs into his neighbour's garden,
   And smiles, and says, 'I beg your pardon;'
   He bows and grins a friendly grin,
   And calls his hungry family in;
   He grins, and bows a friendly bow;
   'So sorry, this my garden now.' (1961: 169)
3. The long hours of more of less intensive work to which they (the Germans) are accustomed, enable them to attend numerous discussions without difficulty: the discipline to which they have been seasoned in military service inclines them to submit easily to cartel regulation: and what is perhaps equally important, the semi-military organization of cartels is well adapted to the purposes of autocratic rule (Marshall 1923: 50-51).
4. The trouble with the Japanese is that they have never really caught up with Adam Smith ... They believe – like Mao unleashing the Cultural Revolution and all other good Confucianists – that you cannot get a decent moral society, not even an efficient society, simply out of the mechanisms of the market powered by the motivational fuel of self-interest, however clever of even divinely inspired, those mechanisms may be (Dore 1986: 1).
5. Theda Skocpol (1980) provides an interesting analysis of the Meiji Reformation using the idea that change was fostered by a faction of the ruling class.
6. Those unfamiliar with the way in which the Japanese understand industry policy might find Komiya (1988) instructive.
7. The remark came during an interview with *Business Week* (Neff 1997: 21-22)with Sekimoto providing a more optimistic spin on the economic future of Japan while still admitting a need for deregulation. The relevant interchange is as follows:

   Q: *Have Japan's economic problems been exaggerated?*
   A: Yes, by Japanese academics, economists, and the media. Who needs these economists? The media are masochists. Their exaggerations are creating misunderstandings outside Japan. Some have been saying that Japan's economy is on a permanent downward slide. But if the Japanese people were assured that they have a future and will continue to get raises, consumption would rise, and the economy would strengthen. They need encouragement (Neff 1997: 21-22).

Perhaps this is another respect in which Japan is becoming more like other industrialized nations.

8. The need to retain Japan as a post-war strategic partner meant that the US occupying forces looked the other way as many of the pre-war institutions were re-established within the seemingly reform minded constitution drafted by Roosevelt-type New Dealers.

> Management had won; it could not go back to pre-Macarthur days, when there were no unions at all, but it had defined labor on its own terms, incorporated labor into the company itself, and ended any possibilities of labor as an adversarial force within (Halberstram 1986: 183-84).

9. See Dore (1986) for this particular insight into the structure of the Japanese economy.
10.

> For him [the 'purposive' man] jam is not jam unless it is a case of jam to-morrow and never jam to-day. Thus by pushing his jam always forward into the future, he strives to secure for his act of boiling it an immortality (Keynes 1963: 370)

The jam allusion refers to Alice's conversation with Humpty Dumpty in Carroll's *Through the Looking Glass.*

11. For a useful introduction to the issue that is sympathetic to the practical policy of managed trade see Stokes (1990). Saxonhouse's article indirectly also provides a very good introduction to the subject though from a very different perspective. Stokes (1990) does not paint the differences in quite the same contrasting tones as Saxonhouse, choosing instead different shades of gray. Supporters of managed trade don't deny that free trade provides a first best solution. They would in fact claim that countries operate in the realm of the second best which makes any simple policy prescription impracticable. Laura Tyson contends that 'The goal of intervention is not simply to improve the trade balance or to address external barriers abroad, but to secure a share of world production and employment in [high-tech] industries with the local knowledge, skills and spillover benefits which they generate (quoted in Stokes 1990:23).
12. An interesting aspect of this debate can be seen in the articles by Saxonhouse (1993) and Lawrence (1993a) analysing whether there is anything distinctive about Japanese trade structure and trade policy. Both look at the same empirical evidence and arrive at distinctly contrasting conclusions.
13. Krugman (1997) evaluates some of the political economy context to the arguments for managed trade and their potential reach.
14. Here it might be wise to remember George Stigler's very strong pronouncement on economists as political appointees:

> I conclude - and perhaps I am alone in concluding - that when an economist goes to Washington, he deserves no more credence, and no less, than any other political appointment, and it is mildly deceptive to address him as Doctor or Professor (1988: 135).

15. Seven of the twenty largest commercial banks in the world are still Japanese (*The Economist* July 19th 1997:99) but only one of the top five. The Japanese banks have the lowest return on assets of any of the other top twenty banks.

REFERENCES

Dore, R. (1986), *Flexible Rigidities*. London: The Athlone Press.

Encarnation, D.J. (1992), *Rivals Beyond Trade: America versus Japan in Global Competition*, Ithaca: Cornell University Press.

Halberstram, D. (1986), *Day of Reckoning*, New York: William Morrow and Company.

Keynes, J.M. (1963), 'Economic Possibilities For Our Grandchildren', *Essays in Persuasion*, New York: W.W. Norton & Company.

Komiya, R. (1988), 'Introduction', in Ryutaro Komiya (ed.) *Industrial Policy of Japan*, Tokyo: Academic Press, 1–12.

Krugman, P. (1997), 'What Should Trade Negotiators Negotiate About?' *Journal of Economic Literature*, **35**, 1: 113–20.

Lawrence, R.Z. (1993a), 'Japan's Different Trade Regime: An analysis with Particular Reference to Keiretsu', *Journal of Economic Perspectives*, **7**, 3: 3–19.

Lawrence, R.Z. (1993b), 'Japan's Low Levels of Inward Investment: the Role of Inhibitions on Acquisitions', in Kenneth A. Froot (ed.), *Foreign Direct Investment*, Chicago: University of Chicago Press.

Marshall, A. (1923), *Industry and Trade*, London: Macmillan and Co.

Mason, M. (1992), *American Multinationals and Japan: The Political Economy of Japanese Capital Controls 1899–1980*, Cambridge, MA:Harvard University Press.

Nash, O. (1961), 'The Japanese', in *Collected Verse from 1929 On*, London: J.M. Dent & Sons, p. 169.

Neff, R. (1997), 'The Economy is in a Recovery Mode', *Business Week*, 23 June 1997, 21–22.

Saxonhouse, G.R. (1993), 'What Does Japanese Trade Structure Tell Us About Japanese Trade Policy?' *Journal of Economic Perspectives*, **7**, 3: 21–43.

Skocpol, T. (1980), *States and Social Revolutions: A Comparative Analysis*, Cambridge: Cambridge University Press.

Spinoza, B. de (1951), *Theologico-Political Treaties*. R.H.M. Elwes (trans.), *The Chief Works of Benedict De Spinoza* Vol. 1, New York: Dover Publications.

Stigler, G.J. (1988), *Memoirs of an Unregulated Economist*, New York: Basic Books.

Stokes, B. (1990), *The Inevitability of Managed Trade*, New York: Japan Society.

PART ONE:

Main Issues Facing Japan's Economy

2. The Japanese Economy at a Historical Crossroads

Yoshio Suzuki

2.1 INTRODUCTION

This chapter starts with a brief sketch of the stagnant Japanese economy in the 1990s, and then goes on to the structural economic reform needed to enable the Japanese economy to make a breakthrough to a new stage of development. I shall also discuss the political situation as it affects the outlook for economic reform. Finally, I shall touch on how the unique systems of the Japanese economy could be transformed. Let me start with the economic trend in the 1990s.

2.2 FIVE YEARS OF STAGNATION IN THE 1990s

The Japanese economy plunged into a growth recession in the second quarter of 1991 (Table 2.1). From fiscal 1992 through 1994, the annual average growth rate remained at the zero per cent level. In fiscal 1995, it recovered to 2.3 per cent, and the government's official forecast for fiscal 1996 is 2.5 per cent (Table 2.1). The economy seems quite likely to achieve such growth, as private sector forecasts also range between 2 and 3 per cent.

The speed of the recovery, however, is very moderate. After 18 years of high growth averaging 10 per cent per annum, the Japanese economy's annual growth rate had declined to 4 per cent between fiscal years 1976 and 1990. However, this was still the highest growth rate among major industrial countries. The potential growth rate of the Japanese economy today, which may have further declined during the five years of stagnation in the 1990s, is still estimated to be at least 3 per cent. As the annual average growth rate between fiscal years 1991 and 1995 stood at only 1.3 per cent, the current GDP deflationary gap is estimated at 7 per cent or so.

Table 2.1 Major economic indicators

	FY1990	FY1991	FY1992	FY1993	FY1994	FY1995	FY1996 (Govt. forecast)
Private consumption	4.2	2.80	1.2	1.7	1.5	2.7	2.3
Residential investment	4.9	–12.3	–3.5	4.9	8.6	–6.7	2.2
Plant and equipment investment	11.3	2.7	–7.2	–10.5	–3.5	5.1	4.1
Private inventory	–14.6	44.1	–80.1	11.9	–105.4	–	
Government consumption	2.2	1.4	2.1	2.4	2.5	1.6	1.5
Public works investment	4.6	7.2	16.6	12.6	–1.0	10.0	
Exports of goods & services	6.6	5.4	4.4	0.4	5.7	4.7	5.6
Imports of goods & services	3.7	–3.4	–1.5	3.5	10.2	15.1	8.2
Real GDP	5.6	3.1	0.4	0.2	0.5	2.3	2.5
Current account balance (trillion yen)		11.3	15.0	14.2	12.4	9.5	9.7
Unemployment rate (%)	2.10	2.09	2.22	2.63	2.92	3.23	3.49 (June)
No. of corporate bankruptcies	7 157	11 557	14 569	14 580	14 201	14 058	
Profit growth rate(%) (NRI400 excl.financials)	1.8	–17.0	–25.2	–18.1	8.7	18.5	15.2 (NRI forecast)

Source: Economic Planning Agency, Business and Investment Survey of Incorporated Enterprises, March 1996.

It follows that during the five years from 1996 to the threshold of the twenty-first century, the Japanese economy has the potential to grow at an annual average rate of 4 per cent. The question is whether or not there will be sufficient demand growth to realize this potential.

It is not difficult to cite superficial reasons for the five years of stagnant demand. Let me point out the four main factors (1 to 4).

1. Capital investment declined sharply between 1991 and 1994, bottomed out in 1995 and has been recovering moderately since the second half of that year (Table 2.1). However, the pace of recovery is very slow, so that the economy has not achieved sustainable growth led by private-sector demand. The reasons for weak capital investment are: (a) a reaction to excessive investment during the boom years of 1987 through 1990; (b) negative wealth effects resulting from the bursting of the asset-price 'bubble'; and (c) a shift to overseas production bases in manufacturing industries, prompted by the yen's steep appreciation.
2. The rapid contraction of the current account surplus since 1995 has acted as a drag on growth. In fact, while domestic demand contributed 3.3 per cent to the 2.3 per cent economic growth realized in fiscal 1995, external demand made a 1.0 per cent negative contribution.
3. The Japanese people feel that they cannot expect economic stimulus on either the fiscal policy or monetary policy front. This is because between fiscal years 1992 and 1995, the government sought to trigger sustainable growth, led by private-sector demand, by increasing public works investment by a cumulative total of 37 trillion yen and cutting income taxes by 5.5 trillion yen. As a result, Japan's ratio of budget deficits to GDP, along with that of Italy, is the worst among the G7 nations in terms of both flow and stock. Consequently, the public cannot pin much hope on additional fiscal measures. On the monetary policy front, the official discount rate has been reduced to 0.5 per cent, the lowest figure ever recorded in Japan or elsewhere, and there is no room for further easing. Under this 'ultra' low interest rate, broad money growth has been a mere 3 per cent, while the growth of narrow money stands at 15 per cent. This situation is exactly what Keynes calls a 'liquidity trap'.
4. Due to these limitations on macroeconomic policy and the continuing stagnation of private expenditure, the growth rate expected by the business sector stands at 1–2 per cent, well below the potential growth rate of 3 per cent. This is responsible for the weak recovery of capital spending and the continuing weakness of land prices, which are in turn prolonging the economic stagnation. The situation is indeed a vicious circle.

2.3 STRUCTURAL ECONOMIC REFORMS TO PROVIDE A BREAKTHROUGH

These reasons for the five years of stagnation (1 to 4) were culled from superficial observations. However, behind these superficial reasons, there exists a more fundamental factor that runs through all of them. This fundamental reason is that, in spite of the fact that Japan is now at a historical crossroads, there is no political leadership in sight that would bring about the necessary structural economic reforms. Because of this lack of leadership, business people are uncertain about the medium-term outlook for the economy. To them, therefore, investment looks risky. This is why there is no vigorous capital spending on a scale that is sufficient to sustain medium-term growth at the potential growth rate.

It would not be an overstatement to say that Japan is now at a historical crossroads comparable to the Meiji Restoration of 130 years ago and its defeat in World War II 51 years ago. At the time of the Meiji Restoration, Japan underwent a radical transformation by adopting science and technology, a market economy, and legal and political systems, all of which gave birth to modern Western civilization. After World War II, Japan adopted a new Constitution, which replaced the old Constitution written at the time of the Meiji Restoration, and adopted democratic institutions. On the economic front, the old *zaibatsu* were dismantled, while a land reform programme distributed agricultural land to tenant farmers to make them into land-owning farmers. Thanks to these steps, Japan succeeded in promoting competition and expanding domestic markets. It achieved postwar reconstruction in eight years and high economic growth at an annual average rate of 10 per cent for as long as 18 years, helped also by the introduction of technology from Western nations. By 1970, Japan had caught up with the advanced industrialized nations of the West in terms of macroeconomic indicators. The event that symbolizes Japan's success is the start of the appreciation trend that has more than tripled the yen's value *vis-à-vis* the US dollar since the 'Nixon Shock' of August 1971.

The previous two historical transformations were 'top–down reforms' in that they were initiated by the government. In the post-World War II era, in particular, under the continuous one-party rule by the Liberal Democratic Party, which is often referred to as the 1955 system, a stable 'Iron Triangle' of politicians, bureaucrats and businessmen led Japan's economic development. Today, however, systems like the 'Iron Triangle' and 'top–down' approaches to reform have themselves reached the limit of their effectiveness. Unless these systems and methods are reformed, Japan has no prospect for new growth. I shall elaborate on this situation in more detail from two aspects, namely industrial structural reform and administrative and fiscal reforms.

2.3.1 Industrial Structural Reform

During the 51 years since the end of World War II, Japan's industrial development has come through two stages. The first stage, which ran from 1945 to 1973, was the period of postwar reconstruction and high economic growth. During this period, Japan took advantage of improvement in its terms of trade brought about by faster growth in the prices of industrial products relative to those of raw materials. It grew by building heavy and chemical industries, which consumed large amounts of raw materials, along its coasts, and exporting their products. Typical examples of such industries are steel, natural fibre textiles, petrochemicals and non-ferrous metals. Japan imported technology from advanced Western nations to develop these industries.

The second stage ran from 1973, when two oil crises triggered a surge in international raw material prices, and when the terms of trade began to deteriorate. During this stage, technology-intensive industries that produce high value-added output without consuming too much raw material led Japan's industrial development. These are typically processing and assembly industries, such as semiconductors, computers, watches, cameras, automobiles and machine tools. Much of the technology required by these industries has been developed domestically.

During these two stages of development, labour productivity in heavy and chemical industries and in processing and assembly industries improved phenomenally, strengthening Japan's international competitiveness and boosting its exports. On the other hand, productivity improvement in the rest of the manufacturing sector and non-manufacturing industries has been slow. Advanced manufacturing industries have caused Japan's trade surplus to expand sharply, and the trend toward a higher yen has taken root. However, other manufacturing industries (including many non-durable consumer goods industries) and non-manufacturing industries, especially distribution and services, have experienced little productivity increase while their wage costs have risen sharply, resulting in a large differential in prices in Japan and abroad. This is why today, at 180 yen to the dollar, the purchasing power parity of the yen is 60 per cent lower than the market exchange rate.

Because of this wide gap between Japanese and overseas prices and high Japanese wages in terms of the market exchange rate, those manufacturing industries that have led the nation's growth have found it to their advantage to shift production offshore and have begun to expand internationally. The question now is 'What will be the new sector that will lead Japan's economic growth in the third stage?'

In present-day Japan, the industries that invest most heavily in plant and equipment are mainly in the non-manufacturing sector, such as electric power, telecommunications, leasing and software services. These industries invest between 3 and 7 trillion yen. The only manufacturing industry to undertake capital investment on a comparable scale is electronic and electrical machinery. The automobile and steel industries once led capital investment in Japan, but now they are spending less, only about 1 trillion yen, on domestic facilities, compared with the above-mentioned non-manufacturing industries.

Here, we can see signs of what the leading industries will be in the coming third stage. There are two main strategies to encourage this industrial structural reform toward the third stage. The first strategy would be to expand new business frontiers through deregulation in the non-manufacturing sector, such as telecommunications and broadcasting, distribution, software services, financial services and housing construction, and to stimulate capital investment in these industries by keeping real interest rates low and providing financial facilities to venture businesses.

The second strategy would be to promote a new type of public works investment to encourage the development of emerging industries. Consideration is now being given to the use of public funds to build the infrastructure required for the creation of high-tech telecommunications networks and to support technological innovation in the area of multimedia equipment to serve as terminals for such networks.

With these two strategies, we must encourage investment in information technology and system building in the non-manufacturing sector and raise its ratio of capital equipment to labour input in order to increase labour productivity and reduce costs. This is the key to industrial structural reform which leads toward the third stage of development.

However, the bureaucracy, which has promoted 'top–down reform' over the past 51 years, is not willing to take the initiative in deregulation that would end its role of intervention in the private economy. Business groups with vested interests, which have long been protected by government's excessive intervention, are also against deregulation that would promote competition. Among the politicians, who along with the bureaucracy and business have preserved the 'Iron Triangle', there are those who want to cling to the *status quo* and are having second thoughts about breaking up the 'Iron Triangle' and implementing deregulation that might threaten their constituencies. This, indeed, is the major problem that must be solved in order to realize structural economic reform in Japan.

2.3.2 Administrative and Fiscal Reforms

This problem may appear to be very difficult and hard to solve. However, there is another reason why urgent action is needed to reform an administrative system that intervenes excessively in private economic activities and to end the 'Iron Triangle' and 'top–down' approach to reform. That is the sheer magnitude of Japan's budget deficits, which I mentioned earlier. In order to reduce the budget deficits, the Ministry of Finance is contemplating increases in the consumption tax, starting with a hike in the tax rate from 3 per cent to 5 per cent in April 1998, and curtailing increases in social security expenditure by reforming the pension insurance and health insurance systems. Given the ageing of the Japanese population, these two measures are inevitable in order to reduce budget deficits. However, they are not sufficient to ensure the reduction of Japan's budget deficits.

In an economy characterized by a high savings rate like Japan, there will be an inclination toward an excess of savings over investment in the domestic economy, which will expand the current account surplus and cause the currency to overshoot unless (1) government debt is sufficiently large or (2) the government implements a medium-term policy to expand domestic investment opportunities through deregulation and promotion of technological innovation to absorb excess domestic savings. During the five years of stagnation in the 1990s, Japan lacked both, namely (1) a large public deficit and (2) ample opportunities for private investment. Therefore, the decline in prices resulting from an oversupply of goods and services stemming from excess domestic savings, combined with a drop in the prices of imported goods due to the overshooting of the yen rate stimulated by an expanding current account surplus, has depressed domestic prices and caused 'real deflation', in which the nominal economic growth rate is lower than the real growth rate.

This low nominal growth rate is reflected in growth rate forecasts, causing asset prices, including land and share prices, to remain weak despite the fact that the bursting of the bubble has already come to an end. This is having an adverse effect on investment decisions by businesses and individuals and is at the same time responsible for expanding banks' non-performing loans.

Inflation targeting to keep inflation rates low and fiscal discipline to contain public-sector deficits have become matters of common interest for the international circle of policy makers. In Japan, however, we are suffering from a negative inflation rate, or small government deficits *vis-à-vis* large domestic savings.

Japan has a high savings rate and needs to continue public-sector deficits. Unless the government implements a medium-term policy to expand domestic investment opportunities, fiscal consolidation will cause such an economy to stagnate in the medium term.

Deregulation and the promotion of technological innovation centring on the non-manufacturing sector, in combination with consumption tax increases and the curtailment of growth in social security outlays, will therefore create conditions suitable for successful fiscal consolidation in Japan.

Furthermore, deregulation will allow the administrative system to be slimmed down, thereby leading to the reduction in budget deficits from this aspect, too. The Japanese public will accept increases in the consumption tax rate and a curb on the growth of social security expenditure only when the bureaucracy, which has long intervened excessively, is pared down, and administrative reform will create a simple watchdog organization that ensures that the rules of the market economy are being adhered to. In this sense, administrative reform to tear down the 'Iron Triangle' must be the starting-point for efforts to reduce the budget deficits.

2.4 OUTLOOK FOR THE POLITICAL SITUATION

So far, I have discussed the nature of the transformation facing Japan from the aspects of industrial structural reform and administrative and fiscal reforms.

Today, all Japanese politicians say that they are in favour of such reforms. However, the ruling coalition of the Liberal Democrats, Social Democrats and New Party Sakigake members is often divided, faces internal conflicts and has been postponing the implementation of necessary reforms. For example, the lifting of the ban on stock-holding companies, which is necessary for the deregulation of the scope of the financial business, has been postponed due to opposition from the Social Democratic Party. The plan for the organizational reform of the Ministry of Finance has not been worked out due to opposition from the Liberal Democratic Party. The only work that is in progress now is that on the reform of the Bank of Japan Law to enhance the independence of monetary policy, but there is no telling what will happen at the last minute.

Even among Liberal Democrats and Social Democrats, there is a minority of people who are eager to promote reforms. However, the majority, as supporters of the 'Iron Triangle' over the past 51 years, want to preserve the *status quo*. By contrast, the majority of the members of the New Frontier Party and the New Party Sakigake clearly want to promote reforms, but they are no match for the coalition of Liberal Democrats and the Social Democrats in terms of the number of Diet members.

There is no doubt that the House of Representatives, the dominant of Japan's two chambers, will be dissolved some time between October 1997 and January 1998. The first general election to be held under the revised Public Office Election Law and Political Funds Regulation Law will then take place. These two laws were revised as part of the political reforms implemented in 1994 by the Cabinet led by Mr Morihiro Hosokawa, who is now a member of the New Frontier Party. The aim of these revisions is to ensure that differences in party platforms are clearly presented to the electorate for judgment by the public under a small constituency system combined with proportional representation. They also aim at meting out severe punishment to vote-buying candidates by strengthening the guilt-by-association system.

It is widely expected that none of the parties will be able to win a majority single-handedly. The focuses of attention, therefore, are which of the two conservative parties, the Liberal Democratic Party and the New Frontier Party, will win the largest number of seats, and whether a reformist coalition will emerge. The new political scene may see not just a coalition of existing parties, but a complete restructuring of the political world, including the splitting of the Liberal Democratic Party and the New Frontier Party.

In any event, we shall know for certain by the beginning of 1997 whether there will emerge a political force strong enough to lead the third historical transformation of Japan after the Meiji Restoration and the end of World War II, and whether the Japanese will regain confidence in their long-term economic outlook to enable the Japanese economy to get on a sustained growth path led by private demand.

2.5 HOW WILL JAPAN'S ECONOMIC SYSTEM CHANGE?

It will be very unfortunate for Japan if the administration tries to stall the reform process. Although such an eventuality may delay structural changes in the Japanese economy, there will still be spontaneous progress to a certain extent in certain fields. Later in this section, I shall discuss how economic systems that are unique to Japan will inevitably change.

First, I would like to look at the Japanese-style employment system, which includes lifetime employment and seniority wage systems. These systems have the advantages of making it possible for companies to rotate their employees flexibly and invest in human capital to nurture multi-skilled workers. However, with manufacturing industries moving their production activities overseas and non-manufacturing industries replacing manufacturing industries as the leading industries of the nation, the value of company training that enables workers to acquire special skills that are useful only in domestic factories has diminished. The relative decline in the number of young workers resulting from the ageing of society is also flattening the wage pyramid based on seniority. Moreover, due to rapid technological innovation, an increasing number of companies are recruiting people with special expertise or skills in mid-career by setting annual salaries.

These are a few signs that Japanese-style employment systems are breaking down. However, we cannot assume that these systems will eventually collapse. The systems will no longer work for people with special professional knowledge and skills. However, for most people, although the lifetime employment and seniority wage systems may become more flexible, they will not break down completely. This is because these systems will continue to be convenient and stable alternatives for both companies and unskilled workers.

The next topic is the Japanese practice of mutual ownership of stocks. This practice has the advantages of defending companies from attempts to corner their shares, confirming the intention of maintaining long-term business relationships, and sharing the risk of bankruptcies among enterprises. These advantages will not change in the future. The practice is therefore likely to continue. However, cross-shareholdings that exist only because of inertia are being dissolved, as companies review their portfolios as part of their restructuring efforts in a stagnant economic environment. When the ban on holding companies is lifted in the future, stock ownership will be used for new objectives, such as the formation of universal banking groups and the creation of venture businesses spun out from existing businesses.

Finally, I would like to mention the main bank system in Japan. This system's advantages are: (1) the reduction of agency costs stemming from the asymmetry of information; (2) insurance against risks, such as the provision of relief during business crises and the alleviation of interest rate fluctuations; and (3) the ease with which various types of information can be shared. However, the significance of the main bank system is diminishing as a result of the emergence of a wide variety of methods for fund raising due to the securitization and globalization of financial activities. Nevertheless, its significance will not disappear completely.

From now on, businesses will choose their own main banks very carefully. Financial administration based on the 'convoy system', whereby the speed of the entire convoy is determined by that of the slowest member, was dropped in 1994, erasing the myth that deposit banks will never fail. As a result, businesses are paying increasing attention to the volume of non-performing loans and profit-earning capability of banks. As the deregulation of areas of financial business proceeds and banks dispose of their non-performing loans, the number of Japanese deposit banks will decrease due to mergers and liquidations. There will also be restructuring of agricultural and forestry financial institutions and government-owned financial institutions. As part of the above-mentioned transition of the Japanese industrial structure to its third stage, these developments in the financial service industry will help to increase productivity in the Japanese non-manufacturing sector.

3. Structural Reforms Proposed in the Japanese Government's Mid-term Economic Plan

Takafumi Kaneko

3.1 INTRODUCTION

In December of 1995, the Japanese government published its 'Social and Economic Plan for Structural Reforms Towards a Vital Economy and Secure Life', a new medium-term economic plan covering the period from FY 1995 through FY 2000. In this chapter I attempt to explicate the basic ideas of this new plan to proceed with structural reforms.

The Japanese government's two previous medium-term economic plans – 'Economic Management Within a Global Context', published in May 1988, and 'The Five-Year Economic Plan – Sharing a Better Quality of Life Around the Globe', published in June 1992, aimed at responding to frustrations, both within Japan and abroad, with the state of the Japanese economy.

Many Japanese had been exasperated with their current situation in which their standards of living did not match their increased income levels. The lack of decent housing was one main source of this frustration. Those outside Japan had been frustrated with the various difficulties of entering the Japanese market. Japan's huge current account surplus testified to this. Therefore, both plans aimed at creating an improved quality of life and harmonizing more closely with the global community. Fortunately, it was possible to address these two goals simultaneously. For example, measures to promote imports of inexpensive goods had the dual effect of increasing the purchasing power of Japanese consumers and reducing Japan's external surplus. The two plans implicitly assumed that the measures aimed at enhancing the quality of life of the Japanese, reducing working hours for example, would result in diminished international competitiveness of the Japanese economy. This would in turn reduce economic friction with the rest of the world. The plans thus reflected the Japanese government's confidence in the vitality of the Japanese economy.

Today many Japanese who have watched Japan's low growth over the past four years are losing confidence in their economy. They are worried about their ability to create new dynamism in the domestic economy. As is illustrated by the recent downgrading of Japan by an international ratings firm, the Japanese economy, the vitality of which used to be feared as a threat to the world economy, is now looked upon apprehensively. Many are worried that Japan will fail to cope with the problems of its financial system. This would lead to a worldwide disruption of financial markets. Within this context, the new plan endeavours to respond to these anxieties. It focuses on the creation of new vitality in the Japanese economy, with a solid emphasis on structural reform as the means to achieve this.

3.2 FOUR MAJOR TIDE SHIFTS

The new plan starts with the recognition that Japan is faced with four major shifts in the tide of domestic and world events:

1. The continued spread of globalization
2. The transition to an advanced, mature economy and society
3. The trend toward an ageing society with fewer children and longer lives
4. Advances in information and telecommunications.

The plan presumes that the current social and economic structure of Japan has been unable to cope with these tidal shifts, causing such problems as retardation of new industries, industrial hollowing out, anxieties over job security, anxieties about life in a greying society with fewer children, and dissatisfaction with the failure to experience affluence in any meaningful way.

3.2.1 The Progress of Globalization

An important issue raised at the 22nd G7 Summit Meeting held in Lyon in June 1995 was how to respond positively to the globalization of individual economies. One manifestation of the globalization of Japan's economy is the surge in Japan's outward direct investment, particularly to East Asia. The considerable appreciation of the yen, improvements in the infrastructures of East Asia, and the adoption of a growth strategy driven by foreign direct investment in East Asia have accelerated the relocation of the production bases of Japanese manufacturing firms to that region. Hitachi and Toshiba no longer doggedly adhere to Japan as their production base. They now choose countries that provide the most favourable business environment. While they have enhanced their competitiveness by extending their activities globally, it has resulted in reductions in Japanese employment.

The number employed in Japan's manufacturing sector decreased by 370 000 in FY 1995 from the previous year (Table 3.1). Because one ultimate objective of a national government is to create conditions in which its people can enjoy a respectable quality of life, provision of decent job opportunities is one of the most important tasks of a national government. Today, it is not only companies that compete on a global scale. National governments too are engaged in global competition for provision of favourable business environments for companies.

Table 3.1 Employment by industry

[figures in 10^3]

Fiscal year	Agriculture, forestry fishery, mining	Construction	Manufacturing	Services	Others
1980	580.9	547.4	1371.0	2843.4	197.6
1981	563.7	544.6	1386.1	2893.3	193.8
1982	557.5	544.1	1384.6	2968.9	194.6
1983	533.8	534.7	1410.0	3043.6	196.3
1984	522.1	524.3	1447.3	3072.8	197.2
1985	475.9	531.5	1454.8	3097.8	197.5
1986	501.5	534.3	1435.0	3169.8	196.3
1987	494.1	540.2	1431.8	3248.1	196.3
1988	479.5	564.3	1456.6	3310.3	196.5
1989	469.9	579.8	1482.4	3407.7	190.3
1990	449.2	593.7	1518.2	3488.5	203.2
1991	432.1	603.8	1562.5	3565.8	201.0
1992	410.4	627.2	1557.6	3608.5	204.4
1993	385.9	647.3	1519.8	3670.3	212.9
1994	373.7	661.3	1489.3	3715.0	216.9
1995	374.6	658.2	1452.2	3693.3	214.0

Sources: Statistics Bureau, Management and Coordination Agency, 'Annual Report on the Labour Force Survey' (1980–1995) and Statistics Bureau, Management and Cordination Agency, 'Monthly Report on the Labour Force Survey' Jan. 1996–Mar. 1996)

When the production bases of Japanese companies were limited to Japan's borders, industrial policies which aimed at increasing the international competitiveness of these companies were effective in creating jobs for the Japanese. The growth of these companies led to an increase in Japanese employment. But in this age of global competition, policies that strive to increase the competitiveness of Japanese companies no longer automatically lead to the creation of Japanese jobs because Japanese companies might move their production bases abroad in pursuit of more favourable business conditions. Thus, the days of industrial policies, based on the notion that the nationality of companies is meaningful, are over. In this context, it is significant that the Inward Direct Investment Board of the Japanese government announced in April 1997 that the Japanese government would, in effect, welcome M&As by foreign companies.

3.2.2 The End of Catch-up-type Growth

By the early 1980s, Japan had become a front runner in the global economic race. But this period also spelled the end of the catch-up-type growth that previously characterized the Japanese economy. It could no longer grow by pursuing the efficient production of standardized and high-volume products based on imported fundamental technologies. But Japan didn't seem able to replace this catch-up-style growth with something more suitable. The emergence of the bubble economy in the late 1980s was partly due to the fact that a lack of new promising industries resulted in pouring money into real estate investment. Even today, the Japanese economy is still groping for a new type of growth.

The group-centred and company-centred thought and behaviour of many Japanese has provided a solid base for effective achievement in high-volume, production-driven, economic growth. Now, however, these characteristics are increasingly recognized as impeding the development of new industries by suppressing creativity.

3.2.3 Longer Life, Fewer Children

As shown in Figures 3.1 and 3.2, the trends of longer life expectancy and fewer children have changed the demographic structure of Japan from its previous pyramid shape into the rectangle we see today. Accordingly, companies are beginning to find it difficult to maintain the traditional labour practices of lifetime employment and the seniority system, both of which are based on the pyramid type of demographic structure.

The elderly – those age 65 and over – will probably account for 17 per cent of the total population in the year 2000, and 25.5 per cent in 2020 (Table

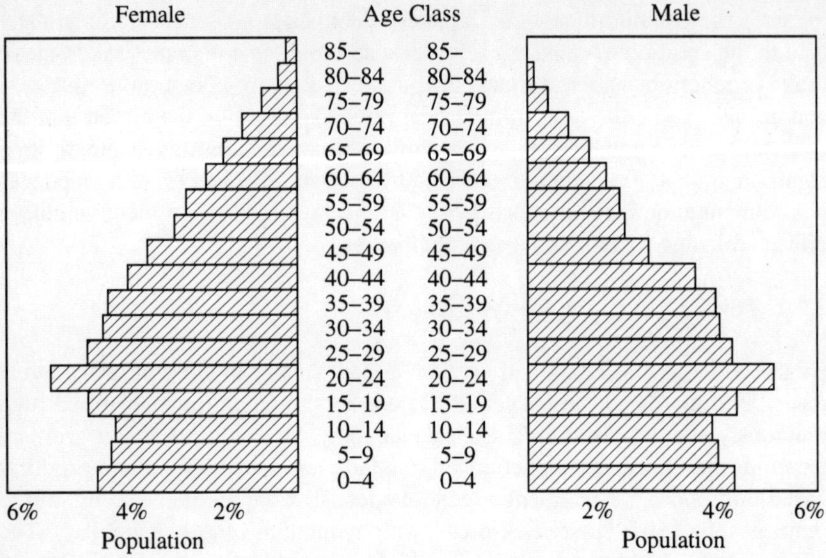

Figure 3.1 Demographic structure (1975)

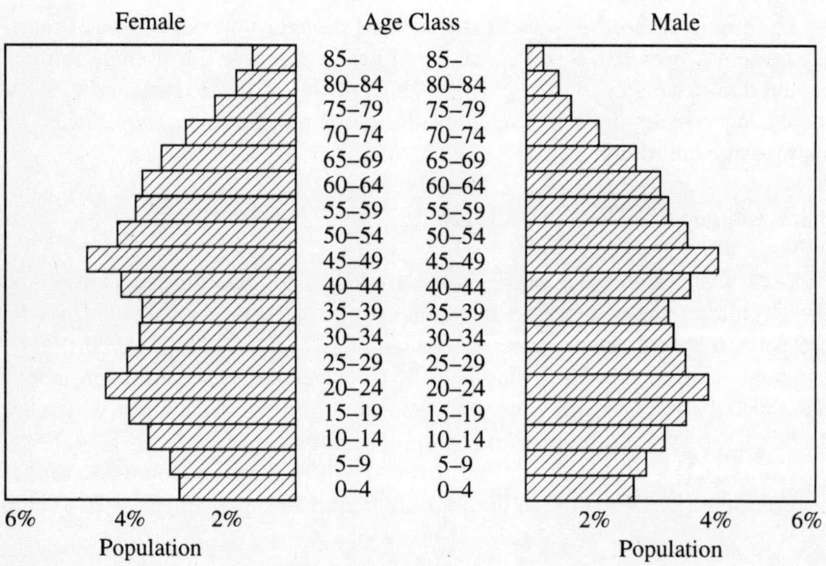

Figure 3.2 Demographic Structure (1995)

Note: Each ratio is the proportion of population in the age class to total population.
Source: Management and Coordination Agency, 'Population Census' (1975,1995)

3.2). On the other hand, the ratio of the population that is of working age – those between age 20 and 65 – to the elderly is projected to decrease from 3.6 to 1 in 2000 to 2.1 to 1 in 2020. This rapid aging of the population will with this increased burden on society as a whole is causing widespread anxiety.

The Japanese working-age population started to decline in 1996. The labour force will begin to decrease at the beginning of the twenty-first century, and the population will start to decline around 2010. These future population trends are causing many in Japan to doubt the Japanese economy's ability to maintain its vitality.

Table 3.2 Transition and estimation of population by age class

[percentages]

	0–14	15–64	65+	75+
1970	24.0	68.9	7.1	2.1
1975	24.3	67.7	7.9	2.5
1980	23.5	67.3	9.1	3.1
1985	21.5	68.2	10.3	3.9
1990	18.2	69.5	12.0	4.8
1995	15.9	69.2	14.8	5.9
2000	15.2	67.8	17.0	6.9
2005	15.6	65.2	19.1	8.5
2010	16.4	62.4	21.3	10.0
2015	16.3	59.5	24.1	11.2
2020	15.5	59.0	25.5	12.5
2025	14.5	59.7	25.8	14.5

Sources: Statistics Bureau, Management and Coordination Agency, 'Population Census' for the period before 1970–95 and Institute of Population Problems, Ministry of Health and Welfare, 'Projections for Japanese Population' (Projections on September 1992) for the period on and after 2000.

3.2.4 Advances in Information and Telecommunications

Advances in information and telecommunications will change the way people live through increased choices and freer participation. These advances will also bring about new industries and further productivity gains by offering more efficient production and distribution, faster decision making, and new corporate and home services. The advances in these areas are expected to become a driving force of new development in the Japanese economy. However, the picture of a society and economy based on advanced information and telecommunications is not yet clear. This lack of clarity contributes to the present uncertainties the Japanese economy now faces.

3.3 STRUCTURAL PROBLEMS

The shifting tides mentioned above are now wreaking havoc on Japan's traditional rigid socioeconomic structure. The country finds itself facing difficult structural problems.

3.3.1 Delay of New Industries, Hollowing Out

The overseas relocation of Japanese manufacturing bases should be seen in the positive light of the formation of a more efficient international division of labour in the globalizing economy.

However, the high-cost structure of the Japanese economy, brought about partially by the persistence of non-competitive sectors protected by excessive regulations and traditional business practices, has the effect of accelerating overseas relocation by making the location of production bases in Japan less favourable.

In addition to the uncertain future prospects of Japanese industry, brought on by the ambiguous nature of a society based on advanced information and telecommunications, excessive regulations are also impeding the development of new industry by deterring individuals and companies from using their creativity to start up new businesses.

The continuing overseas relocation of the production bases of Japanese companies therefore creates apprehension in many Japanese, who increasingly fear that Japanese industry will hollow out, taking with it job opportunities.

3.3.2 Anxieties Regarding Employment

The erosion of Japanese labour practices especially affects the middle-aged generation adversely. They can no longer expect automatic promotions and yearly rising wages as rewards for sticking with the same company. Moreover, companies are tending to dismiss, in the process of restructuring, middle-aged workers whose wages are above the marginal productivity of their labour. Anxieties over job security are spreading throughout the middle-aged generation. These anxieties are exacerbated by the overseas relocation of production bases and the delay in the development of new industries.

3.3.3 Anxieties about Life in an Ageing Society with Fewer Children

As the population ages, the costs associated with pension payments, medical treatment and welfare are expected to increase. Simultaneously, as the number of children declines, the tax base ultimately shrinks. The ratio of working-age to elderly population is projected to continue to fall to 3.6 to 1 in 2000 and even further to 2.1 to 1 in 2020. This forecasted trend has generated a vague but widespread anxiety. No obvious or agreed upon solution exists as of now. The decline in the labour force is also giving rise to the fear of weakened dynamism in the Japanese economy.

3.3.4 Dissatisfaction with Life

Many Japanese feel that miserable residential environments are the prime reason why their everyday life seems to lack a sense of achievement. Equally many seem to be increasingly aware that self-fulfilment through active social participation is important in achieving a degree of satisfaction. It was surprising to learn that so many of the members of the Aum cult, who perpetrated the Tokyo subway sarin attack and other serious subversive activities, were young intellectuals. Aum had organized a Japanese government-like administrative system: each member belonged to one of the ministries (such as the Ministry of Construction, Ministry of Finance, and so on). It may be that these young intellectuals, who could not find opportunities to make full use of their abilities, felt a sense of fulfilment by participating in the pseudo-governmental activities of the cult.

To take another example, a large number of young Japanese became involved in volunteer activities to help those who suffered from the great Hanshin-Awaji earthquake, something way beyond the expectations of most middle-aged Japanese. These phenomena suggest that social participation has become increasingly important as a component of feeling fulfilled, particularly among young Japanese.

3.4 DIRECTION OF STRUCTURAL REFORM

3.4.1 Enhancement of Market Mechanism

Japan must proceed with structural reforms to cope with these problems. The first structural reform aims at fostering a new and creative dynamism in the Japanese economy.

As mentioned above, as the nationality of companies becomes less and less relevant, industrial policies are no longer effective in creating better job opportunities for the Japanese by increasing the competitiveness of Japanese companies. The government can no longer play the role of responsible pilot in guiding Japan's economic development. Japan's previous model of development is no longer relevant. The Japanese economy has finished the process of catch-up-type growth. The future direction of the industrial structure itself is opaque because the picture of a society based on information and telecommunications is still unclear.

It is vital for individuals and enterprises to exercise their creativity freely and responsibly in order to produce a new dynamism in the Japanese economy. Only when the market mechanism works properly do people who bear risks gain the full rewards of their own initiatives. Establishing conditions that allow the market mechanism to flourish is critical. It can be done by actively proceeding with deregulation, by developing proactive competition policies, and by rectifying impediments to competitive business practices.

Aiming to initiate structural reforms, an 'Action Plan for Rectifying High-cost Structures and Promoting Dynamism' was formulated while the economic plan was still being drafted. The Action Plan covers ten areas:

1. physical distribution;
2. energy;
3. wholesale/retail distribution;
4. telecommunications;
5. financial services;
6. passenger transport services;
7. agricultural production;
8. standards, certification and import procedures;
9. public works; and
10. housing construction.

Each of the above incorporates five policy areas: deregulation, development of proactive competition policies, rectification of business practices, enhancement of infrastructure, and improvement in information disclosure.

3.4.2 Organization of Flexible Labour Markets

Structural reforms accompany industrial adjustments. This may in turn cause unemployment problems due to increased mismatches between labour supply and demand. One important structural reform is to create a labour market that can respond flexibly to industrial adjustment and thus help prevent unemployment problems. One classic characteristic of the Japanese labour market is the transfer of redundant company workers either to other sections in the same company or to a subsidiary, thus preventing workers from losing their jobs.

But it has become increasingly difficult to expect companies, many of which are attempting to maximize their flexibility in dealing with increased uncertainty, to continue to follow traditional employment policies. According to a recent survey conducted by the Ministry of Labour, 50.5 percent of polled companies said that they no longer adhere to the lifetime employment system, as opposed to 31.8 percent who said so in 1993 (Figure 3.3).

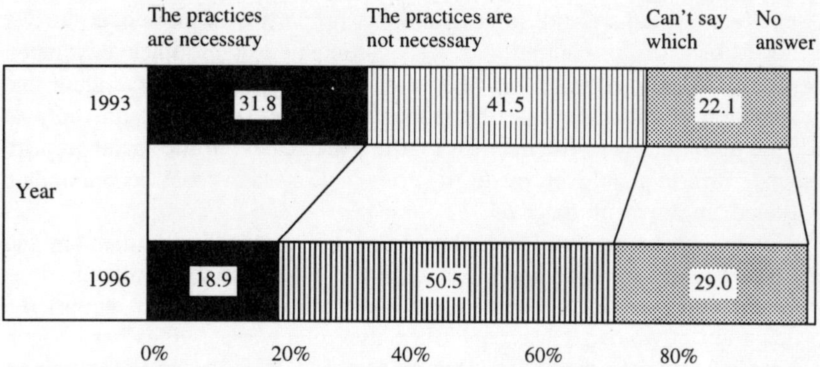

Source: *Ministry of Labour, "Personnel Management Survey" (1993, 1996)*

Figure 3.3 Japanese companies views on lifetime employment practices

With traditional labour practices changing, workers are becoming keener on the idea of switching companies. They have also begun to realize the need to acquire specific industry skills, as opposed to company-specific skills. In this context, measures that encourage workers to move in the labour market must be implemented. Deregulation of fee-charging employment agencies and temporary employment agencies should be promoted. Since the present employment systems, including the tax-qualified pension plan, lump sum retirement payments and welfare programmes, are based on the criteria of continuous employment which impede labour market mobility, a complete review should be undertaken of systems that hinder the movement of labour.

3.4.3 Building a Society that Allows Participation by All

Because a growing number of Japanese are beginning to perceive that participation in society is an important element of the quality of life, it is essential to build a society that respects the uniqueness of each individual and ensures that individuals have the option to play a variety of roles in society according to their wishes and abilities.

Expansion of the types of participation in society is desirable not only because it enhances the quality of life, but also because it is very effective in coping with the problems that accompany the ageing of the population. Japan's working population will start to decline at the beginning of the next century. Increased participation of women and the elderly in the labour market is thus indispensable to enhancing the growth potential of the Japanese economy. The expected rise in the ratio of elderly to working-age population presents serious problems for the increasingly burdened social security system. However, if more and more elderly continue to work, the burden will lessen. Because Japan tends to have a higher proportion of those over the age of 60 who wish to continue to work (compared with other developed countries, as shown in Table 3.3 and 3.4), measures to facilitate the participation of the elderly in the labour market are desirable, not only to increase their quality of life but also for the management of the social security system. Efforts should be made to promulgate systems that accommodate continued employment to age 65.

With the increasing trend toward nuclear families, care for children and the frail elderly have become impediments to the employment of women. It is important to implement integrated and systematic policies that support the participation of women. Moreover, because volunteer activities have begun to seem attractive to many Japanese as a means of social participation, an environment conducive to such volunteer activities should be created.

3.4.4 Building Social Assistance Systems

With the advent of an ageing population, support for the elderly to lead self-reliant lives has become increasingly important. The combination of larger numbers of elderly people (aged 75 and over) and progressively fewer children makes it more and more difficult for families to take care of their frail parents. The social assistance system for the feeble elderly has to be expanded if women, the traditional caregivers of family elders, are to enjoy increased social participation.

Social assistance systems must be built by the cooperation of individuals, corporations and government (self-help, mutual help and public help) in order to hold down management costs.

Table 3.3 Labour force participation rates for elderly male workers (percentages)

Year	Japan			US			Great Britain			Germany		
	55–59	60–64	65+	55–59	60–64	65+	55–59	60–64	65–	55–59	60–64	65+
1980	91.2	77.8	41.0	81.7	60.8	19.0	90.1	71.2	10.3	81.9	44.3	6.8
1985	90.3	72.5	37.0	79.6	55.6	15.8	82.5	55.5	8.5	80.0	34.6	5.1
1990	92.1	72.9	36.5	79.8	55.5	16.4	81.4	54.4	8.8	78.5	34.8	4.6
1993	94.1	75.6	37.7	78.2	54.1	15.6	75.7	52.2	7.4	–	–	–

Year	France			Netherlands			Sweden		
	55–59	60–64	65+	55–59	60–64	65+	55–59	60–64	65+
1980	81.0	47.9	8.4	74.8	48.8	4.8	87.7	69.0	14.2
1985	67.8	30.8	5.3	64.8	27.8	3.5	87.6	65.1	11.0
1990	67.7	22.8	3.7	66.3	22.7	0.0	86.7	63.3	12.4
1993	67.8	19.0	3.2	62.2	23.8	0.0	82.8	57.6	13.2

Source: OECD, 'Labour Force Statistics', (1985, 1994).

Table 3.4 Employment situation for the elderly (1992) (percentages)

			Total		55–59		60–64		65–69	
			1988	1992	1988	1992	1988	1992	1988	1992
	Employed	Total	73.8	76.6	88.4	92.9	67.9	71.6	54.5	58.6
	Unemployed	Total	26.2	23.4	11.6	7.1	32.1	28.4	45.5	41.4
Male			(100.0)	(100.0)	(100.0)	(100.0)	(100.0)	(100.0)	(100.0)	(100.0)
		Want to work	(50.9)	(48.1)	(60.4)	(63.3)	(56.5)	(55.1)	(40.3)	(37.9)
		Do not want to work	(49.1)	(50.7)	(39.6)	(35.7)	(43.5)	(43.6)	(59.7)	(61.0)
		Don't know	(–)	(1.2)	(–)	(1.0)	(–)	(1.3)	(–)	(1.1)
	Employed	Total	41.4	43.7	51.8	56.1	39.7	39.8	28.9	32.1
	Unemployed	Total	58.6	56.3	48.2	43.9	60.3	60.2	71.1	67.9
Female			(100.0)	(100.0)	(100.0)	(100.0)	(100.0)	(100.0)	(100.0)	(100.0)
		Want to work	(32.2)	(32.4)	(41.8)	(39.7)	(32.0)	(33.5)	(23.1)	(25.2)
		Do not want to work	(67.8)	(66.5)	(58.2)	(59.3)	(68.0)	(65.3)	(76.9)	(73.8)
		Don't know	(–)	(1.1)	(–)	(1.0)	(–)	(1.2)	(–)	(1.0)

Note: Employed means to have worked with earnings in September.
Source: Ministry of Labour, 'Survey on Employment Situations for the Elderly' (1992).

3.5 ESTABLISHING A DEVELOPMENT BASE

In an increasingly globalized economy, the government should set the stage in creating a business environment that encourages companies, irrespective of nationality, to choose Japan as their production base. The government will thus provide a basis for new development while proceeding with economic reforms.

3.5.1 Human Resources Development

Japan's traditional, egalitarian-oriented education system greatly contributed to its successful growth in the catch-up phase, which focussed on high-volume production. This growth has been achieved by fostering conformist-oriented individuals through the process of a uniform education. However, it is clear that creativity and the risk-taking ability of individuals are the driving forces that will bring about new and much-needed development, given Japan's heightened uncertainty generated by increased economic globalization. The vague and undefined future that will accompany the further advancement of information and telecommunications, in addition to the end of catch-up-style growth, can only strengthen this conviction. Schools should emphasize the development of creativity and independence.

Universal skills are also increasingly important, given the erosion of lifetime employment practices. Support for human resources development based on individual initiative, such as paid educational training leave systems, should be expanded.

3.5.2 Enhancement of Scientific and Technological Creativity

To maintain its dynamism, Japan needs to create new industries which make full use of the existing international division of labour, especially that available in the fast-growing East Asian region. Japan should thus actively promote scientific and technological development, with priority given to basic and original research, which can be utilized globally as international public goods.

In this context, the Japanese government will formulate a 'Science and Technology Basic Plan' that will include comprehensive guidelines for research and development and provisions for research facilities. The Japanese government will seek to double government investments in research and development as quickly as possible.

3.5.3 Advances in Information and Telecommunications

Advances in information and telecommunications, which bring about drastic changes in the *modus operandi* of both people and corporations, are a basis for new development. Expediting the transition to an information and telecommunications-driven economy and society is of critical importance.

However, there are many administrative systems and practices that impede the advancement of information and telecommunications by making it mandatory to keep documents in the form of paper, or to appear in person for simple applications. The government will review these systems and practices with an eye toward a fast transition to the electronic processing of information. This should create incentives for households and companies to introduce equipment and software that can exploit the advantages of information and telecommunications, and should in turn help accelerate the advent of an economy and society driven by information and telecommunications.

Because low telecommunications costs are necessary to make this transition, the government seeks lower telecommunications fees by establishing fair and effective conditions for competition in the area of telecommunications through deregulation.

3.5.4 Improvement of Social Overhead Capital

Superior social overhead capital is a basis for development in the globalized economy because it determines (along with the equality of human resources) the location that companies choose for their bases of operation. Although the Japanese government will continue to give priority to investments that will directly improve the quality of life, including the building of sewer systems, urban parks, disposal facilities, and the development of housing and residential land in accordance with the 'Basic Plan for Public Investment' (published in October 1993), it will place a renewed emphasis on the improvement of infrastructure related to the advancement of information and telecommunications and to the rapid ageing of the population.

3.6 PROMOTING ADMINISTRATIVE AND FISCAL REFORM

In pursuing the above structural reforms, the government should accelerate the reforms of its own system to establish an administration that can more flexibly adapt to changes in the economy and in society. The general direction of the reform should be 'from the bureaucracy to the private sector, from the central government to the local community'. Thus, the three major areas of administrative reform are deregulation, decentralization of authority, and disclosure of information held by government.

Because the ratio of general government gross financial debts to GDP is projected to be 89 per cent in 1996 (Table 3.5), significantly higher than the average 74 per cent of G7 countries, public finance is growing structurally more stringent. Debt payments are heavily impinging on discretionary expenditures. It is therefore urgent to improve the fiscal structure and responsiveness in order to be able to use fiscal resource allocation functions effectively. During the course of the plan, the government will seek to create a fiscal structure that does not accumulate outstanding government bonds by reducing its dependence on national bond issues.

Table 3.5 General government gross financial liabilities (as a percentage of GDP)

		Projections
	1995	1996
United States	64.3	64.1
Japan	81.3	88.8
Germany	61.6	64.4
France	57.9	60.3
Italy	1233	123.1
United Kingdom	57.6	60.7
Canada	99.1	99.4
Total of above countries	71.9	73.9
Total of OECD countries	72.4	74.2

Source: OECD, 'OECD Economic Outlook 59' (1996).

3.7 OUTLOOK FOR THE ECONOMY

The plan projects an average annual economic growth rate of approximately 3 per cent between fiscal 1996 and the final year of the plan (fiscal 2000). Unemployment is projected to decline to 2.75 per cent in fiscal 2000 from the present level of 3.5 per cent (Table 3.6). This scenario is possible only if the structural reforms proposed in the plan are implemented. The plan also presents an alternative scenario in which little or no progress is made with structural reforms. Economic growth could end up as low as 1.75 per cent, while unemployment would remain as high as 3.75 per cent by the final year of the plan.

Since labour inputs are expected to decline, with the labour force starting to decrease from 1996, and working hours continuing to decrease, realization of a 3 per cent increase in the growth rate will be impossible without a concomitant rise in labour productivity.

Table 3.6 The outlook for the Japanese economy under the new economic plan (fiscal 1996–2000)

Real economic growth rate	Approx. 3%	(Approx. 1 ¾%)
Of which, contribution from domestic demand	Approx. 3%	(Approx. 1 ½%)
Nominal economic growth rate	Approx. 3 ½%	(Approx. 1 ¾ %)
Consumer price growth rate	Approx. ¾%	(Approx. ½%)
Wholesale price growth rate	Approx. - ¼%	(Approx. –¾%)
Full unemployment rate (final year)	Approx. 2 ¾ %	(Approx. 3 ¾%)

Notes:
Figures in parentheses ( ) indicate what the economy can expect if little or no progress is made in structural reform.
Real and nominal economic growth rates are for GDP (gross domestic product).
Given the many fluid elements in domestic and international conditions, the figures above should be taken as approximations with a certain margin for error.
The economic growth rates and price growth rates indicated are annual rates for fiscal 1996–2000, inclusive.

Source: Economic Planning Agency, 'Social and Economic Plan for Structural Reforms Towards a Vital Economy and Secure Life' (1995).
Since labour inputs are expected to continue to decline, with the labour force starting to decrease from 1996, and working hours continuing to decrease, realization of a 3 per cent increase in the growth rate will be impossible without a concomitant rise in labour productivity.

In this context, deregulation in low-productivity areas, in line with an 'Action Plan for Rectifying High-Cost Structures and Promoting Dynamism', is indispensable. Moreover, the 3 per cent growth rate will be impossible without associated demand. Deregulation in information and telecommunications is thus necessary to create new demands by improving lifestyles and by creating new businesses.

3.8 CONCLUDING REMARKS

Deregulation and changes in business practices are needed if Japan is to proceed with structural changes. Although the speed of deregulation may not be as fast as expected, changes in both business practices and consumer behaviour, brought on by the globalization of the Japanese economy, have been working to bring about changes in Japanese economic structures.

Japanese consumers have been deemed too fussy about quality and insensitive to prices. These characteristics of Japanese consumers have helped prevent the global market mechanism from working in the Japanese economy. But after experiencing extreme spending sprees during the bubble economy and thrift in the wake of its subsequent burst, Japanese consumers have again begun to change. They now tend to be more sensitive to prices and more rational in judgment on quality of goods and services. Brand-name French companies such as Chanel and Cartier, whose prices in Japan used to be more than double those in France, have changed their price strategy. The price differential on Chanel lipstick, for example, between Tokyo and Paris has been reduced to 12 per cent. With the increased price sensitivity of consumers, sales of these brand-name products have been expanding rapidly in Japan. These changes in behaviour of Japanese consumers are helping the cause of structural reform by furthering Japan's integration with the global economy.

Faced with global competition, Japanese companies can no longer maintain the inefficient business practices that have been retained under the pretext of managing from a long-term perspective. Large-scale manufacturing companies are now often quick to sever relations with the small and medium-sized companies that have been their long-time subcontractors when they find more competitive ones. Such changes in the behaviour of Japanese companies are working to enhance the function of price mechanisms. These are the types of structural reforms sought by the plan.

Changes in consumer behaviour and business practices are thus helping to reform the Japanese economy by strengthening the market mechanism, but they alone are hardly sufficient. Sweeping deregulation is necessary to accomplish the structural reforms the plan hopes to achieve. Strong initiatives from politicians are also required for deregulation to be carried out. Although many have criticized the slow speed of deregulation in Japan, new initiatives for deregulation from politicians have only now begun to emerge. Mr Shusei Tanaka, Minister for Economic Planning, recently presented to the Cabinet his own package of deregulation covering six areas, including information and telecommunications, financial services and physical distribution without traditional *nemawashi* (prior consultation with the ministries concerned). Although it remains to be seen how successful this new strategy will be, it does signify increasing deregulation initiatives by politicians.

4. Theoretical Approaches to the Japan–America Security Alliance

Daniel I. Okimoto

4.1 HISTORICAL SIGNIFICANCE

The formation of the Japan–America Security Alliance (JASA) will go down in history as one of the most seminal developments to have taken place in the second half of the twentieth century. It is comparable in historic significance to the establishment of the North Atlantic Treaty Organization (NATO) in 1949, a breakthrough development on the European continent. What JASA and NATO succeeded in creating was the framework for the postwar security systems in East Asia and Western Europe following the catastrophe of World War II. Thanks largely to the two alliance systems, East Asia and Western Europe have enjoyed more than half a century of peace, stability, and prosperity – the longest period of stability East Asia has known since the Opium War (1842) and the longest stretch of tranquillity in Europe since the Crimean War (1854–56). For both regions, the second half of the twentieth century deserves to be described as truly a 'golden age', an era of unprecedented economic growth, political stability and international coexistence.

To appreciate the significance of JASA, compare current conditions with those of prewar Asia when the region was racked by Japanese military expansion, colonial competition over control of Asian territories, China's dismemberment, Japan–America and Japan–Soviet rivalries, the Pacific War, and a staggering cumulative toll of death and destruction. For more than a century – from the mid-nineteenth to the mid-twentieth centuries, Asia had to endure the turbulence of chronic instability, colonial exploitation, political upheavals and revolution, grinding poverty, and almost constant warfare.

Viewed against this historical background, JASA is a watershed institution. It is the bedrock of stability in postwar East Asia. Thanks largely or in part to JASA, the following crucial developments have stabilized postwar Asia:

- Japan and America, deadly enemies in the Pacific War, bury the hatchet.
- America sets up military bases in key strategic locations in and around Japan's archipelago.
- JASA is the anchor for a network of bilateral, US military alliances extending throughout the region with South Korea, Taiwan, the Philippines, Australia and New Zealand.
- Japan undergoes a metamorphosis from military to merchant state.
- Japan concentrates all its energies on economic recovery and growth; and becomes the world's second largest producer of economic goods and services.
- Japan refrains from converting its economic power into military firepower.
- A stable democracy takes root in Japan.
- Dynamic economic development sweeps through East Asia.
- Democracy also spreads through the region (albeit more slowly and not along a linear pathway).
- Robust capitalist performance in Japan and Asia helps to undermine and ultimately destroy the socialist paradigm and the communist bloc.
- Within the JASA framework, economic ties of interdependence expand, bringing the United States and Japan into ever widening and entangling webs of cooperation and conflict.

For Japan and the United States – not to mention East Asia as a whole – JASA's importance would be hard to exaggerate. JASA can be called a 'system-shaping' institution, the cornerstone of the postwar security system in East Asia. It would be hard to imagine where East Asia would be without it. If JASA disappeared, the costs and consequences would be monumental.

4.2 COSTS/RISKS/BENEFITS

There is no doubt that JASA and NATO are the two most successful alliances in modern times. Those belonging to the alliances (as well as many non-member states) have benefited immensely.

The costs, risks, and benefits of membership in the two alliances, however, are neither symmetrically designed nor fairly distributed. Indeed, Japan and the European states, the protected members, have arguably reaped a larger harvest of benefits from the alliances than the United States; and on top of that, the United States, the guarantor, has had to shoulder a disproportionate share of the costs and risks.

To cite a few of the benefits in the case of JASA that have accrued lopsidedly to Japan's advantage:

- Security without domestic political polarization or turmoil;
- The lightest burden of defence spending in the advanced industrial world: 1 per cent of GNP for Japan compared to 5 to 6 per cent for the US;
- Dramatic gains in relative economic power *vis-à-vis* the United States over most of the postwar period;
- Access to America's lucrative market – in contrast to the relative inaccessibility of Japan's own market;
- Utilization of the world's most advanced technology and scientific knowledge with comparatively little replenishment by Japan;
- A long period of healing in Asia and Japan's commercial advance into Asia (made possible, to a considerable extent, by JASA).

Conundrum

Why has the United States, the most powerful partner in the security alliance, accepted what appears to be the short end of the JASA relationship? Why is it willing to pay more of the burdens while receiving fewer of the benefits? If the United States is indeed the dominant power, what has prevented it from dictating more advantageous terms? Isn't Japan the weaker, more dependent partner?

4.3 THREE THEORIES

Three theories can be used to shed light on the conundrum. The orthodox answer is derived from the realist school of international relations – specifically, the *theory of hegemonic stability*.[1] It posits that the hegemonic state has an overriding stake in upholding a global balance of power favourable to its interests. Since the security stakes are so high, the hegemonic state is willing to pay a premium (in economic currency) to maintain a favourable politico-military balance. In return, the United States receives a bigger voice in matters related to the alliance. It is thus an implicit bargain that is struck: America's willingness to pay a disproportionate share of the costs in exchange for the right to hold and to wield disproportionate influence and power.

An alternative explanation emerges from the *theory of public or collective goods*.[2] This theory argues that the weaker state has a strong incentive to 'free-ride' – that is, to get away with paying as little as possible for as long as possible because the security made available through the alliance is a 'collective' or 'public' good. There are two defining properties of collective goods:

1. Every alliance member shares in the benefits of security, regardless of how much of the costs each member bears; and
2. when the collective good (that is, security) is made available to one member of the alliance (the strongest state), it is also available to other members at little or no marginal cost.[3]

Thus, there is a rational, built-in propensity for nation-states to maximize their self-interests by minimizing what they pay, since the marginal costs of distributing security to member states are minor and there is no depletion of the security good provided.

A third explanation is suggested by the *theory of economic institutions or path-dependency*.[4] In relationships of long standing, the calculus of costs extends well beyond surface numbers, such as defence expenditures. The calculus must encompass, for example, the hidden costs of what might happen if security were provided on a one-shot, spot-market basis: namely, the likelihood of disloyalty, defiance, opportunism and other acts of irresponsible behaviour on the part of the weaker alliance state. To ensure loyalty, conformity, compliance, honesty and responsible behaviour over time, it is less costly for the dominant state to pay more of the upfront costs of the alliance than to bear what would amount to far larger costs and more damaging consequences later on. Moreover, once the security alliance is put in place, with an asymmetric distribution of costs and benefits, and once a structure of institutions emerges to administer the alliance, the asymmetry of the initial bargain is very hard to correct, because the extant structure has staying power and is resistant to change. Accordingly, the dominant partner is bound to encounter resistance in its attempts to force its weaker partner to pay a larger share of the burdens, even if the weaker state becomes capable of paying a great deal more. There is an institutional 'lock-in' effect.

Each of the three theories is plausible. Each sheds light on the classic conundrum of trying to explain glaring asymmetries in the distribution of costs/risks/benefits in military alliances like JASA. Each theory leads to a different set of predictions about where JASA is headed. Will JASA hold together in the face of the asymmetries? Can the United States prod Japan into shouldering a larger share of the burdens? Will Japan continue to resist – even at the risk of antagonizing the United States or exposing the alliance to crises that might lead to its unravelling? What are the biggest threats to JASA's survival? How will Japan cope with these threats, according to the three theories?

No single theory offers a comprehensive explanation of JASA's evolution over time. JASA has changed far too much over the past half-century for one theory to capture its full multidimensionality and complex dynamics. If, however, JASA is divided into three stages or periods of development, the three theories can be applied to each of the stages, making it easier to understand what has happened and why. The three stages cover the following time periods:

Phase I: Cold war containment: 1952–71
Phase II: Escalating conflicts: 1971–89
Phase III: Post-cold war challenges: 1989–

Phase I: Cold War Containment: Hegemonic Stability

The theory of hegemonic stability offers the best explanation of why JASA was formed and how it functioned from 1952–71, when the cold war divided the world into two contending blocs. When the United States and the Soviet Union demarcated the boundaries of their respective blocs, the establishment of JASA marked the northeastern perimeter of America's arc of containment running through the Asia–Pacific. Locked in a deadly confrontation with the Soviet Union, the United States had a far higher stake in containing communism than Japan; it also had a much more productive economy to pay for the costs of JASA (remember that from 1951–62, Japan was still struggling to recover from the devastation of the Pacific War). Furthermore, owing to the dangers of domestic instability arising from Japan's economic backwardness (for example, the spread of communism and political upheavals), the United States also had a compelling interest in accelerating the pace of Japan's economic recovery and growth (and not having the weight of heavy defence spending slow it down). Hence, the United States was willing to pay a disproportionate share of JASA costs while facilitating Japan's economic development and giving Japan access to America's vast market and state-of-the-art technology.

Phase II: Escalating Conflicts: Collective Goods

From the end of the Bretton Woods system in 1971 until the end of the cold war in 1989, the theory of collective goods probably provides a better explanation of what transpired. As Japan rapidly closed the GNP gap with the United States, ringing up huge bilateral trade surpluses in the process, the United States grew less forgiving of Japan's low share of alliance burdens and less tolerant of its trade and economic practices. During this period, the chorus of complaints about Japan's incorrigible propensity to 'free-ride' grew louder as the US government turned up pressures on Japan (*gaiatsu*) to contribute more to the provision of the collective good. In the face of mounting US pressures, Japan shouldered a progressively larger share of costs; but incremental increases in Japan's share of the burdens failed to keep pace with its rapidly expanding economic output and failed to mollify American resentments. The theory of collective goods is helpful in understanding why Japan resisted mounting US pressures. Such behaviour is not unique to Japan; it is characteristic of alliance states faced with the same set of incentives created by the nature of collective goods.

Phase III: Post-Cold War Challenges: Path Dependency

The third phase of JASA begins with the fall of the Berlin Wall (1989), a momentous event that dramatically transformed the structure of the world system (as well as the dynamics of JASA). The end of the cold war altered national incentives for both the United States and Japan. The dismemberment of the Soviet Empire removed the most dangerous common threat that had brought the two nations together in common defence. Not having to worry about the Soviet threat, the United States took off its gloves and used bare-knuckles diplomacy to coerce Japan into altering its mercantilist trade practices. Japan responded by resisting US blandishments and seeking to curtail America's unilateral power by insisting that the United States abide by the multilateral rules and procedures as set forth under GATT. Though strained by economic spats, JASA has remained intact. One reason is that the security picture in Northeast Asia is ominously uncertain, and both Japan and America are worried about the danger of instability on the Korean peninsula and the far-reaching implications of China's rise as a military power. Whether JASA can survive and adapt to the ever-changing circumstances of the post-cold war environment is open to question. The theory of path-dependency provides perhaps the most pessimistic forecast of JASA's future capacity to adapt.

4.4 HYPOTHESIS

This chapter draws on all three theories cited above. It argues that JASA is a combination of elements from all three theories but that the alliance's evolving nature makes a separate theory the best explanation and predictor for each of the three specific phases. It advances the hypothesis that security alliances involving partners of unequal power are fraught with tensions arising from a basic clash of incentives and from disparities in power and roles. The weaker partner will seek to minimize the costs and responsibilities associated with its own national security while simultaneously seeking to reduce its dependence on the protector and to curtail the protector's capacity unilaterally to impose its will. Similarly acting on self-interest, the stronger state will seek to shift more of the burdens of the alliance on to its dependent partner while simultaneously trying to retain its power to dictate outcomes. The incompatibility of national incentives will give rise to complaints about 'free-riding' on the part of the protector and about 'arbitrary unilateralism' on the part of the protected. The complaints will grow louder as the relative power of the two allies shifts, with the weaker state making significant gains relative to its dominant partner.

Over time, the incentive structures and relative national power capabilities are bound to change, and so too is the external security environment. If the changes are major, they will necessitate modifications in the structure and function of the alliance; otherwise, the alliance may cease to be effective. But the need to modify the terms of the alliance will run into the problem of path-dependency, especially the obstacle of inertia stemming from domestic structures largely put in place during the formative years of the alliance. The term, path-dependency, refers here to embedded institutions, routine practices, vested interests, ingrained expectations, ideological doctrines, legal constraints, and inertia. Owing to path-dependency, major modifications of the alliance will be difficult to administer, even though incremental changes may be possible. To make major changes, a serious external crisis or series of crises will be needed as catalysts and justification. Even if national incentives change from free-riding to more equitable cost-sharing, and even if the gap in relative power is narrowed, accordingly, the capacity of the two allies to transform the nature of the alliance will be limited by the 'lock-in' effect of path-dependency.

4.5 PHASE I: 1952–71

To understand the evolving nature and dynamics of JASA within the context of the ever-changing security environment requires that several key variables be analysed over the course of JASA's existence. This section will divide JASA into three periods and seek to answer the basic conundrum – namely, why the asymmetry in the distribution of alliance costs, risks, and rewards persists – in terms of the following factors:

- Relative US and Japan economic capabilities
- External security environment
- Incentive structures
- Safety mechanisms
- Main threats to JASA's continued existence.

Legacy of the Cold War: 1952–71

The conundrum is easy to explain for the first phase of the US–Japan alliance, 1952–71. This was the height of the cold war and the golden age of American hegemony. US supremacy was embodied in the Bretton Woods system of fixed exchange rates pegged to the US dollar. The United States possessed both the incentive and economic capacity to accept the asymmetry inherent in its alliance with Japan. In the arc of containment against communism that the United States drew in the Asia–Pacific, running from Hokkaido down through Australia and New Zealand, Japan functioned as the linchpin both in terms of geo-strategic location and politico-economic centrality.

The location of the Japanese archipelago off the Asian continent gave the United States an ideal geo-strategic position to deploy air, naval and marine forces. US naval facilities in Sasebo and Yokosuke allowed the Seventh Fleet to patrol the Pacific Ocean without having to return all the way to Guam or Hawaii to refuel and to undergo servicing and repairs. Japan's location also offered the US and Japanese navies the opportunity to control what can be called 'strategic choke points' in the Pacific Ocean – that is, entry ways to the deep waters of the Pacific for Soviet ships and submarines leaving from bases in the Far East, such as Vladivostock and Petropavlovsk. The 'choke points' include the Soya Straits (between Hokkaido and Sakhalin), Tsugaru Straits (between Hokkaido and Honshu), and the Tsushima Straits (between Japan and South Korea). In theory, the three entry ways provide the American and Japanese navies with the possibility of bottling up the Soviet Far Eastern fleet during a military crisis or war.

Thanks in part to the existence of key naval bases in Japan, the US Seventh Fleet ruled the Pacific both during and after the cold war. No foreign power in modern history – not Spain, Russia, or Japan – not even Great Britain, dominated the Pacific as did the US Navy.[5] Indeed, from 1945–96, it was no exaggeration to call the Pacific Ocean an 'American lake'.

Nor was Japan's strategic value for the United States confined to the navy. From air bases in Kadena (Okinawa), Misawa, Atsugi and Yokota, the US Air Force was in striking distance for missions to Korea and Taiwan and even as far away as Vietnam and the Middle East. Moreover, from forward bases in Okinawa, US marine troops could be deployed rapidly to most hypothetical 'hot spots' in Northeast Asia; as the first wave of troops arriving on the scene, they could hold on until reinforcements arrived from San Diego and other bases in the United States.

Thus, from a military point of view, Japan was of extraordinary geo-strategic value. No country in Asia could have offered the prime location that Japan offered for America's East Asian arc of cold war containment – not

Korea, Taiwan or the Philippines (though they also offer strategic positions). Japan's location is comparable to that of the United Kingdom, which stands astride Europe's gateway to the Atlantic. Japan's geo-strategic value is arguably even greater than that of the UK, not only because of the proximity of the major communist powers – the Soviet Union, China and North Korea – but also because of the much greater length of Japan's archipelago (comprising roughly 7 000 islands) – stretching over 3 000 kilometres, from Hokkaido all the way down to the China Sea (close to the Tropic of Cancer). This stretch represents a total land area 1.5 times the size of the United Kingdom.

Paying the lion's share of costs associated with the US–Japan alliance in exchange for the right to deploy US forces in critical locations along the arc of containment in Northeast Asia had to be worth the fiscal outlays, however heavy. Never mind Japan's political and economic importance as America's closest ally in Asia; US bases in Okinawa and Japan were of sufficient strategic value to the United States that they justified the payment of disproportionate costs.

The onset of the cold war in the late 1940s prompted American government officials, like John Foster Dulles, who was appointed to negotiate peace and security treaties with Japan, to press Prime Minister Yoshida Shigeru in 1950 to establish a defence force of 325 000 to 350 000. Although Yoshida agreed that Japan would have to have its own self-defense force (SDF), he resisted Dulles's proposal that an SDF of 350 000 be organized. That figure was far too large. Yoshida cited a variety of reasons for rejecting it:

1. Domestic political opposition by leftist forces
2. Questions about the SDF's constitutionality
3. The need to uphold the principle of civilian control over the military
4. Negative reactions throughout East Asia to Japan's mobilization of such a large SDF
5. The low likelihood of an external invasion or attack
6. The fear of being pulled into participation in the Korean War
7. The big economic burdens that such an SDF force would impose on Japan at a time when Japan desperately needed to pull itself out from the rubble of the Pacific War.

Of the above reasons, the final one was paramount. Economic recovery and growth constituted the *sine qua non* for political stability in Japan. Yoshida argued that Japan lacked the fiscal flexibility to underwrite so large an SDF organization. A heavy budgetary burden would undermine Japan's efforts to get back on its economic feet, and economic recovery had to be regarded as the country's highest priority. If Japan remained an economic basket case, Japan would always be prone to instability and its volatility would pose a constant threat to American national interests.[6]

Yoshida's argument carried the day. John Foster Dulles and the US government backed off their initial demands; but the US government expressed a wish that Japan gradually expand the SDF over time in accordance with an expansion of its economic output. The United States, in short, was willing to accept a low level of burden-sharing by Japan for longer-run economic and political goals; and over the short run, the US could reap the immeasurable benefit of having military base facilities, equipment, and troops stationed in Japan.

During its first phase, 1952–71, the biggest threat to JASA's existence resided in Japan: specifically, leftist opposition to the initial signing of the treaty, revision of the treaty in 1960, and its extension in 1970. It even took deft political handling by Prime Minister Yoshida to secure parliamentary ratification of the security treaty in 1951.[7] In 1960, leftist students and labour unions led mass demonstrations in the streets of Tokyo, protesting forcible passage of the revised security treaty. Not only did the demonstrations bring down Prime Minister Kishi Nobusuke and his Cabinet; it also made the Japanese and American governments wary of taking future steps that might rekindle mass protests. From 1960 until 1996, the United States and Japan adopted a low profile with respect to JASA, eschewing any moves that might give leftist forces justification to re-ignite protests.

From 1952–71, there was little chance that political opponents in the United States would act unilaterally to abrogate the treaty. Because US leaders were well aware of the strategic importance of US military bases in Japan, JASA enjoyed strong bipartisan support. The only threat to JASA emanated from ideologically driven, Marxist opponents in Japan. The United States had strong incentives, accordingly, to do everything possible to avoid stepping on the dragon's tail. Such incentives represented another reason why America was willing to shoulder the lion's share of alliance burdens without complaint.

Japan's Political And Economic Importance

As essential as the military bases in Japan were during the cold war, the political and economic benefits of entering into an alliance with Japan were at least as great, if not greater. Bear in mind the historical context within which JASA was established. The Cold war began in the late 1940s and spread rapidly to East Asia. By 1952, the communist tide appeared to be rising. The communists had won control of China in 1949; the Korean War erupted in 1950; communist insurgencies threatened to oust existing regimes in such pivotal countries as Malaysia, the Philippines and Vietnam. In Japan, the Communist and Socialist Parties, allied with militant labour unions and left-wing student groups, had become powerful forces.

Facing the communist tide, the United States hastened to sign defence treaties with Japan, South Korea and SEATO (Southeast Asian Treaty Organization). Not only did the security treaties provide defence assurances for Japan and South Korea; they also placed the two countries firmly in the Western camp, foreclosing any possibility that they might join the communist camp.

From the outset, Japan behaved as a loyal ally. It demonstrated fealty to the United States by recognizing Taiwan, not the People's Republic, as the legitimate government of China, despite considerable sentiment within Japan that it should not take steps that would turn the People's Republic needlessly into an adversary. Japan also kept a discreet distance from the Soviet Union and other satellite states in the communist orbit. And on a variety of controversial foreign policy fronts, Japan lined up next to the United States. For example, Japan took a pro-Israel stance in the Arab–Israel conflict; it refused to recognize the Democratic People's Republic of Korea; and unlike France under De Gaulle, Japan seldom voiced open criticisms of the United States.

In the high-stakes game of cold war chess, Japan was without question the prize in East Asia. The United States could not stand idly by and let postwar Japan fall into the hands of a hostile power, like the Soviet Union; nor could it allow Japan to feel so vulnerable that Japan would comply with Soviet blandishments and external intimidation (the so-called problem of 'Finlandization'). In the minds of key American strategists, like George Kennan, Japan not only had to be given credible assurances about its national security; the United States also had to extend a helping hand so that Japan could become prosperous and democratic.[8]

Japan's political and economic centrality was based on the perception that it represented the one indigenous nation in East Asia capable of rebuilding its industrial infrastructure and dominating the region. To prevent a revanchist Japan from re-emerging as a destabilizing force in the region (as happened in interwar Europe), it was absolutely essential that Japan grow economically and transform itself into a stable, capitalist democracy, a full-fledged member of the non-communist camp. If Japan's economy failed to recover quickly from the devastation wrought by the Pacific War, its political system might have trouble trying to cope with such unsettling problems as high unemployment, labour strife and low disposable income. Political instability would turn Japan into a fertile breeding ground for extremism – either communism or right-wing nationalism.

Think about the impact an unstable Japan would have had on South Korea, Taiwan and other countries in East Asia, which were struggling mightily to dig themselves out of the rubble of war. To achieve prosperity and peace, East Asia needed a catalyst, a pacesetter, a model of economic development to emulate (the so-called 'demonstration effect'). Given its proven track record as the first latecomer outside the West to industrialize, Japan held out the best hope of kick-starting economic recovery and industrial growth throughout East Asia. Rapid growth, in turn, would create optimal circumstances for the liberalization of trade and investments, a high-priority goal for the United States in restructuring the global economic order.

Another reason why the United States was eager to see Japan's economy back on its feet again was to ensure that the United States would be spared the onerous burden of supplying foreign aid to keep Japan solvent, a per the Marshall Plan. From 1945–48, the US government had provided Japan with more than $750 million in direct assistance. By the end of the Occupation in 1952, the cumulative figure is estimated to have reached $2 billion.[9] No wonder sentiment in the US Congress supported Japan's reintegration into the world economy. With the task of rehabilitating Western Europe as the highest priority, American legislators did not want the federal budget to strain under the weight of Japan's economic hardships.

American Support

Direct aid was not the only form of American assistance. The United States also interceded on Japan's behalf to moderate demands put forth by East Asian countries which had suffered from Japanese military occupation. John Foster Dulles believed that, in order for Japan to have a fair chance of recovering from the war, the East Asian victims of Japanese aggression had to scale back their reparation demands. He argued that excessive demands might boomerang if Japan had to default on payments.[10]

Whether America's support was decisive or not, the level of demand for war reparations was reduced sharply. Japan got off the hook lightly. It wound up paying a total of $1.15 billion. While the amount may seem large, given the devastated state of Japan's economy, $1.15 billion was not an onerous burden, because it consisted mainly of the provision of capital goods manufactured in Japan (with raw materials supplied from the recipient Asian countries). Japan also extended $707 million in loans, most of which were tied to the purchase of Japanese goods.[11] War reparations thus had the effect of stimulating the Japanese economy and helping it secure economic footholds in Southeast Asia.

Of greater assistance than its intercession on demands for war reparations was America's assistance in Japan's on going efforts to cope with its balance of payments problem. For Japan, a country lacking in natural resources and severely strapped for capital in the early postwar years, the need to keep the current account deficit within an acceptable range posed a chronic problem. Because Japan was unable to balance its international payments through normal channels of merchandise trade, the United States agreed in 1953 to offer military procurement orders as a mechanism to ease the squeeze of current account deficits. Military procurements and spillover spending connected with the Korean War generated much-needed foreign exchange as well as a substantial impetus for Japan's economic recovery.

America's willingness to use military procurements and other forms of security assistance to help Japan get back on its economic feet and its reluctance to impose an excessive burden on Japan's economy were written into the text of the Mutual Defense Assistance Agreement, signed in 1954. The language of the Agreement makes explicit reference to the relationship between defence and economics: 'In the planning of a defense assistance program for Japan, economic stability will be an essential element for consideration in the development of its defense capacities, and ... Japan can contribute only to the extent permitted by its general economic conditions and capacities.'[12] Clearly, the United States assigned a high *security* priority to Japan's return to sound *economic health.* Acting out of its own national interests as the hegemonic state in East Asia, the United States willingly administered a variety of policy measures – ranging from direct foreign assistance to military procurements – to facilitate Japan's economic recovery.

Alliance Burdens and Benefits

In its initial phase, JASA is best explained by the theory of hegemonic power. To construct the edifice of a preponderant power in East Asia, the United States was willing to take on the lion's share of costs of an alliance with Japan, including the burdens of helping Japan recover from the ravages of war and sustain full-speed economic growth. Having neither the capacity nor the will, Japan was in no position to shoulder an equitable share of the costs. In exchange for assuming the lion's share of costs, the United States reaped significant benefits, including:

- A dominant voice and influence *vis-à-vis* Japan
- Preponderant political and economic power in East Asia
- A peaceful, non-threatening Japan (the one country in East Asia with the industrial potential to build itself back into a potent military power).
- Japan's unwavering membership in the Western camp

- Japan's willingness to centre its foreign policy around the axis of the US–Japan relationship and to 'follow the American leader' on most foreign policy issues (including non-recognition of the PRC and DPRK)
- A key ally in America's political–diplomatic struggles against communism and communist ideology and a pivotal economic actor in capitalism's competition against socialism
- Japanese economic development as the trigger for economic recovery and growth throughout East Asia (a catalyst)
- Japan became a showcase for the viability of capitalist democracy in East Asia (undergoing a paradigm shift)
- Japan's successful integration in a world economic system based on liberal norms, rules and ideals.

If the United States realized substantial benefits that justified the assumption of significant costs, what can be said about the advantages to Japan, the other side of the alliance equation? What benefits accrued to Japan as a result of JASA? For Japan, the package of benefits was enormous, especially considering the low costs and risks incurred and the lack of viable alternatives to JASA. The advantages to Japan included:

- A secure position under the foreign policy umbrella of the strongest nation-state in the world:
- The spillover benefits of US global leadership on matters related to the international political economy and especially with respect to specific international economic organizations, such as the OECD, IMF, World Bank and GATT
- Alleviation of Japan's prewar anxieties concerning its economic security as a resource-poor island nation, especially access to overseas resources and raw materials as well as access to overseas markets for Japan's manufactured products
- Optimal circumstances for rapid economic growth and democratization
- American intercession to moderate Asian demands for Japanese wartime reparation payments
- A major infusion of American foreign aid during a time of dire need
- Substantial military procurements designed to boost Japan's economy (as part of the US–Japan Mutual Defense Assistance Agreement)
- A comparatively light fiscal burden for national defence
- Time for Japan to develop a national consensus on its postwar international orientation – leading to the formulation of the so-called 'Yoshida Doctrine'

- The luxury of side-stepping domestic controversy and possible polarization over contentious foreign policy choices and national security demands
- Time to allow Asian countries that had suffered from Japanese military aggression to heal their wounds and normalize postwar relations with Japan.

What made Japan's package of benefits so substantial was not only the low costs and risks incurred, but also Japan's lack of viable alternatives to alliance with the United States. While allying with the United States meant the acceptance of certain constraints, such as conforming broadly to America's cold war containment policies, there were no alternative powers with which Japan could align – not Great Britain or other European states and certainly not the Soviet Union or China. No other country measured up to the United States in terms of military, political and economic clout. From 1952–71 America was clearly the hegemonic power. No other potential ally offered the same generous package of advantages. Neutrality may have been an alternative; but neutrality probably would have required a more rapid pace of rearmament than Japan was willing to undertake (or the region prepared to accommodate).

Thus, JASA came into being and functioned as an alliance that benefited the United States and Japan immeasurably. True, from JASA's inception through the period of early development (1952–71), the United States bore a disproportionate share of the costs; but that was the price of building a regional system that institutionalized America's preponderance. As the hegemonic power, America had both the capacity and the will to take on the alliance burdens. Until the 1970s, Japan was limited in what it could contribute by the overriding priority given to economic reconstruction and growth. Fortunately for Japan, the United States understood and accepted this priority. During JASA's initial phase, in short, the United States willingly paid the asymmetric costs of the alliance as the price of establishing a hegemonic presence in East Asia.

4.6 PHASE II: 1971–89

The Power Shift

JASA's second phase, 1971–89, saw the relative power positions of the United States and Japan shift dramatically. America's imperial power declined steadily while Japan's economy continued to climb. In statistical terms, the regression towards the mean was not surprising, given the opposite poles from which the two economies started out; but the sheer speed of Japan's growth exceeded expectations. Between 1952 and 1971, Japan grew twice as fast as the United States (though Japan began from a much lower base). This led to a sharp narrowing of the US–Japan power gap. In 1952, Japan's economy was 7 per cent the size of the US economy; but by 1970, it had climbed to 35 per cent. Japan was no longer the small, fragile economy that had to be nursed back to health in 1952. Its GNP in 1970 ranked as the world's third largest.

By 1980, Japan had expanded to 45 per cent the size of the US economy, making Japan's GNP the world's second largest. In 1987, Japan's GNP reached half the size of that of America. So from 1952–89, covering the first two phases of JASA, Japan took giant strides forward (Figure 4.1). Its economy went from 7 per cent to 50 per cent the size of America's; and bear in mind that during this period, the US economy was hardly standing still. The gap between Japan and the United States continued to shrink. Japan moved from 53 per cent in 1990 to 68 percent in 1994 (but the shrinkage was largely a result of the yen's steep appreciation relative to the dollar).

In 1971, President Nixon abandoned the Bretton Woods system of fixed exchange rates and moved to a system of floating exchange rates. The value of the US dollar fell from 360 yen to 310 yen and continued its free fall over the next two decades. The Plaza Accord in 1985 pushed the weakening dollar farther downward; the dollar–yen exchange dropped from 240 (1985) to 180 (1986). The collapse of the Bretton Woods system in 1971 marked the end of the era of American hegemony. The dollar devaluation undercut America's relative standard of living. And in spite of the higher price tag of imported goods, American consumers continued buying Japanese automobiles and consumer electronics, leading to ballooning trade deficits.

In the realm of national security, America's failure to win the war in Vietnam represented another, more graphic illustration of the relative decline in American power. In spite of its vast superiority in military firepower, the US could not subdue the Vietnamese communists. This dealt a serious blow to US credibility. America's intervention in Vietnam was also costly in a fiscal sense, opening the floodgates of deficit spending that over the years reached the swollen, cumulative level of $5 trillion (1995), roughly 70 per cent of America's GDP. The combination of costs associated with the Vietnam War and the inauguration of the Great Society sent the United States sliding down a slippery slope from which it has yet to recover.

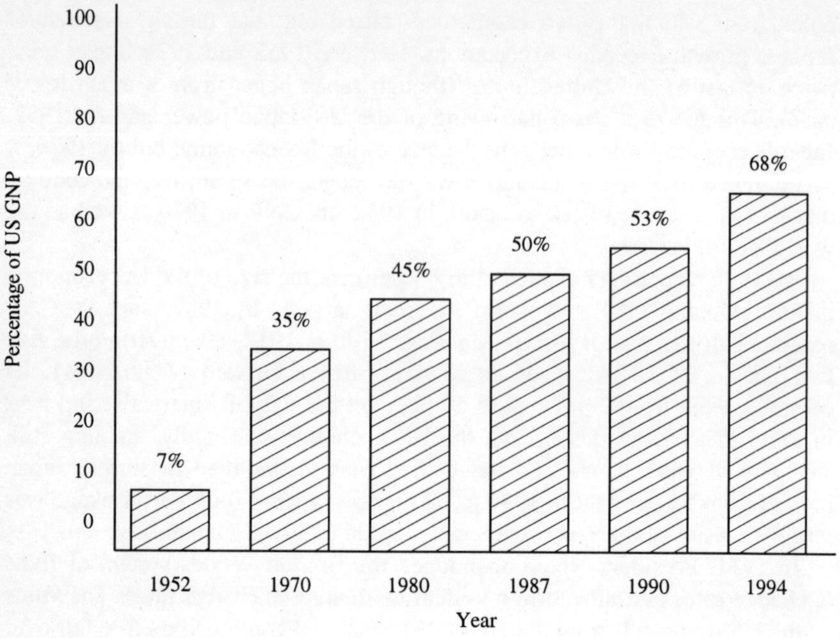

Figure 4.1 Relative size of the Japanese economy

But America's setback in Vietnam led, ironically, to a series of adjustments that softened the full force of America's humiliation. To make up for the damage done to its credibility, to restructure the security system in East Asia, and to strengthen its position *vis-à-vis* the Soviet Union, the United States pulled off a diplomatic coup – namely, normalizing ties with China. In a single bold stroke, the United States set up the framework for a new and more stable security system in East Asia. In the wake of the communist victory in Vietnam, ASEAN also took steps to solidify its ranks. And alarmed by the prospect of a possible US withdrawal from Asia, Japan sought ways of strengthening JASA, including expanding joint military manoeuvres. Thus, the communist victory in Vietnam set off a chain reaction of diplomatic manoeuvres that counteracted the most damaging consequences. But these compensating steps could not mask the stark reality that the United States had suffered a costly setback and that the curtain had fallen on the old era of American hegemony.

Japan's rapid rise and America's relative decline altered JASA's structure and underlying dynamics. It changed the way Americans looked at the initial bargain struck in JASA, Phase I. It prompted Americans to demand that changes be made in the original bargain. The power shift also gave rise to a chorus of complaints about the 'unfair' distribution of costs and benefits associated with JASA. Because Japan had risen out of the ashes of war, taking its place as the country with the second biggest GNP in the world, Japan clearly had become capable of assuming more of the burdens of its own national defence. Certainly it was in a position to contribute a lot more than it could have in 1952.

Bilateral Trade Imbalances

During JASA's second phase, 1971–89, US–Japan trade captured the limelight as the most riveting and contentious issue on the bilateral agenda. From 1970, Japan's trade balance with the United States turned from a ledger of chronic deficits to surging surpluses. As the bilateral trade imbalance grew progressively larger, more and more American leaders came to voice criticisms of Japan's trade practices. US trade officials came up with a growing list of grievances against Japan, ranging from export dumping and protection of domestic markets to industrial policy targeting and non-level playing fields. The complaints rose to acrimonious and loud levels. The governments of the two countries engaged in protracted negotiations, leading to a variety of bilateral agreements, such as voluntary export restraints (VERs) on Japanese automobiles.

The size of America's trade deficit with Japan, multiplying from $2.5 billion in 1971 to $52 billion in 1987, became politically hard to manage. Although many Americans understood that focusing on the bilateral deficit made no sense within a system of multilateral trade, the size of the bilateral deficit came to be viewed as the sole barometer of 'fairness' in trade. Japan came to be seen as an 'adversarial' trade partner, a predatory power intent on achieving the goal of displacing the United States as the *numero uno* in the world. Japan's image in the United States underwent a change. It came to be seen less as a strategically pivotal ally and more as a pernicious commercial rival and potent threat to America's economic supremacy.

Japan's emergence as an economic superpower and America's struggle to cope with an array of vexing and seemingly insoluble problems such as huge fiscal and trade deficits, plummeting public trust in government, skyrocketing divorce rates, and uncontrolled drugs and crime gave rise to an intellectual climate receptive to the articulation and spread of 'revisionist' ideas. The revisionists took exception to mainstream images of Japan offered by traditional interpreters of that country.[13]

From the early 1950s to the mid-1980s, American attitudes toward Japan were influenced by scholars, like Edwin Reischauer, who had grown up in Japan as children of Christian missionaries or who, like Chitoshi Yanaga, were *nisei* (second-generation Japanese Americans) at first-rate American universities or who, like Robert Scalapino, were recruited for Japanese language training by the US military during World War II. Labelled 'traditionalists', these scholars prided themselves on their deep immersion in, and subtle understanding of, Japanese history, culture, and society. The image of Japan that they portrayed was positive: dynamic, democratic, responsible, adaptive and loyal – a constructive force in world affairs. The message that the traditionalists preached, over and over again, was simple: the US–Japan relationship is the most important bilateral alliance in the world. It is absolutely essential that the two allies work to keep the alliance strong. Regional peace and prosperity hinge on it. Until 1985, this sermon was accepted as gospel.

Japan In Revisionist Eyes

The traditional image of Japan came to be challenged around 1985 by a small, heterogeneous group of 'revisionists', most notably James Fallows and Karl van Wolferen, who painted a more cynical picture. The revisionists portrayed Japan as quasi-democratic, passive-aggressive, protectionist, collusive, a free-rider, and motivated less by loyalty than by the force of powerful national self-interest. Breaking with the old orthodoxy of traditional assumptions, revisionism offered several new propositions to guide America's interactions with Japan:

- Japan poses a serious threat to American interests.
- The national interests of Japan and America are compatible in some areas but clash in others.
- Where national objectives clash, the United States must be vigilant to defend and promote its own interests.
- Ignore what neoclassical economists say; bilateral trade deficits do matter, and Japan's lopsided surpluses are inflicting significant damage on the US economy and America's quality of life.
- The United States must overcome a natural propensity to give top priority to national security and to sacrifice economic interests for the sake of military security.
- As an insular nation-state, having had only a brief interlude of 'normal' contact with the West, Japan is a unique and prickly country to deal with.
- In its eagerness to maintain alliance solidarity, the United States has been exceedingly naive in its assessment of Japanese intentions, behaviour, goals and strategies.
- The only effective way of dealing with Japan is to focus on a set of specific issues and to apply sustained pressures to achieve desired outcomes, backed by credible threats of sanctions.

- Practising a modern version of mercantilism, Japan is taking unfair advantage of the United States by penetrating open US markets, keeping Japan's own markets closed, free-riding on basic research at American universities, and relying on the United States to provide the basic collective goods such as global leadership and military protection.
- The Japanese are masters at resisting foreign pressures; they are skilled at stonewalling, spending huge sums for lobbying in Washington, using abstract macroeconomic theory as a cover for mercantilist practices, claiming that their hands are tied by domestic constraints, making last-minute concessions only grudgingly, and then dragging their feet on implementation, hoping that bilateral agreements will be forgotten.
- Considering its high degree of dependence on the United States, and the limited alternatives to JASA, Japan has still managed to extract much of what it has wanted from the United States.
- Insisting that Japan rectify unfair commercial practices does not jeopardize JASA; external pressures can be applied on the economic front without destroying security cooperation.

The main tenets of revisionist doctrine raise questions about how the United States should be dealing with Japan, a military ally but also at the same time a formidable commercial rival. Probably the biggest impact that revisionist notions have had on US policy has been to elevate the priority given to trade issues and to favour a hard-line stance in negotiations with Japan, insisting on concrete results and the use of quantitative indicators to measure progress made (such as market share expansion). This approach, subsequently adopted by the first Clinton Administration, came to be called derisively 'managed trade'.

Japan Bashing

Although the revisionists cannot be accused of irresponsible journalism, the criticisms levelled at Japan by other, less reputable writers went to emotional extremes, taking rhetorical forms that bordered on racism and demagoguery. A whole new popular genre sprung into existence, called 'Japan bashing'.

Japan became the favourite whipping-boy of individuals and groups with specific axes to grind. There were popular books and articles written about Japan's plot to conquer the world, to re-establish the Greater East Asia Co-Prosperity Sphere, and to turn the United States into a Japanese colony. There was even a prediction that another war with Japan was looming on the horizon.

Japan bashing reached a low point when a few US Congressmen gathered on Capitol Hill to smash consumer electronic products made in Japan as a message of protest. Appalled by the ugly episode, Japanese television stations broadcasted the event repeatedly so as to let the mood of anti-Japanese racism sink in. The Japanese reacted to Japan bashing with their own form of 'America bashing'. Thus, emotions ran high on both sides of the Pacific – though public opinion as a whole remained remarkably even-keeled amid the nastiness of the verbal exchanges.

Members of the US Congress voiced shrill complaints about unfair trade practices and Japan's free security ride. While the US federal government was sinking 25 per cent of its budget into defence (neglecting urgent social needs), Japan was spared the burden of having to allocate more than 6 per cent of its budget, thanks to protection provided by the US military umbrella. The inference was simple but inaccurate: the US taxpayer was having money taken out of his pocket and placed directly into the hands of the Japanese taxpayer. It was a transfer payment. The United States was being taken for a ride – a free ride.

National Incentives

The shift in relative power capabilities altered the incentive structure for the United States. The desire to off-load alliance costs grew stronger during the second phase of JASA because America was feeling the pain of fiscal overstretch and because the Japanese economy had grown so big that it clearly could afford to absorb the costs of its own defence. Indeed, Japan's rapid rise as an economic power became the source of some resentment and fear. To alarmists in America, Japan seemed hell-bent on establishing dominance in nearly all sectors that mattered – automobiles, consumer electronics, construction, information technology, biotechnology and financial services. And what was galling to Americans was the perception that the Japanese were refusing to play by universal rules of fair competition. Thus, the US moved to implement a two-track strategy:

1. seeking to curb unfair practices and level the non-level playing field while
2. persuading Japan to accept more of the burdens of the security alliance. The political mood in the US demanded greater hard-headedness in both the economic and security domains.

For Japan, by contrast, the set of incentives remained largely the same. Even though it had climbed to second place among the world's economic giants, Japan still wanted to entrust its security to JASA and to extend the initial bargain struck in 1952: namely, having the United States pay for the favourable balance of power in East Asia (sustained by Japan's membership in the Western camp) and to pay a premium for Japan's yielding of voice and influence to the United States. What Japan wanted, in short, was to extend the free ride for as long as possible.

Since, however, the US was turning up the heat on Japan to assume more of the costs (in keeping with its rising economic affluence), Japan could hardly expect the original bargain to hold up indefinitely – not when the US–Japan power shift had altered the foundations on which JASA rested; and not when severe trade conflicts had forced their way on to the alliance agenda. Consequently, if Japan's hands were tied on military expenditures, as Japan repeatedly claimed, what could Japan do to mollify American demands for more equitable burden sharing? What 'side payments' might Japan make to ease tensions? What 'safety valves' could be opened to release pent-up pressures?

Safety Valves

To minimize conflicts with opposition parties over military matters, the ruling conservative party in Japan placed a *de facto* cap on defence spending at 1 per cent of GNP. The hard ceiling has had the desired effect of defusing the volatility of an issue that had the potential of turning into a highly confrontational problem. Since the mid-1960s, all Japanese Cabinets have adhered to the 1 per cent ceiling. In consequence, few political battles have broken the truce in the Diet.

In partial response to US accusations that Japan is guilty of free-riding, the Japanese have pointed out that very rapid rates of economic growth have lifted the absolute amount of money spent on national defence (see Figure 4.2). The 1 per cent ceiling, they maintain, is misleading. It masks the steady climb in absolute levels of spending. In dollar amounts, Japan spent more for defence in 1985 than either Italy or China. Indeed, according to government statistics, Japan ranked seventh in the world in terms of actual money spent. By 1993, Japan had moved up to third place – behind only the United States and Russia and well ahead of France, Germany and the United Kingdom. But this line of argument has failed to mollify free-ride critics.

The mechanism that has released the most pent-up pressure has been host-nation support. Host-nation support covers maintenance costs for US base facilities as well as salaries for Japanese employees working on US bases. The expenditure passes Diet scrutiny as a line item on the budget; the expenditures are 'civilian' in the sense that they are not being used to purchase military hardware or to underwrite military exercises and operations.

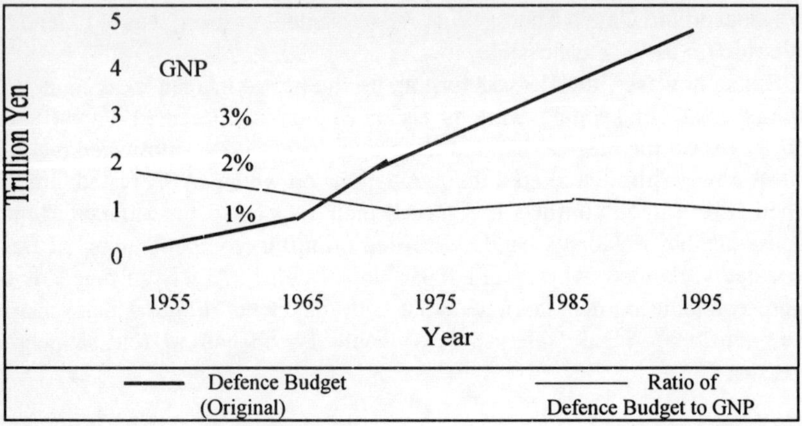

Figure 4.2 Defence spending in Japan

Japan began giving host-nation support in order to offset the rising costs of operating US base facilities (owing to rising labour and material costs and yen appreciation). From a low baseline, the amount has risen steadily over the years, reaching $2.4 billion in 1987 and covering 39 per cent of the total costs of maintaining US bases in Japan (see Figure 4.3). If the $2.4 billion had been added to Japan's defence expenditures (and it is factored into defence spending data for NATO countries), Japan would have broken the 1 per cent ceiling.

Japan has gained a lot of political mileage out of host-nation support. Japan's willingness to open its wallet to facilitate US forward deployments has probably done more to appease angry hawks on Capitol Hill than any other policy measure. Japan has been hailed as the country that pays more host-nation support than other ally – Germany, other NATO members or South Korea. Pentagon officials highly appreciated Japan's contribution. They said that it made forward deployments in East Asia sufficiently cost-effective that cost-cutting measures, such as troop reductions or withdrawal, did not have to be carried out. It was cheaper to maintain strong force deployments in East Asia as a deterrent than it would have been to deal with conflicts that broke out (in the absence of a credible deterrent). Thus, host-nation support has functioned not only as a safety valve to ease bilateral tensions but also as a justification to continue forward deployments in East Asia. No wonder host-nation support has pleased the US Department of Defense.

Procurements of American military hardware is another safety valve that Japan has utilized to keep the bilateral alliance harmonious. Over the years, Japan has purchased missiles, fighter jet aircraft, helicopters, AWACs and other advanced weapon systems. Under the Carter Administration, the two countries agreed to adopt common technical standards so as to achieve inter-operability of military equipment. The plan, aimed at facilitating coordination of American and Japanese forces, has yielded the spillover benefit of locking the JDA into acquiring US military hardware. As a result, nearly all of Japan's arms imports come from the United States. The amounts spent have helped, modestly, to reduce America's trade deficit with Japan (see Figure 4.4).

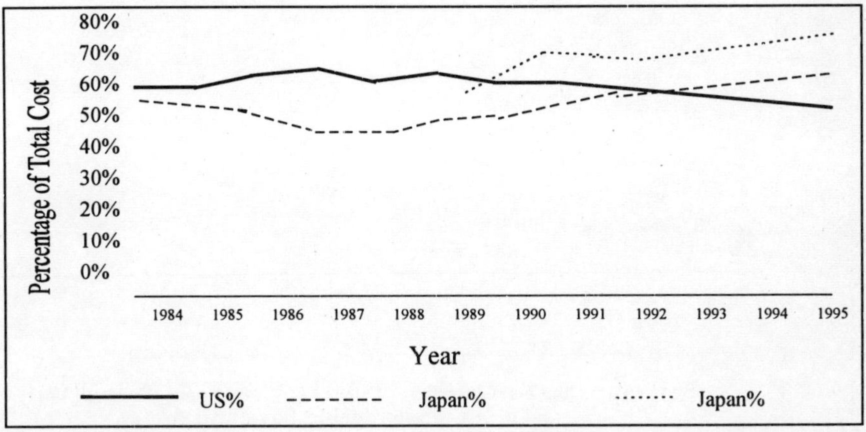

Source: A Strategic Framework for the Asian Pacific Rim, *Report to Congress*, Department of Defence.

Figure 4.3 Japanese host nation support

As manufactured imports from the United States, Japanese military procurements have served three purposes:

1. responding constructively to free-ride accusations;
2. advancing the goal of equipment inter-operability; and
3. contributing to the reduction of the US–Japan trade imbalance. Like host-nation support, arms purchases are a timely and useful safety valve mechanism. Without such mechanisms bilateral tensions might have reached levels that inflicted serious damage on JASA.

Unlike host-nation support, however, military procurement can produce undesirable outcomes. If certain expected purchases fail to be made or if procurements lead to the transfer of state-of-the-art, dual-purpose technology, which is then used for commercial products, the whole area of military procurements can backfire. It can breed disillusionment, resentment and mistrust.

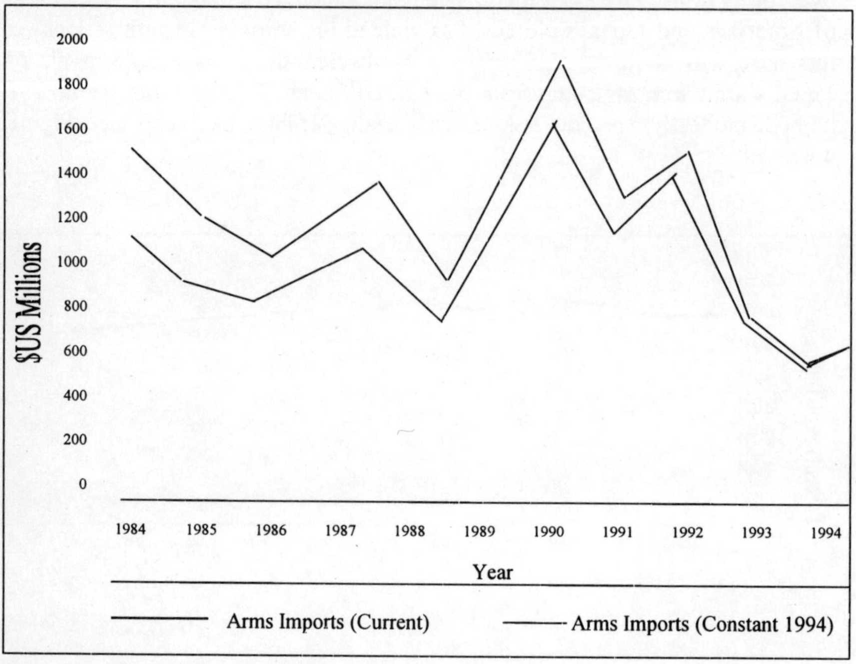

Source: ACDA World Figures

Figure 4.4 Arms imports to Japan

This is exactly what happened in the controversial case of the FSX programme.[14] JASA came to the brink of a potential rupture when the United States thought Japan should purchase the F-16 US fighter jet aircraft off the shelf as the most cost-effective option; but Japan wanted to design and build its own fighter jet aircraft in order to develop its own autonomous base of technology. Under heavy pressure from the US, which urged Japan to do everything within its power to lower the trade imbalance, Japan decided to compromise by manufacturing its next generation of fighter aircraft, FSX, under licence from the US, with the promise of giving US aerospace companies a large slice of the production pie. But a number of US policy makers saw the compromise as a Japanese stratagem to obtain state-of-the-art, dual-purpose technology, which Japan would turn around and use to further its own commercial interests. The cynics believed that the FSX programme revealed Japan's true colours: a callous disregard for the trade imbalance and a lack of loyalty. Their opposition very nearly succeeded in killing the compromise that Japan proposed. Only a razor-thin margin of support in Congress pulled the two countries back from the brink of what might have been a disastrous turn of events.

Non-Military Safety Valves

To curb growing US complaints about Japan's free ride, Prime Minister Ohira, in 1978, floated the idea of 'comprehensive security' as a framework for defining and expanding Japan's role in world and regional affairs. What Ohira had in mind in bringing up the concept of comprehensive security was for Japan to concentrate on contributing to the non-military aspects of national security, such as foreign assistance to developing economies (especially ODA, official development assistance), energy security, environmental protection and health care. He believed that the non-military areas of national security were as vital to peace and stability as military manpower and hardware. Japan happened to be in a strong position to answer criticisms of free-riding by stepping up its contributions to the non-military areas of national security.

Comprehensive security is based on an explicit division of labour: the United States would continue taking responsibility for maintaining the military balance of power in East Asia; and Japan would step up to the plate and play an expanded role in the vital economic areas of national security. The division of labour appeared to make sense because the United States and Japan would do what they were especially qualified to do (the concept of comparative advantage). For Japan the goal was to raise its contribution to comprehensive security to 3 per cent of GNP: 1 per cent for its own military defence, and 2 per cent earmarked for non-military security, especially foreign aid. The United States would still be spending twice as much as Japan; but Japan would raise its overall contribution and future increases would be politically possible.

During Phase II of JASA, Japan has raised its ODA level. From $2.2 billion in 1980, Japan more than doubled its ODA by 1986, lifting the contribution to $5.6 billion. Japan simultaneously raised its contributions to a variety of multilateral financial institutions like the World Bank and Asia Development Bank. It also became a central actor in the high drama of international debt relief. So Japan began to show signs of shedding the free-rider label.

But the concept of comprehensive security never took hold. It failed to win over the American sceptics who saw the strategy as little more than a PR campaign to place a good face on Japan's attempt to continue skirting hard international responsibilities, especially military and political tasks. They saw

Japanese foreign aid, even ODA, as a self-serving instrument that tied East Asian recipients to the purchase of Japanese goods and services. Instead of promoting local development, therefore, Japanese foreign aid was designed to help Japanese corporations establish beach-heads in booming East Asian markets. Even though Japanese ODA rose to impressive levels, therefore, the political impact in terms of changing the American image of Japan's free-rider behaviour turned out to be limited.

Japan made other noteworthy contributions, especially its donation of $13 billion to underwrite the costs of the Persian Gulf War. The donation was the largest sum contributed by an OECD state. But here again Japan's generosity failed to win international gratitude or respect. It took time to persuade Japan to come up with the money, and even when Japan made the commitment, the impression conveyed was largely negative. It was perceived as a grudging concession made in order to deflect criticism away from Japan for refusing to dispatch Japanese volunteers to the Persian Gulf. Indeed, Japan appeared to be a rich, spoiled nation willing to hire foreign mercenaries to fight in the Persian Gulf, where Japan had vital interests at stake, but unwilling to get involved in any proactive way. Thus, the Persian Gulf donation turned out to be a PR fiasco confirming the image of Japan as a free-rider and ostrich state.

Phase II: Summary

Phase II of JASA, 1971–89, saw the economic capabilities of the United States and Japan move in opposition directions. The power shift – Japan's economic ascension and America's relative decline – was by far the most consequential development during Phase II. It changed US incentives – from providing paternalistic protection for a ravished Japan to applying pressures on a rich and mercantilist Japan to jettison its free-rider approach.

Japan's incentives remained more or less the same. Japan continued to place top priority on economic interests while relying on JASA to provide security insurance. To shield itself from political attack (stemming from the bilateral trade imbalance), Japan felt compelled to turn on a number of safety valves so as to release political pressures that had built up. This suggests that the theory of collective goods offers the best explanation of JASA developments during Phase II. The United States sought to push a larger share of JASA burdens on to Japan's shoulders, since Japan's emergence as an economic power meant that it had developed the capacity to pay for the common defence. American and Japanese incentives, which co-existed in an uneasy symbiosis in Phase I, came into direct conflict during Phase II, erupting regularly into pitched political battles.

There was no stable point of equilibrium. Once relative power capabilities shifted, underlying tensions stemming from conflicting national incentives came to the surface. The United States grew less tolerant of Japan's unique characteristics as a 'non-normal' nation. Bilateral problems became harder to manage, as trade negotiations prodded their way on to the bilateral agenda, monopolizing the spotlight.

In Phase I, the main threats to JASA's existence came from Japan. Leftist organizations possessed the political clout to mount mass movements capable of destroying JASA. There was always the danger that a dramatic event, like an explosion on a US nuclear submarine ported in Yokosuka, might ignite a massive protest that would cause the Diet to terminate the Security Treaty. There was almost no chance that the US Congress would vote to abrogate the Security Treaty. Nor was there much chance that the Soviet Union, China, or North Korea would attack US bases in Japan – not when China and North Korea lacked the requisite amphibious capabilities and not when US forces commanded a preponderance of power in East Asia. The only real danger – and a highly improbable one at that – resided in the possibility that opposition groups in Japan might seize upon an unexpected crisis to abrogate the Security Treaty.

In Phase II, JASA was beset by political conflicts brought on by fundamental shifts in relative power capabilities, conflicting incentive structures, divergences of national interests, and the intrusion of nasty economic disputes. As long as there was a common security threat to bring the two partners together – the 'evil empire' – economic disputes, no matter how bruising, could be handled without damaging JASA irreparably. But the conflicts threatened to get out of hand when the cold war ended, and the menacing 'evil empire' broke into a jigsaw puzzle of smaller, less menacing republics.

4.7 PHASE III: 1989–

End of the Cold War

The defining event in JASA's third and last phase, 1989–, was the abrupt, unanticipated end to the cold war and the subsequent collapse of the Soviet empire. The denouement to the cold war drama, arguably the single most seminal event since the Russian Revolution, not only realigned the global balance of power but also caused a major shift in the tectonic plates underpinning the world system. An earthquake of such magnitude was bound to have an impact on JASA – an ongoing impact given the series of smaller after-shocks that followed in its wake. Recall that the onset of the cold war gave birth to JASA. With the end of the cold war, the US and Japan had to search for a new rationale to replace the containment doctrine that had served for so long as JASA's conceptual framework.

The central question that faces JASA in Phase III, the post-cold war era, is whether, in what form, and for how long, JASA can survive, now that its old *raison d'etre* has disappeared. What are the main threats to JASA's existence? How has the end of the cold war and the new balance of power altered US and Japanese incentives? Are national incentives drifting further apart? In what ways, if at all, is JASA adapting to the new and continuously changing external environment?

During JASA's history, the relative weight of independent variables has shifted with certain variables (like the external security environment) rising in salience and others (like Japan bashing) receding from the spotlight. From 1952–89, the central independent variables were endogenous. Changes in relative power capabilities supplied the kinetic energy behind changes in JASA structure and dynamics. Exogenous variables, like the regional balance of power (BOP), exerted much less influence, because the BOP fluctuated relatively little and the Western alliance enjoyed a preponderance of power throughout the cold war era.

With China's rapid economic development and its big power ambitions, however, exogenous variables have acquired significantly greater weight. Chinese power and China's international behaviour will have a profound long-term impact on JASA. So will other external variables. What happens on the Korean peninsula, for example, is also bound to test JASA's operational effectiveness. It is therefore clear that East Asia has evolved to a point where the most salient independent variables affecting JASA are now exogenous. Of course, exogenous factors interact with, and affect, domestic variables that give shape, in turn, to JASA policies.

China And Korea: New Threats?

Over the second half of the twentieth century, US hegemony in East Asia and the existence of JASA have kept Japan safe from external aggression - far safer, indeed, than Japan has ever experienced since its opening to the outside world in 1854. After its crushing defeat in the Pacific War, Japan's national security has never been seriously threatened. None of its East Asian neighbours has had the audacity or the requisite power to attack. Nor have they had reason to. Japan has posed no threat to its neighbours. If, in a fit of irrational behaviour, a neighbour ever launched an attack on Japan, it would have faced the prospect of withering retaliation from the United States.

But a preponderance of power cannot be sustained for ever. There are indications that it may not extend beyond the first quarter of the next century. China's high-speed development means that it will have the economic wherewithal to build a powerful military machine, featuring naval and air strike capabilities as well as land-based nuclear weapons to go along with its veritable 'sea' of army soldiers. If and when China acquires the capacity to project power, it will bring about a fundamental realignment of power in East Asia. JASA may unravel. Even if it does not, Japan will never feel the same sense of security that it has enjoyed over the past half-century.

Consider also the impact of a unified Korea. A unified Korea would take its place in East Asia as a major military power, a formidable commercial competitor, and an influential state. There is no doubt that Japan would view Korea as a significant threat to its national security. If Korea kept a stable security tie to the United States, the connection would mitigate Japan's threat perception. But the strength of historical antagonisms between Korea and Japan would not dissipate. A seemingly insignificant event or an off-hand statement could ignite an explosion of national anger. And just as Japan would see Korea as a threat, so too would Korea view Japan as a menacing neighbour. A vicious cycle of negative reinforcement could complicate Korea–Japan relations, leading to an arms build-up on both sides of the Japan Sea.

Viewed from the long-run perspective, therefore, regional trends – China's rise and Korea's unification, not to mention the spectre of a revanchist Russia in the Far East – are bound to affect JASA and pose the first real threats to Japanese national security in postwar history. Such developments might render JASA ineffective. They would cause Japan to reassess its security options. They might even drive Japan or the United States to exit from JASA. JASA's collapse, though inconceivable in Phase II, cannot be ruled out in Phase III. The security environment in East Asia is evolving at such speed that institutional carryovers from the cold war might be rendered obsolete.

National Incentives

For the United States, the set of national incentives that motivated it during Phase II remains basically the same for Phase III. The overriding objective is still to hold JASA together. The US is still bent on coaxing and cajoling Japan to accept more of JASA's burdens, whether in the form of higher defence expenditures or larger 'side payments'.

For Japan, some incentives remain the same while others have changed. Its incentive to resist US pressures has not changed. Nor has its desire to contain the damaging fallout effects of its lopsided trade surplus. What has changed is Japan's desire to neutralize the appeal of neo-isolationism in the United States. Many Japanese have doubts about the staying power of America's commitment to Japan. They want to keep the United States constructively engaged in East Asia, fully committed to JASA, and capable of maintaining credible forward deployments. In Phase I, leftist opposition in Japan posed the greatest threat to JASA's existence; today, in Phase III, there is a fear of US isolationism – or at least some degree of US disengagement – at a time of critical transition in the region.

Japan is well aware that there would be problems and bottlenecks if it tried to activate JASA agreements when external crises visit East Asia, like a war on the Korean peninsula. Many operational questions would have to be answered. Would US forces be given full use of bases in Japan to fight a war in nearby Korea? Would Japan provide logistical back-up support? If the answer is no, the American public might react so angrily that there would be a sudden upsurge of demand for JASA's immediate termination. Accordingly, Japan has an incentive to fine-tune JASA in ways that heighten the chances of an effective response to the test of external crises.

At the same time that it wants to keep the US engaged and JASA operationally effective, Japan seems intent on curbing America's coercive power so that the US cannot impose its will unilaterally on Japan. There are strong incentives at work as well to begin fallback preparations for the day –it is hoped a long time from now – when JASA is no longer effective or is terminated. To prepare for that day, many Japanese feel that it would be wise to strengthen Japan's own power base, scale back its dependence on the United States, and expand its capacity to take autonomous action.

Several of these incentives are pulling Japan in opposite directions. On the one hand, Japan places the highest priority on consolidating and fine-tuning JASA to make sure that the US stays actively engaged in East Asia; but on the other hand, Japan needs to protect itself against the possibility of a US cutback or troop withdrawal. Japan must also be prepared to act if JASA fails to pass its first operational test. Not that these incentives are necessarily contradictory or that they are working at cross-purposes. Indeed, Japan's cultivation of a stronger, independent power base and its assumption of a more activist international role may turn out to be mutually reinforcing. But the indications are that incentive structures have become multidimensional and complex.

Path-dependency

There is another key factor that comes into play: path-dependency. It is a mediating variable that affects a nation's capacity to convert incentives into concrete policies. Japan's incentive to free-ride is not simply the result of rational choice. Over the years of JASA's existence, Japan's free ride has come to be embedded in a dense cluster of institutions, procedures and doctrines that function as a powerful brake on new policy initiatives designed to encourage bold action, such as constitutional revision and Japan's transformation into a 'normal' state.

The dense network of institutions, doctrines and precedent-setting practices – constituting the essence of path-dependency – includes, for example, Article Nine of the 'Peace' Constitution, the 1 per cent ceiling on defence expenditures, the three non-nuclear principles, the Yoshida Doctrine, the ban on arms exports, the legacy of Hiroshima and Nagasaki, the low prestige and muted voice of the Japan Defence Agency, and other institutions unique to Japan. The density of these institutions and practices suggests that any attempt to diverge from past policies will require high levels of political power, shrewd policy strategy, and effective organization simply to overcome the inertia. If Japan decided to ramp up its military power to ease US burdens, path-dependency would make that decision hard to implement.

If exogenous factors – specifically developments in the external security environment – are now the driving forces behind changes in JASA, then the reality of path-dependency will have to be taken into account as a constraining factor in JASA's future. This is especially the case if changing circumstances require that major adaptations be made. Path-dependency is a key variable intervening between changes in the external security environment and JASA's capacity to adapt. It is apt to delay, distort or limit JASA's capacity to adapt and perhaps precludes the possibility of creating new, multilateral institutions for regional security (to replace the current network of separate, bilateral defence arrangements). There is thus a high cost to JASA's remarkable longevity. It takes the form of path-dependency and leads to a loss of significant degrees of freedom.

Reduced Tensions

The acrimonious trade disputes that sent political temperatures soaring and prompted Japan to turn on various safety valves in Phase II have not disappeared in Phase III; but the raw intensity of emotions has abated, thanks to several recent developments. The myth of Japan as *numero uno* has been exploded. Japan's mighty economic machine has not laid American competitors to waste in key sectors like the information industries, biotechnology, and financial services. Quite the contrary, US producers have not only held their own; they have actually widened their lead in many product markets. Having gone through the pain of downsizing and re-engineering, US corporations have gained renewed confidence in their ability to compete against the Japanese. Of course, the bursting of Japan's speculative bubble and the economic doldrums from which Japan has failed to lift itself have had a lot to do with the reduced threat perception and the lower level of tensions.

The rise of industrial Asia is another development that has deflected attention (and criticism) away from Japan. East Asia's rising stars – China,

Taiwan, South Korea, and the ASEAN economies – have rung up large trade surpluses with the United States – larger as a whole than Japan's. Owing to the absence of well-developed legal systems 'unfair' practices. and rampant corruption, the rising NICs of East Asia have drawn attention to themselves as prime targets of America's wrath. US officials have not forgotten about Japan. But the bruising US–Japan battles waged from 1985–95 have probably come to an end, at least for the time being. The truce now in effect will reduce US pressures on Japan to make greater side payments by turning on all available safety valves.

Safety Valves

It is a good thing that political temperatures have fallen. The use of safety values has reached a point somewhere near saturation. Japan has already extracted as much value out of the available safety valve mechanisms as could have been extracted. If excess pressures build up again, they will have to be managed by other means. How much higher can Japan boost host-nation support? It currently stands at 75 per cent of the costs of US bases (minus salaries for US personnel). Even if it were pushed all the way up to 100 per cent, would the added increment make much of a difference? Probably not. As for ODA, the level is high enough already to place Japan at the top of all donor nations. The only change that might enhance Japan's image is to free Japanese aid completely from the procurement of Japanese goods and services. If Japan actually implements its rhetoric about 'untied' aid, it will enhance the political value of Japan's programme of foreign assistance.

Constraints On US Unilateralism

Having been the object of unrelenting American pressure (bordering on coercion), Japan has explored ways of curbing US unilateral power. Perhaps the surest way is to develop the capacity to act autonomously. There are several noteworthy areas in which Japan has acted autonomously – even against the direct wishes of its patron, the United States. The first time Japan struck out on its own was in 1974, when it shifted its diplomatic stance in the Middle East, switching from a pro-Israel policy (following America's lead) to a neutral position (under the threat of an Arab oil embargo). Since then, the cases of autonomous action have multiplied, especially over the past decade. To cite one example: Japan has taken a less doctrinaire position than the United States on the issue of human rights in developing countries. It is not as insistent as the US that developing states like China adhere to certain standards of human rights set by affluent Western nations. It is less inclined, therefore, to apply the same stringent sanctions to human rights violations.

Other issues over which Japan has struck out on its own include: the right to life (abortion), energy (nuclear reprocessing), carbon dioxide emissions and the environment, agricultural liberalization, immigration, Iran and the Middle East, a timetable for APEC liberalization, and China (for example over Tibet, arms sales, intellectual property). As East Asia changes and power capabilities continue to evolve, Japan's perceptions of what lies in its own interests are apt to drift even farther apart from America's.

China and Korea pose the most troublesome cases. To coordinate Japanese and American policies toward China and Korea will be enormously time-consuming and difficult. It will require regular communication, a common strategic vision, tactical coordination, and constant fine-tuning. In addition to very different historical legacies, Japan and the United States must deal with different dynamics at work in their respective political systems.

Japan has also pursued a strategy of what might be called the 'multilateralization' of bilateral conflicts – with surprisingly favourable results. The strategy is to push bilateral differences through multilateral channels of conflict resolution, such as GATT and the WTO (World Trade Organization). Japan has used this approach primarily for economic disputes. The WTO option was used as a negotiating lever for both Japan and the United States when they reached an impasse over automobiles in 1994–95. The Fuji–Kodak dispute in 1996 was sent to the WTO for resolution.

Over the past several years, MITI bureaucrats have learned how to deal with America's unilateral demands. The idea is to enmesh the United States in a binding web of multilateral norms, rules and procedures (that America itself had a large hand in creating). Multilateralization allows Japan to take the high road by demonstrating a willingness to accept and abide by multilateral rules and norms. So far, at least, the strategy has worked. Whether it will continue to work remains to be seen, since the WTO, as a fledgling institution, is still struggling to establish its identity. An overload of contentious cases might cripple the WTO permanently.

For security-related conflicts, multilateralization is not as useful, because there are not as many international organizations through which disputes can be channelled. There are, to be sure, a variety of specialized organizations for nuclear energy, nuclear weapons, arms control and disarmament, technical verification, and so forth. There is also the United Nations as a general forum for conflict resolution. In East Asia, the Asia Regional Forum (ARF) has been organized as a forum for deliberation and confidence-building initiatives. But East Asia as a region has fewer established multilateral institutions than Europe. This means that Japan will not be able to implement the same strategy of multilateral enmeshment that it has pursued in cases of economic disputes. Fortunately, there are not as many bilateral bones of contention in the security domain. The absence of a NATO-like organization in East Asia may allow the United States to exercise dominant power in bilateral relationships over the short run; but it may weaken US influence over the long haul.

Alliances in East Asia

JASA has served as the cornerstone of the East Asian security system that the United States put in place at the early stages of the cold war. As noted at the start of this chapter, JASA can be compared to NATO in terms of historical significance. It remains a crucial part of the post-cold war security system. In some respects, JASA is as essential today for Japan, the United States, and East Asia as it was during the cold war.

Remarkably, JASA, like NATO, has survived as a working alliance for a half-century. It has passed the twin tests of time and periodic crises – with resilience and staying power. To appreciate what JASA represents, bear in mind the brief history of alliances in East Asia. The region has seen the establishment of only a handful of alliances in modern history. Among the best known in the twentieth century are the Anglo-Japanese Alliance (1902) and the Sino-Soviet Alliance (1950). Put East Asia in comparative perspective. Western Europe has had a long history of security alliances, growing out of the violent struggles of nation-building from the seventeenth through the nineteenth centuries. East Asia lacks a similar tradition. Most other regions – Africa, the Middle East, Latin America – also lack such a tradition. Of the small number of security alliances set up in East Asia, nearly all have met the same fate: birth defects and premature death.

Some might argue that the secret of JASA's longevity has been the involvement of the United States as the senior partner – specifically, its liberal values and hegemonic power. The argument has some merit. The United States has provided the cohesion and stability so essential for alliances to endure. No alliance in East Asia has lasted long without American involvement. But there is also empirical evidence that disproves the argument. Several American alliances in East Asia have failed. SEATO was still-born and US alliances with the Philippines and Taiwan died before reaching maturity.

JASA and the US–ROK alliance have lasted longer than any alliance in East Asian history. Clearly, America's involvement as the senior partner has had a lot to do with their longevity. But even though the United States has been associated with all cases of alliance successes, it is still not the whole story. There has to be a relatively stable regional environment within which to operate the alliance; a common enemy against which to rally; and a fairly close convergence of national interests and common values binding allies together. JASA has incorporated all these ingredients. This is why it has staying power.

But as JASA heads into the twenty-first century, it will surely have to adapt to cope effectively with East Asia's rapidly changing environment. If the theoretical explanations offered for each of JASA's three phases is accurate, the dead weight of path-dependency could hamper JASA's capacity to adapt effectively. For a half a century, JASA has demonstrated remarkable resilience. It has survived the loss of American hegemony, a big relative shift in national power capabilities, the onslaught of economic conflicts, and the end of the cold war. But will JASA be able to shed the shackles of path-dependency and address the first serious threats now being posed to Japan's national security? The answer is not clear. Whether it be yes or no, East Asia is certain to feel the reverberations well into the next century.

NOTES

1. Stephen D. Krasner, *Defending the National Interest* (Princeton: Princeton University Press, 1978); Robert Gilpin, *War and Change in World Politics* (New York: Cambridge University Press, 1981); Charles P. Kindleberger, *Power and Money* (New York: Basic Books, 1970).
2. Mancur Olson Jr, *The Logic of Collective Action* (Cambridge: Harvard University Press, 1965); Mancur Olson and Richard J. Zeckhauser, 'An Economic Theory of Alliances,' *Review of Economics and Statistics*, **48**:266–79.
3. Olson and Zeckhauser, 'An Economic Theory of Alliances', *Review of Economics and Statistics* 48: 267; John G. Head, 'Public Goods and Public Policy', *Public Finance*, **XVI1**:3 (1962): 197–219.
4. Oliver E. Williamson, *Markets and Hierarchies* (New York: The Free Press, 1975); and *The Economic Institutions of Capitalism* (New York: The Free Press, 1985).
5. For a historical overview of America's role in the Pacific, see Walter A. McDougall, *Let the Sea Make a Noise* (New York: Basic Books, 1993).
6. John W. Dower, *Empire and Aftermath* (Cambridge: Harvard University Press, 1979), pp. 369–400.
7. Takeshi Igarashi, 'Peace-Making and Party Politics: The Formation of the Domestic Foreign-Policy System in Postwar Japan', *Journal of Japanese Studies*, Vol. 2 (Summer 1985) pp. 323–56.
8. George F. Kennan, *Memoirs 1925–1950* (Boston: Little, Brown, 1967), p. 376.
9. Frederick S. Dunn, *Pacemaking and the Settlement with Japan* (Princeton: Princeton University Press, 1963), p. 123.
10. Ibid.
11. Richard B. Finn, *Winners in Peace* (Berkeley: University of California Press, 1992), p. 299.
12. Ibid.
13. Cf. Karl van Wolferen, *The Enigma of Japanese Power* (New York: Alfred Knopf, 1989); James Fallows, 'Containing Japan', *Atlantic Monthly,* May 1989, pp. 40–54.
14. Jeff Shear, *The Keys to the Kingdom* (New York: Doubleday, 1994).

[illegible]

[illegible]

NOTES

1. Stephen D. Krasner, [illegible]
2. [illegible]
3. [illegible]
4. [illegible]
5. [illegible]
6. [illegible]
7. [illegible]
8. [illegible]
9. [illegible]
10. [illegible]
11. [illegible]
12. [illegible]
13. [illegible]

PART TWO:

Foreign Trade and Investment

5. Japan and the 1994 *Economic Report of the President*

Gary R. Saxonhouse

5.1 INTRODUCTION

On Friday, 11 February 1994, amidst an avalanche of publicity, the US–Japan Framework for a New Economic Partnership negotiations collapsed following a summit meeting between President Clinton and then Prime Minister Morihiro Hosokawa. On the first working day following the Framework talks, Monday, 14 February, the Clinton Administration's first *Economic Report of the President* and its first *Annual Report of the Council of Economic Advisers* were released to the public. These *Reports* are mandated by the Employment Act of 1946 and have appeared annually since that time.[1]

The first *Economic Report* of any president is an event of considerable interest. President Kennedy's 1962 *Economic Report* made a historic case for the application of Keynesian economics. Twenty years later, President Reagan's 1982 *Economic Report* made an equally historic case for supply-side economics. Coming immediately after the breakdown of the Framework talks, a very close examination of what President Clinton's 1994 *Report* had to say about Japan and about US–Japan economic relations was inevitable. While any *Report* is cleared through an inter-agency process, with many different government agencies contributing comments and alternative perspectives, it is the Council of Economic Advisers' basic views which prevail in the final document. What would a Council of Economic Advisers chaired by Laura Tyson, who had come to President Clinton's attention as a critic of Japan's trade policies, have to say now that the Framework talks had broken down?[2]

5.2 JAPAN IN THE PRE-TYSON ECONOMIC REPORTS

Until the early 1980s, Japan, despite its importance in the global economy, rated scarcely a mention in the *Economic Report*. This was not because there was no trade friction or even because there were no significant ongoing trade negotiations between the US and Japan. Far from it. Major disputes regarding textiles, steel, colour television sets and automobiles, to name just a few sectors, quite apart from major disputes regarding macroeconomic policy, were ongoing in the 1960s and 1970s.[3] Rather there was little mention of Japan because, in principle, bilateral trade disputes were seen as an aberrant departure from the multilateralism that was the cornerstone of the postwar international economic system. Writing in the summer of 1945, Howard Ellis noted:

> There are good reasons for believing that no device portends more restriction of international trade in the postwar setting than bilateral trade arrangements.[4]

It was only in the 1983 and 1984 *Economic Reports*, prepared by the Martin Feldstein-chaired Council of Economic Advisers, that US–Japan economic relations finally emerged as a special topic. Japan's appearance did not reflect a change in outlook so much as an opportunity, in the face of much popular misunderstanding, for the Feldstein Council to make the case once more against bilateralism. The 1983 *Report* noted:

> Japan runs a huge surplus in its manufactures trade, while the United States runs only a small one, and Japan also has a large surplus in its bilateral trade with the United States. The main explanation of Japan's surplus in manufactures trade and in trade with the United States is that Japan, with few natural resources, incurs high deficits in its trade in primary products, especially oil and with primary producers. Looking at Japanese-US trade in isolation is misleading. The Japanese surplus in trade is largely a response to the rise of OPEC.[5]

The 1983 *Report* also broke new ground by stressing that Japanese trade restrictions do not affect either Japan's trade surplus or America's trade deficit:

> trade restrictions probably do not lead to an overall larger trade surplus. If they were removed, the yen would depreciate and increased Japanese imports in the currently protected sectors would be offset by reduced deficits or increased surpluses elsewhere.[6]

> Large trade deficits are not the result of unfair foreign competition. Large projected US trade deficits are a result of macroeconomic forces, particularly large budget deficits. The main sources of the US trade deficit are not to be found in Paris or in Tokyo, but in Washington.[7]

The 1984 *Report*, while continuing to emphasize both how misleading it may be to look at trade relations bilaterally and the lack of any obvious connection between trade barriers and overall trade balances, went on to discuss how to measure the degree of protection afforded to any particular sector. The 1984 *Report* explicitly rejected import shares as a measure of protection:

> Import barriers in every country protect those sectors that would not have the comparative advantage in a fair fight, at the expense of those sectors that would. In the Japanese case, it is agriculture that is easily the least competitive sector and therefore the most protected. ... Japan already imports lots of agricultural products, indeed it is the largest customer of US agricultural exports. But, in general, a high observed degree of 'import penetration' does not preclude the existence of a high degree of protection. In fact, import penetration is often the cause and protection the effect, rather than the other way around.[8]

5.3 JAPAN IN THE TYSON *ECONOMIC REPORT*

In so far as Japan is concerned, the Tyson *Economic Report of the President* does stand in dramatic contrast to previous *Reports*. Where once bilateralism was an embarrassment, the Tyson *Economic Report* devoted more space to US–Japan economic relations than it did to the Uruguay Round.[9] Where once great pains were taken to stress the absence of any significant connection between trade barriers and overall trade imbalances, the Tyson *Economic Report* noted that the US trade deficit with Japan accounted for more than 60 per cent of the overall US trade deficit and then emphasized that uniquely restrictive Japanese trade barriers were responsible for a significant share of this bilateral deficit.[10]

The Tyson *Economic Report*'s view that Japanese trade barriers were uniquely restrictive was bolstered with arguments a number of which ran directly counter to the arguments and evidence presented in earlier *Economic Reports*. Where the Feldstein *Economic Report* took such pains to reject import shares in domestic consumption as a measure of protection, the Tyson *Economic Report* in discussing Japanese trade policy noted:

> Manufactured imports play a relatively small role in the Japanese economy, with the share of manufactured imports in consumption less than half that of the other advanced industrialized economies.[11]

This is important to Tyson because when low import shares co-exist with:

> an unusually low share of intra-industry trade, an unusually small stock of inward foreign investment, an unusually low small share of domestic sales accounted for

> by foreign owned firms and an unusually high share of intrafirm trade, which is predominantly controlled, moreover, by Japanese rather than foreign-based firms.

The Tyson *Economic Report* found it possible to conclude that 'the preponderance of evidence points to the closed nature of the Japanese market'.[12]

The 1994 *Economic Report* stressed that it was not only the Tyson Council of Economic Advisers that found the Japanese market closed to imports. In direct contradiction of the 1990 *Economic Report*, prepared by the Council of Economic Advisers and chaired by Michael Boskin, which found that:

> Some statistical studies have concluded that this trade pattern might be expected of a country with Japan's resource endowments; however, others do not share this finding,

the Tyson *Economic Report* concluded that:

> studies have been virtually unanimous in their conclusion that Japan's low volume of manufactured imports cannot be entirely explained by economic fundamentals.[13]

The Tyson *Economic Report* was willing to go beyond just concluding that the Japanese market was closed. After noting that the closed nature of the Japanese market was reflected in price differentials between Japan and other countries, it mentioned that:

> Japanese manufactured imports might increase by more than 20 percent if the price differentials were eliminated

and that

> if Japan were to eliminate all formal and informal barriers to trade, US exports to Japan would initially increase by somewhere in the range of $9 billion to $18 billion per year.[14]

Having taken great pains to establish that Japanese trade patterns and practices were highly distinctive, the Tyson *Economic Report* lauded the ongoing bilateral US–Japan Framework talks as the appropriate vehicle for changing Japanese policies. The *Report* noted that the Framework would make

> use of 'objective criteria' to assess progress. The Framework agreement states that 'assessment will be based upon sets of objective criteria, either qualitative or quantitative as appropriate' upon which the two governments will agree. The

> negotiation is results-oriented, with both governments agreeing that 'tangible progress must be achieved.'[15]

The use of 'objective criteria' is not the only purported innovation of the Framework. According to the *Report:*

> The other innovation of the Framework talks is procedural: By explicitly incorporating biannual meetings between the President of the United States and the Prime Minister of Japan, the Framework dramatically raises the political profile of the negotiations.[16]

5.4 EVALUATING THE TYSON *REPORT*

Compared to past *Reports*, the Tyson *Economic Report* presented a new view of Japan and, on this basis, advocated new policies for dealing with US–Japanese economic relations. Was the evidence and argument in the Tyson *Economic Report* correct? Was this a solid foundation for what came to be the Clinton Administration's initial Japan strategy?[17]

There can be little question that the Tyson *Economic Report*'s effort to link the bilateral US–Japan trade and current account deficits with the overall trade and current account deficit was ill-considered. The best critique of this position so painstakingly laid out in Chapter 6 of the *Report* was Chapter 1 of Tyson's own *Report*. There, echoing the Feldstein *Economic Report*, the US current account deficit was linked to the US budget deficit:

> If private saving is insufficient to cover ... private investment and the combined deficit of all levels of government we must borrow the difference from abroad. Such a shortage of saving has characterized the United States for about a decade now.
>
> When Americans borrow from foreigners we run a surplus in our international capital account. ... The mirror image of this capital account surplus is an equally large current account deficit. Thus, a country that saves less than it invests and runs a budget deficit is bound to have a large current account deficit. Indeed, chronic, large current account deficits date from precisely the time that the United States started running huge budget deficits.[18]

If the relationship between American saving and American investment was responsible for America's trade deficit, adjusting the bilateral trade imbalance with Japan would have little impact except in so far as savings and investment relationships were affected. Improving US access to the Japanese market and/or restraining Japanese access to the American market might change investment and savings relationships in both countries, but it is by no means obvious in which direction. In an influential study published in 1988, Jeffrey

Sachs and Peter Boone found that the long-term impact of a removal of Japanese restrictions on agricultural imports might well be to increase rather than to decrease Japan's trade surplus.[19]

Should reducing the Japanese bilateral trade surplus with the United States have no net effect on savings and investment flows, there would be an equivalent increase in US trade deficits with other countries and/or an equivalent decrease in the US trade surpluses with other countries. For example, even today, the easiest way for the United States to reduce its bilateral trade deficit with Japan is not through international diplomacy. Recognizing this, the Clinton Administration has worked with Congress to pass legislation that would remove the embargo that has been in force since 1973 on the export of Alaskan oil. On 28 November 1995, President Clinton signed legislation lifting the 22-year-old embargo.[20] It is variously estimated that removal of this embargo will result in time in an increase of American exports to Japan of anywhere between $2 billion and $16 billion.[21] Critics of US trade policy towards Japan can argue that such a step confers comparatively little benefit. New American oil exports to Japan will be offset by new American oil imports from Mexico or some of the OPEC countries. Meanwhile, Japan, with new imports from the United States, will reduce imports from these same suppliers. Such criticism is correct but it is important to appreciate that it applies equally well to the removal of any of Japan's trade barriers that might influence the bilateral trade imbalance without having any net effect on the relationship between investment and savings in the United States or in Japan.

5.5 THE TYSON *REPORT*'S EVIDENCE

While the first Tyson *Economic Report*'s embrace of bilateralism can be rejected on theoretical grounds, Japanese trade barriers, to the extent that they exist, can have significant consequences for US and Japanese welfare even while they may have no effect on the overall trade balance of each country. For this reason, the case the Tyson *Economic Report* made that Japanese trade barriers were distinctively restrictive must be directly addressed.

Much of the evidence assembled in the Tyson *Economic Report*, even where correct, was hardly decisive for and largely irrelevant to the point it wished to make. Consider the stress placed by the *Report* on the prominent role played by intra-firm transactions in US–Japanese trade.

As seen from Table 5.1, while an unusually large share of Japanese exports to the United States in 1992 were intra-firm transactions, it's not clear that this represents a policy problem of any particular significance. Unsurprisingly, in 1992, Japanese exports to the United States were either intermediate products, capital equipment or consumer products. For consumer products it surely makes little difference whether the retailer from which an American household ultimately purchases a Japanese-made product imported it directly from Japan, purchased it from an American-owned wholesaler, or finally purchased it from a Japanese-owned wholesaler.[22]

Table 5.1 Intra-firm trade as a share of total US exports to and imports from Europe and Japan, 1992 (per cent of total)

Region	US exports to region	US imports from region
Europe	32.4	46.3
Japan	36.2	73.0
World total	30.6	45.0

Source: *Economic Report of the President*, 1994.

What's true for American imports of Japanese-made consumer products was also clearly true for the purchase by American-owned companies of Japanese-made capital equipment and intermediate products. In and of itself, whether the wholesaler was American-owned or Japanese-owned, and whether title was taken to the products in Tokyo or Los Angeles would not seem to be a matter of great substance.

What was thought to be a matter of greater significance was the import of Japanese-made capital equipment and intermediate products by American-based, Japanese-owned companies. It was argued that in making such purchases Japanese companies were behaving in a discriminatory fashion.[23] Whether Japanese companies were discriminating is difficult to say, but it is true that in 1992 42.1 per cent of the procurement by American affiliates of Japanese companies came from Japan.[24] This may seem like a large proportion, but consider that General Motors at that time was purchasing no less than 75 per cent of its inputs from its own divisions.[25] General Motors' procurement behaviour may have been discriminatory but it was not a violation of US antitrust statutes. If General Motors or a Japanese-owned company based in the United States discriminate in favour of long-time, but high-cost suppliers, the competitive American markets in which they sell their products will penalize them.

While the unusually large share of Japanese exports to the United States in 1992 that were intra-firm transactions does not suggest discriminatory behaviour that was distinctively Japanese, what about trade flow going in the other direction? What about the US exports to Japan that were intra-firm transactions by Japanese-owned companies? In the first place, as is clear from Table 5.1, most US exports to Japan did not fall into this category at all. Only about one-third of US exports to Japan were intra-firm transactions by Japanese-owned companies. It should be kept in mind that, for the most part, these transactions did not represent backward integration in the way that term is normally understood. These intra-firm transactions, by and large, were neither the purchases of Japanese manufacturers, nor of Japanese retailers of goods produced by their subsidiaries and overseas affiliates. While this may change in the late 1990s, by comparison with firms in other major industrialized countries, firms with established positions in the Japanese market have found it less profitable to integrate backwards into production entities abroad. In 1993 only 10.5 per cent of Japanese imports were intra-firm transactions of goods produced by Japanese entities abroad.[26] By contrast, 15.5 per cent of US imports were goods manufactured by American-owned firms abroad.[27]

The relatively large role played by intra-firm transactions in US exports to Japan, in and of itself, does not mean that goods produced by American-owned firms have not been reaching the Japanese market. Quite the contrary. Until very recently almost all US exports to Japan were goods produced by American-owned companies. Between 1985 and the time the Tyson *Report* was issued US exports to Japan doubled. US-owned firms were responsible for virtually all this increase.

The Tyson *Economic Report* examined intra-industry trade flows as well as intra-firm transactions in its efforts to demonstrate that Japan is economically distinctive. As seen in Table 5.2, Japan's participation in intra-industry trade in 1990 appeared to be less than that of other advanced industrialized economies. By itself, this is not a significant matter. In any sample of countries one must have the lowest measure. Japan's measure is not so out of line that any strong conclusion can be drawn.[28] Japan's measure is closer to Italy's than Italy's is to any other country. Were the Japanese and Italian markets in 1990 together far more closed than those of other countries? Is it true, as this metric implies, that the German market was more protected in 1990 than the American market?

In fact, factor-endowment-based explanations of net trade and import shares can account for inter-country variations in intra-industry trade.[29] It's possible that Japan was a relatively meagre participant in 1990 in intra-industry trade because with its very distinctive pattern of factor endowment it remained quite unlike its trading partners and/or because of its distance from its major trading partners.[30] In recent years, Japan's participation in intra-industry trade has been increasing. This primarily reflects the increasing capital intensity and skill intensity of many of Japan's substantial trading partners in East and Southeast Asia.

Table 5.2 Intra-industry manufacturing trade indices for 1990

	Japan	US	Germany	UK	France	Italy
Intra-industry trade index	.58	.83	.73	.79	.77	.67

Source: Economic Report of the President, 1994.

Just as the low level of Japan's intra-industry trade may reflect distinctive features of the Japanese economy that have nothing to do with government policy, the same might be true of the extremely low levels of foreign investment in Japan. To a considerable degree, the low Japanese numbers presented in Table 5.3 (taken from the Tyson *Economic Report)* reflect the distinctive character of the Japanese labour market. Japan's permanent employment practices make it difficult for foreign firms to hire experienced managers, engineers, salesmen and/or factory operatives. Not only do permanent employment practices make it difficult for foreign firms to hire experienced employees, they also make the acquisition of Japanese firms extremely difficult. Given the absence of an external market for their services, Japanese managers are uniquely resistant to the sale of their companies. Even if Japanese securities statutes were identical with American statutes, as long as permanent employment remains the norm among larger Japanese companies, takeovers of one company by another will remain modest relative to practices of other countries.[31] While structural change in the Japanese economy and demography may alter the character of the Japanese labour market, no one has yet suggested that permanent employment developed in Japan as an institution to inhibit foreign investment or that a modification of permanent employment practices is the proper object of international negotiation.[32]

Table 5.3 The role of foreign investment in six industrialized countries

	Japan	US	Germany	UK	France
Foreign firms' share of domestic sales	1.2	16.4	14.0	24.	28.4

Source: Economic Report of the President, 1994.

5.6 IS THE *REPORT*'S TREATMENT OF JAPAN REPRESENTATIVE?

While it is possible to quarrel with the inferences drawn from them, the data presented in the Tyson *Economic Report* are unimpeachable. By contrast, the Tyson *Economic Report*'s statement that studies by economists have been virtually unanimous in their conclusion that Japan's low volume of manufactured imports cannot be entirely explained by economic fundamentals is incontestably incorrect. No industrialized country's imports can be explained entirely by economic fundamentals. Neither economic theory nor economic data collection are well enough developed for this to be a realistic possibility. The real question is whether the volume of Japanese imports is less well explained by economic fundamentals than is that of other countries. Contrary to the Tyson *Report*'s statement, no less than sixteen studies by eleven different authors find Japanese trade flows just as well explained as those of other countries. As seen in the Appendix, this is more than double the number of studies that find Japanese behaviour distinctive.[33]

Just counting up studies that come down on either side of the issue is not enough. Quality as well as quantity does matter. As Srinavasan and Hamada conclude, the most important criterion for evaluating studies on the terms of access to the Japanese market is whether and which international trade theory is used. Only tightly structured theory can provide a guide as to which variables should be included in a model and which among the many, many possible functional forms should be chosen for the equations.[34] Only a fully articulated theoretical framework can offer any assurance that arbitrary decisions made in the course of empirical work have been minimized. This is the standard by which empirical work on important policy issues should be judged.[35] As seen in the Appendix, Part 2, none of the studies which find Japanese behaviour exceptional meets this standard. By contrast, as seen in Part 1 of the Appendix, studies by Goto, Harrigan, Leamer, Saxonhouse and Takenaka–Ishikawa meet the Srinavasan–Hamada test. All reject the hypothesis that Japanese behaviour is exceptional while making use of structural equations derived explicitly from international trade theory.

5.7 THE QUANTITATIVE IMPACT OF JAPANESE TRADE BARRIERS

As curious as the Tyson *Report*'s unwarranted claim about the conclusions of studies by economists on Japan's trade structure is its observation that, if barriers were removed US exports to Japan would probably increase by somewhere in the range of $9 to $18 billion a year. The finding the Tyson

Report cites was apparently the work of C. Fred Bergsten and Marcus Noland. In a 24 June 1993 press release headlined in part 'Japanese Barriers Block $9–$18 Billion of Annual American Exports', the Institute for International Economics announced that a comprehensive new study by Bergsten and Noland found that:

> Japanese market access barriers are limiting American merchandise exports by an estimated $9-$18 billion annually of which $6-11 billion are in manufactures with most of the remainder in agriculture.[36]

The press release announcing the Bergsten–Noland study provided some estimates, reproduced in Table 5.4, as to the US manufacturing sectors whose imports were being blocked by Japanese barriers. The estimates in Table 5.5 sum to no more than $2.794 billion. Neither the press release nor the actual Bergsten–Noland study itself provided further detail on precisely which barriers in which sectors account for what part of the remaining $3.2 billion to $8.2 billion in allegedly blocked US manufactured goods exports to Japan.[37]

Table 5.4 Bergsten–Noland estimates of potential US gains from liberalization in Japan (millions of dollars)

Computers	$1075
Fuels	785
Wood products	750
Retailing	150
Supercomputers	30

Note: The figure for computers excludes an estimated $1 billion in US firms' foreign-sourced products. The figure for retailing includes only those gains attributable to Toys 'R Us' entry into the Japanese market.

Source: Institute for International Economics News Release 24 June 1992.

Where did the Bergsten–Noland aggregate findings actually come from? Surprisingly, despite the press release issued by the Institute for International Economics, the Bergsten-Noland study was not the source of this estimate. Rather the estimates came from what was at the time an unpublished seven-page paper by Noland entitled, 'Why Are Prices in Japan So High?' Notwithstanding how central these estimates were to their study, notwithstanding the Noland paper being unavailable in published form, notwithstanding the paper's brevity and notwithstanding how common the practice is for Institute of International Economics studies to include detailed technical appendices, unaccountably it was not appended to the Bergsten–Noland study.[38]

Noland estimated Equation (5.1) using data taken from joint 1989 and 1991 studies of US–Japanese price differentials for 159 identical products conducted by MITI and the US Department of Commerce.[39]

$$P_J / P_{US} = 78.21^b - 98.89^a D89 - 57.77 JAPAN^a + 9.08 US + 29.49 EC + 0.65 JTAR \quad (5.1)$$
$$+ 2.05 USAR + JNTB^b - 1.00 USNTB^a + 0.65 HKEI^b + 1.53 VKEI^a$$

$\overline{R}^2 = 0.58$ a ≡ significant at .01 level
b ≡ significant at .05 level

D89	≡	dummy variable indicating 1989 observation
JAPAN	≡	dummy variable indicating good produced in Japan
US	≡	dummy variable indicating good produced in the United States
EC	≡	dummy variable indicating good produced in the European Community
JTAR	≡	Japanese tariff
USTAR	≡	United States tariff
JNTB	≡	Japan non-tariff barrier
USNTB	≡	United States non-tariff barrier
HKEI	≡	share of industry shipments accounted for by bank-centred *keiretsu* member firms
VKEI	≡	share of industry shipments accounted for by industrial firm-centred *keiretsu* member firms
P_J	≡	Retail price of good in Japan
P_{US}	≡	Retail price of good in the United States

No one doubts that, in general, the prices of most foreign products are substantially higher in Japan than in their country of origin. What is surprising is that the 1991 joint survey and its 1989 predecessor did not confirm the existence of the so-called 'Forty-Seventh Street Photo Phenomenon'. In general, the prices of Japanese products were not found to be substantially higher in Japan than were the prices of identical products in American and European markets. The results of these surveys present a problem for the argument that Japan maintains exceptionally protective, if informal trade barriers. If the Japanese market is highly protected, both Japanese as well as foreign products should reasonably be expected to have much higher prices in Japan than abroad. That only foreign products were found to have substantially higher prices in Japan suggests that alternative interpretations need to be considered.

Distribution margins and the cost of distribution as a proportion of the price of goods are not substantially higher in Japan than in the United States.[40] This makes it doubtful whether Japanese distributors are either the primary cause or the primary beneficiaries of the higher prices charged for foreign goods in Japan.[41] If Japanese firms in competing with foreign firms at home and abroad are charging substantially the same prices and if Japanese distributors are neither the prime cause nor the prime beneficiaries of the high prices of foreign products in Japan, it is hard to see what protection is given the Japanese economy. At the same time, neither the profit shares nor the rate of return earned by Japanese manufacturers compared to those of foreign manufacturers was exorbitant. Rather the higher prices in these late 1980s and early 1990s surveys for United States and European products in Japan quite possibly reflect no more than the marketing strategies of foreign oligopolistic firms.[42]

Noland's estimation of Equation (5.1) was to a considerable degree an effort to test whether high prices for foreign goods in Japan in 1989 and 1991 were due to price overcharging by foreign oligopolists. Noland hypothesized that if after other factors have been allowed for, US and European country of origin dummy variables were positive, this would be an indication that strategic behaviour by foreign firms was a cause of high foreign-good prices. Finding, as seen in Equation (5.1), that the coefficients on these dummy variables were statistically insignificantly different from zero, Noland concluded, 'The argument that higher traded goods prices are due to gouging by foreign oligopolists receives no support from these results.'[43]

Unfortunately, Noland drew the wrong inference from his results. In his study the European Community and US country of origin dummy variables were not insignificantly different from zero. Rather they were insignificantly different from the baseline non-European Community, non-US, non-Japanese country of origin dummy variable. Such a result is hardly surprising. *A priori*, there is no reason why US firm and European Community firm behaviour should be different from the strategic behaviour of firms situated in other countries outside Japan. What is more important, Noland's results indicate that the foreign country of origin dummies were statistically significantly greater than the Japanese country of origin dummy variable. In other words, Noland's results were just the opposite of what he thought. They actually indicated considerable support for the hypothesis that the prime determinant of the high prices of foreign products in Japan is the strategy of foreign manufacturers themselves. In addition, the highly negative Japanese dummies once again confirmed the absence of the 'Forty-Seventh Street Photo Phenomenon'.[44]

Noland also attempted to estimate the impact of Japanese trade barriers by first setting the trade policy (*JTAR*, *JNTB*) and *keiretsu* (*HKEI*, *VKEI*) coefficients in Equation (5.1) equal to zero. The resulting price changes were then multiplied by Japanese price elasticities of demand for US imports previously estimated by Noland and by Bergsten–Cline to yield the widely disseminated estimate of $6 to $11 billion in increased Japanese manufactured imports from the US

Deriving estimates of the impact of Japanese trade policies and practices on Japanese imports of manufactures using Equation (5.1) is a dubious exercise. Unfortunately, the 159 products included in the MITI–Department of Commerce price surveys that are the basis of Noland's statistical work in no sense constitute a random sample of the universe of comparable products available in US and Japanese markets. Rather, they were the results of weeks of acrimonious negotiations between Commerce and MITI. Indeed, in the 1991 survey as with the predecessor 1989 survey, the final list could not be agreed upon until the day before the survey started. As can be seen in Table 5.5, the 1991 DOC–MITI sample bears little relationship to the structure of Japanese imports of US products. Even if Equation (5.1) were a sensible structural equation, it makes little sense to use the coefficients estimated from such a highly biased sample to forecast the performance of Japan's entire manufacturing sector.

Table 5.5 *The 1991 DOC–MITI price survey and Japanese imports of US manufactures for 1992*

	Per cent of sample	Per cent of total imports
Electrical & Optical	26.8	13.9
Auto Parts	8.9	0.7
Liquor	8.9	0.5
Autos	6.3	1.6
Capital	17.9	13.0
Miscellaneous	20.5	8.5
Consumer		
Food Products	10.7	23.1

Sources: United States Department of Commerce, 'Results of the 1991 DOC/MITI Price Survey', *US Department of Commerce News* (May,1991); Tsushosangyosho, *Tsusho Hakusho Heisei Go-nen* (Tokyo, 1993).

One result from Equation (5.1) that Noland did not dwell on was the highly statistically significant negative coefficient on US non-tariff barriers. If these results are credible, US non-tariff barriers against Japanese products and the products of other countries appear to be responsible for substantially higher prices for these product lines in the American market than might otherwise be the case. Given the size of this highly significant coefficient on US non-tariff barriers, given the large proportion of US imports from Japan that were covered by non-tariff barriers at the time the DOC–MITI survey was conducted and given the size of the US price elasticity of demand for Japanese manufactures, it's likely that at least as many imports of Japanese manufactures were being kept out of US markets by US trade barriers, as US manufactures were being kept out of the Japanese market by Japanese barriers. This is quite consistent with findings in the vast majority of the studies listed in the Appendix.[45]

5.8 CONCLUSION

There is no question but that the 1994 *Economic Report of the President* marked a break in the Council of Economic Advisers' view of both trade policy, in general, and of Japan, in particular. Instead of a stout defence of the multilateral trading system, even as the ratification of the Uruguay Round agreement remained uncertain there was a preoccupation with bilateral economic relations with Japan. Instead of an effort to explain to the 45 000 readers of the *Report* why bilateral trade imbalances have little or no economic significance, the US–Japan bilateral trade imbalance was highlighted as a serious economic problem. Instead of emphasizing the macroeconomic determinants of Japan's trade surplus and the US trade deficit, as was done in its own macroeconomic chapter, the Tyson *Report*'s trade chapter drew an unwarranted link between Japanese trade barriers and US trade imbalances.

These new positions taken by the Tyson-chaired Council of Economic Advisers appear to have been framed with data which were either irrelevant or incorrect. Neither Japan's low index of intra-industry trade in manufactures, nor the high proportion of its trade that consists of intra-firm transactions is evidence, either singularly or together, that Japan's trade barriers and economic practices were uniquely restrictive. In complete contradiction to what had been alleged in the Tyson *Report*, the overwhelming majority of studies of cross-national trade patterns have not found Japanese trade patterns to be distinctive once allowance is taken of Japan's distinctive factor endowments. Indeed, at the time the *Report* was prepared, there were no studies making use of tightly structured models derived from international trade theory that actually found Japanese trade behaviour at all distinctive. (Nor have any studies with such findings appeared since that time.) Finally, there was no sound basis for the Tyson

Report's suggestion that Japanese barriers might have been keeping some $9 billion to $18 billion of US exports from the Japanese market.

This *Report*'s Japan content might have been of largely academic interest save that its substance undoubtedly helped frame the Clinton Administration's bilateral trade policies with Japan. When the Framework talks broke down with Japan in February 1994, President Clinton himself focused on the '$60 billion bilateral trade deficit with Japan'. Moreover, despite the budget battles of the previous summer, President Clinton appeared to be oblivious to the macroeconomic determinants of the US trade deficit.

The Clinton Administration clearly believed that Japan's economic institutions and policies were so different from those of other major industrialized countries that the traditional standards used to assess compliance with international agreements and norms did not apply. This led the Clinton Administration to attempt to insist that whatever new trade agreements were reached with Japan, they must specify the expected results of the agreements in terms of increased imports into the Japanese market. This demand was found to be unacceptable not only by Japan. US trading partners in Europe and Asia also denounced the Clinton Administration's approach, and the managed trade it risked, as a threat to the welfare of the international economic system.[46] Tragically, this failed policy was framed on premises about Japan which were largely incorrect. In June 1995, at the conclusion of the US–Japan auto parts talks, the Clinton Administration effectively abandoned this policy. The attempt to apply special rules to US–Japan economic relations has all but ended. The 1997 *Economic Report of the President,* the final *Report* of the Clinton Administration's first term, devotes no more than one short paragraph to Japan.

NOTES

1. These two *Reports* are traditionally bound together and known simply as the *Economic Report of the President*. This terminology will be used here.
2. Tyson's *Who's Bashing Whom?* (Washington, DC: Institute for International Economics, 1993) appeared in print just a few weeks after the Democratic presidential victory in November 1992.
3. See the discussion in Gary R. Saxonhouse, 'Textile Confrontation', Jerome B. Cohen (ed.), *Pacific Partnership: United States–Japan Trade* (Lexington, Mass.: D. C. Heath, 1972), pp. 177–200 and in Gary R. Saxonhouse, 'Employment, Imports, the Yen and the Dollar', Henry Rosovsky (ed.), *Discord in the Pacific: Challenges to the Japanese–American Alliance* (Washington, DC: Columbia Books, 1972), pp. 76–116.
4. Howard S. Ellis, 'Bilateralism and the Future of International Trade', *Essays in International Finance* No. 5 (Summer, 1945).
5. *Economic Report of the President*, 1983 (Washington, DC, 1983), p. 56.
6. *Ibid.*, p. 56.
7. *Ibid.*, p. 67.

8. *Economic Report of the President*, 1984 (Washington, DC, 1984), p. 66.
9. *Economic Report of the President*, 1994 (Washington, DC, 1994), pp.215–21; 233–37.
10. *Ibid.*, pp. 215–19.
11. *Ibid.*, p. 216.
12. *Ibid.*, pp. 216–217.
13. *Economic Report of the President*, 1990 (Washington, DC, 1990), pp. 248–9; *Economic Report of the President*, 1994 pp. 218–9.
14. *Economic Report of the President*, 1994, 219. In the absence of trade barriers the *Economic Report* argues that arbitrage should eliminate the difference between the price of the similar product in Japan and elsewhere.
15. *Ibid.*, p. 221.
16. *Ibid.*, p. 221.
17. Some of the issues raised in the Tyson *Economic Report* are examined in detail in Gary R. Saxonhouse, 'What Does Japanese Trade Structure Tell Us About Trade Policy?' *Journal of Economic Perspectives* Vol. 7, No. 3 (Summer, 1993), pp. 21–43.
18. *Economic Report of the President*, 1994, p. 29.
19. Jeffrey Sachs and Peter Boone, 'Japanese Structural Adjustment and the Balance of Payments', *Journal of the Japanese and International Economies* Vol. 2, No. 3 (September 1988). Clyde V. Prestowitz, Jr, Lawrence Chimerine, Saul Goldstein and Andrew Z. Szamosszegi, *Making the Framework Talks a Success* (Washington, DC: Economic Strategy Institute, 1994) found that the better than $50 billion in increased US exports to Japan that they believe should occur if all Japanese trade restrictions were removed increased US savings by more than US investment. At the same time, they found the availability of cheaper foreign products diminishes the Japanese household savings rate.
20. *Yomiuri shimbun*, 30 November 1995.
21. Gary R. Saxonhouse, 'Japan's Intractable Trade Surpluses', *The World Economy* Vol. 9, No. 3 (September 1986), pp. 239–57. Whatever increase in exports will occur will depend heavily on the future price of oil and what share of the exported oil goes to Japan. The immediate impact of the new legislation has been small because of the requirement that all oil exported be shipped in US-crewed and US-flagged vessels.
22. Japanese direct investment in the American retail industry is negligible. There are a number of sectors where Japanese-owned companies are a significant presence in wholesaling. The best example of this is automobiles where Japanese manufacturers such as Toyota have attempted to maintain equity control of regional wholesalers.
23. Mordechai E. Kreinin, 'How Closed is Japan's Market? Additional Evidence', *The World Economy* Vol. 11, No. 4, pp. 529–42.
24. Tsushosangyosho, *Tsusho Hakusho Heisei Roku-nen* (Tokyo, 1994) p. 245.
25. Masahiko Aoki, 'Horizontal vs. Vertical Information Structure of the Firm', *American Economic Review* (December 1986) Vol. 76, No. 5, pp. 971–83.
26. Tsushosangyosho, *Tsusho Hakusho Heisei Hachi-nen* (Tokyo, 1994), pp. 247–58.
27. Gary R. Saxonhouse, 'How Closed is the Japanese Market?: Comment' in Paul R. Krugman (ed.), *Trade with Japan* (Chicago: University of Chicago Press for the National Bureau of Economic Research, 1991), pp. 38–46.
28. The Tyson *Economic Report* (p. 216) characterizes Japan's intra-industry trade as 'unusually low'. C. Fred Bergsten and Marcus Noland, *Reconcilable Differences?* (Washington, DC: Institute for International Economics, 1993, 66) looking at the very same numbers characterize Japan's intra-industry trade as 'somewhat lower' than that of comparable industrial countries.
29. Elhanan Helpman and Paul Krugman, *Market Structure and Foreign Trade* (Cambridge, Mass.: MIT Press, 1985).
30. Gary R. Saxonhouse, 'Economic Growth and Trade Relations: Japanese Performance in Long-Term Perspective' in Takatoshi Ito and Anne O. Krueger (eds), *Trade and*

Protectionism (Chicago: University of Chicago Press, 1993).
31. Gary R. Saxonhouse, 'Japan, SII and the International Harmonization of Domestic Economic Practices', *Michigan Journal of International Law* Vol. 12, No. 2 (Winter, 1991), pp. 450–69.
32. For further discussion of this issue, see David Weinstein, 'Structural Impediments to Investment in Japan: What Have We Learned Over the Last 450 years?' in Masaru Yoshitomi and Edward M. Graham (eds), *Foreign Direct Investment in Japan* (Cheltenham, UK: Edward Elgar, 1996).
33. The Appendix does not include studies by Robert Z. Lawrence, 'Efficient or Exclusionist: The Import Behavior of Japan', *Brookings Papers on Economic Activity* 1991:1 and by Peter A. Petri, 'Japanese Trade in Transition: Hypotheses and Recent Evidence' in Paul R.Krugman (ed.), *Trade with Japan* (Chicago: University of Chicago Press, 1991). Neither of these studies addresses the question whether Japanese behaviour is exceptional. Rather they can be interpreted as explaining the institutional modalities of Japanese trade structure. They are effectively silent on whether Japanese trade structure is the product of comparative advantage or some other factors. The study by Marcus Noland, 'Why Are Prices in Japan So High?' *Japan and the World Economy* Vol. 7 No. 3 (1995) is similarly excluded. For more detailed comments on all three studies see Gary R. Saxonhouse, 'What Does Japan Trade Structure Tell Us about Japan's Trade Policy?'
34. T.N. Srinavasan and Koichi Hamada, 'The US–Japan Economic Problem' (New Haven, Conn.: Yale University, 1989). See also Edward E. Leamer, *The Sources of Comparative Advantage*.
35. Edward E. Leamer, 'Testing Trade Theory', *National Bureau of Economic Research* no.3957 (Cambridge, Mass: 1992); T. N. Srinavasan and Koichi Hamada.
36. Institute for International Economics *News Release*, 24 June 1993.
37. C. Fred Bergsten and Marcus Noland, *Reconcilable Differences* (Washington, DC: Institute for International Economics, 1993).
38. Contrast the appendix-less Bergsten–Noland study with such Institute for International Economics studies as Balassa and Noland, *Japan in the World Economy*, C. Fred Bergsten and William R. Cline, *The United States – Japan Problem*; C. Fred Bergsten, Kimberly Ann Elliott, Jeffrey J. Schott and Wendy E. Takacs, *Auction Quotas and United States Trade Policy* (Washington, DC: Institute for International Economics, 1987), John Williamson and Marcus H. Miller, *Targets and Indicators: A Blueprint for the International Coordination of Economic Policy* (Washington, DC: Institute for International Economics, 1987), and Gary Clyde Hufbauer, *Western Hemophere Economic Integration* (Washington, DC: Institute for International Economics, 1994), all of which have detailed technical appendices to support their specific quantitative findings. A revised version of 'Why are the Prices in Japan so High?' was finally published in *Japan and the World Economy* in 1995, more than two years after the Bergsten–Noland study was published. 'Why are Prices in Japan so High?' was only submitted to *Japan and the World Economy* after the publication of the Bergsten and Noland study.
39. This study and its predecessor are discussed in Gary R. Saxonhouse, 'What Does Japanese Trade Structure Tell Us About Japanese Trade Policy?', and Gary R. Saxonhouse, 'Japan, SII and the International Harmonization of Domestic Practices'.
40. Takatoshi Ito and Masayoshi Murayama, 'Is the Japanese Distribution System Really Inefficient?' in Paul R. Krugman (ed.), *Trade with Japan*; Motoshige Itoh, 'The Japanese Distribution System and Access to the Japanese Market' in Paul R. Krugman (ed.) *Trade with Japan* and Kiyohiko Nishimura, 'The Distribution System of Japan and the United States: A Comparative Study from the Viewpoint of Final Goods Buyers' (Tokyo: University of Tokyo, 1992).
41. As Ito and Murayama, 'Is the Japanese Distribution Really Inefficient' note, allowing for the role played by Japan's trading companies in no way changes these results.

42. William R. Cline, 'Japan's Trade Policies'. It is by no means surprising that American and European firms might choose to set higher relative prices in Japan while Japanese firms reject this strategy. With significant market shares, Japanese firms might well decide they have a particular interest in discouraging the entry of new competitors by maintaining low prices in a contestable market. That foreign firms are able to do this by no means demonstrates the presence of uniquely protective trade barriers in Japan. As Michael M. Knetter, 'International Comparisons of Pricing to Market Behavior', *National Bureau of Economic Research* Working Paper no.4098 (September 1992) notes, pricing to market appears pervasive in all advanced industrial economies.
43. Marcus Noland, 'Why Are Prices in Japan So High?'
44. In 'Why Are Retail Prices in Japan so High?: Evidence from German Export Prices', *National Bureau of Economic Research Working Paper* No. 4894 (October 1994), Michael Knetter found in an analysis of data on 37 7-digit German export industries that prices of German exports to Japan were systematically higher than prices of German exports to the United States, United Kingdom and Canada. It is by no means clear that relatively higher Japanese non-tariff barriers were responsible for these findings. Alternatively, the effect of differences in the composition of exports on unit values and the possibility of non-linear pricing could account for Knetter's findings relative to the United States and the United Kingdom during the period he examines. Knetter, assuming that 1) Japan's lower income would lead it to import relatively lower-quality products and 2) that the Canadian distribution system is separate from the American distribution system rejected both these possibilities. Neither of these assumptions appear warranted for the goods in Knetter's sample, nor was Japan's income per capita lower than the UK's during the years his study covered.
45. In December 1994 the Institute for International Economics released a comprehensive new study, *Measuring the Costs of Protection in Japan,* authored by Yoko Sazanami, Shuijiro Urata and Hiroki Kawai, the results of which appear to confirm the order of magnitude of the Noland estimates of the impact of Japanese trade restrictions. Comparing the results of this new study with the findings in Gary Clyde Hufbauer and Kimberly Ann Elliott, *Measuring the Costs of Protection in the United States* (Washington, DC: Institute for International Economics, 1994), it would appear that the Japanese barriers were five to six times more restrictive than those in the United States. These two studies, however, are not comparable. Hufbauer and Elliott, *a priori*, decided which US sectors had restrictions and then estimated their impact. By contrast, Sazanami, Urata and Kawai assumed that any Japanese sector might be protected by some barrier, visible or otherwise. On this basis they assume that any difference between a sector's ex-factory domestic production unit value, and its import (c.i.f.) unit value is a measure of the degree of protection the sector receives. Had the same criterion been applied by Hufbauer and Elliott to American evidence, the degree of protection found in the United States might well be many times larger than their current estimate. Almost certainly many sectors known to be barrier-free would be identified as receiving considerable protection from foreign competition. For example, applying the Sazanami, Urata and Kawai approach to US international trade data and data taken from the 1987 US Census of Manufacturers yields a tariff equivalent for the colour television set sector for 1987 of 94.7 per cent It is clear that when Sazanami, Urata and Kawai departed from Hufbauer and Elliott in calculating tariff equivalents they biased upward their estimates of the restrictiveness of Japanese trade barriers. This bias was probably exaggerated when in the second step of their estimation procedure they did follow the textbook methods of Hufbauer and Elliott. In particular, Hufbauer and Elliott assumed that, behind the protective barriers a nation erects, perfect competition reigns. This is what permitted Hufbauer and Elliott to assume there exists a supply curve when they calculated the impact of restrictive barriers on imports and consumer welfare. While Hufbauer and Elliott were free to assume perfect competition among domestic suppliers, the whole

rationale for Sazanami, Urata and Kawai's indiscriminate comparison of domestic unit value with imported unit value was that the collusive structure of Japanese domestic markets permitted the successful erection of private barriers against foreign competition. The method Sazanami, Urata and Kawai used to estimate the tariff equivalent of Japanese barriers is inconsistent with the method they used to measure the impact of such barriers on trade flows, except if they believe oligopolistic behaviour will cease once there is unfettered foreign access to the Japanese market. In all likelihood, the methods Sazanami, Urata and Kawai used at both stages of their analysis are flawed and both bias upward the estimated impact of Japanese trade barriers.

46. For a discussion of numerical targets, see Gary R. Saxonhouse, 'The Economics of the US–Japan Framework Talks', *Hoover Essays in Public Policy* no. 53, 1994.

REFERENCES

Balassa, B. and Noland, M. (1988), *Japan in the World Economy*, Washington, DC: Institute for International Economics.

Barbone, L. (1988), 'Trade Imbalances and Import Barriers', Paris: Organization for Economic Cooperation and Development.

Lawrence, R.Z. (1987), 'Imports in Japan: Closed Markets or Closed Minds?' *Brookings Papers on Economic Activity*, Z: 517–54.

Noland, M. (1997), 'Public Policies, Private Preferences and Japan's Trade Pattern', *Review of Economics and Statistics*, 79, 2:May.

Prestowitz, C.V., Jr, Chimerine, L., Goldstein, S., and Szamosszegi, A.Z. (1994), *Making the Framework Talks a Success*, Washington, DC: Economic Strategy Institute.

Sato, K. (1986), *Increasing Returns to Scale and International Trade: The Case of Japan*, New Brunswick, New Jersey: Rutgers University.

APPENDIX

Table A 5.6 Studies on the quantitative impact of Japanese trade barriers, part 1

Author(s)	Time period	Countries in sample	Level of aggregation	Dependent variable	Independent variables	Model	Finding
Bergsten–Cline (1985)	1974–84	11	1 economy-wide sector	Imports/GNP	Log GNP, log crude oil, production per capita, log arable land per capita, transport costs, dummy for iron ore resources	*Ad hoc*	Insignificant dummy variable for Japan
Carliner (1985)	1967, 1972, 1977, 1980, 1982	19	1 economy-wide sector	Index of intra-industry trade, trade balance	Log GNP per capita, log GNP, distance	*Ad hoc*	Insignificant dummy variable for Japan
Cline (1990)	1989	2	69 products	Japanese prices/US prices	US dummy, European dummy, food products dummy	*Ad hoc*	Insignificant dummy variable for Japan

Author(s)	Time period	Countries in sample	Level of aggregation	Dependent variable	Independent variables	Model	Finding
Golub (1994)	1970–89	7	7 industrial sectors, agriculture, total industrial	Net trade/sectoral value-added	Log relative unit labour costs, log relative GNP, log relative GNP squared	*Ad hoc*. Time series inspired by Ricardo	Japan most closely conforms to the Ricardian model
Goto (1991)	1970, 1980, 1983	13	21 industrial sectors	Imports/total domestic use	Export/total OECD use; exports/total OECD production; distance	Helpman–Krugman (1985)	Insignificant dummy variables for Japan
Harrigan (1996)	1985	22	28 industrial sectors	Log bilateral imports/GNP	Log exporter sector output	Helpman–Krugman (1986)	Japan and US equally open to each other's imports; Japan more open to EU imports than EU to Japanese imports
Hosen (1993)	1980, 1985	10	1 economy-wide sector	Intra-industry trade index	Land/labour, energy/labour, log GDP	*Ad hoc*	Insignificant dummy variables for Japan

Author(s)	Time period	Countries in sample	Level of aggregation	Dependent variable	Independent variables	Model	Finding
Leamer (1984)	1958, 1975	60	10 sectors	Net trade	Capital, 3 varieties of labour, 4 varieties of land, coal, oil	Heckscher–Ohlin with factor price equalization	With two minor exceptions, insignificant dummy variables for Japan
Noland (1987)	1980	45	1 economy-wide sector	Log imports, log exports, log trade volume	Log GDP, log GDP per capita, factor endowment similarity index, transport costs	*Ad hoc*. Inspired by Heckscher–Ohlin, Helpman–Krugman	Insignificant dummy variables for Japan
Noland (1997)	1968, 1988	30	46 sectors	Net trade	Capital, 2 varieties of labour, 3 varieties of land, coal reserves, oil reserves, minerals, transport costs	Heckscher–Ohlin with additive factor endowment measurement error	Insignificant mean of studentized residuals for Japan

Author(s)	Time period	Countries in sample	Level of aggregation	Dependent variable	Independent variables	Model	Finding
Saxonhouse (1983)	1959, 1962, 1964, 1967, 1969, 1971, 1973	9	109 sectors	Net trade	Capital, 2 varieties of labour, petroleum reserves, iron ore deposits, arable land, distance	Heckscher–Ohlin with factor price equalization normalized for factor quality	17 significant Japanese dummy variables out of a possible 109 instances; covers 4.9% of Japanese trade
Saxonhouse (1986)	1964, 1971, 1979	22	109 sectors	Net trade	Capital, 2 varieties of labour, petroleum reserves, iron ore deposits, arable land, distance	Heckscher–Ohlin with factor price equalization normalized for factor quality	61 out of 327 possible instances of Japanese trade outside the forecast interval; covers 6.1% of Japanese gross external trade
Saxonhouse (1993)	1979	24	61 sectors	Imports/GNP	Capital, 2 varieties of labour, petroleum reserves, coal reserves, arable land	Helpman–Krugman with factor price equalization normalized for factor quality	8 of 61 possible instances of Japanese imports outside tolerance interval; covers 5.1% of Japanese imports

Author(s)	Time period	Countries in sample	Level of aggregation	Dependent variable	Independent variables	Model	Finding
Takenaka-Ishikawa (1992)	1984-88	19	1 economy-wide sector	Log imports/GNP, imports/GNP	Log GNP per capita, log population, primary imports/total imports, transport costs	*Ad hoc*	Insignificant dummy variables for Japan
Takenaka-Ishikawa (1992)	1984-90	13	5 sectors	Imports/total domestic use	Production/global production, distance	Helpman–Krugman	Insignificant dummy variable for Japan
Trefler (1993)	1983	33	79 sectors	Log wages	Log factor augmentation parameter	Heckscher–Ohlin	Japanese implicit trade in labor services within forecast interval
Wei (1996)	1982, 1986, 1990, 1994	19	one economy-wide sector	Log bilateral trade	Log GDP exporting country, log GDP importing country, bilateral distance remoteness, adjacency, language	*Ad hoc*. Inspired by Deardorff gravity model	Japanese home bias insignificant

Sources: This table is an updated version of Table 9.5 in Gary R. Saxonhouse and Robert M. Stern, 'An Analytical Survey of Formal and Informal Barriers to International Trade and Investment in the United States, Canada, and Japan' in Robert M. Stern (ed.), *Trade and Investment Relations Among the United States, Canada, and Japan* (Chicago: University of Chicago Press, 1989); C. Fred Bergsten and William R. Cline, *The United States–Japan Economic Problem* (Washington, DC: Institute for International Economics, 1985); Geoffrey Carliner, 'Patterns in Japanese and American Trade' (Cambridge, Mass.: National Bureau of Economic Research, 1985); William R. Cline, 'Japan's Trade Policies' (Washington, DC: Institute for International Economics, 1990); Stephen S. Golub, 'Comparative Advantage, Exchange Rates and G-7 Trade Balances' *IMF Staff Papers* Vol. 41 No. 2 (June 1994); Fumihiro Goto, 'Is the Japanese Market Really Closed? A Critical Review of the Economic Studies' (Tokyo: Research Institute of Trade and Industry, 1991); James Harrigan, 'Openness to Trade in Manufactures in the OECD', *Journal of International Economics* Vol. 40 No. 1 (February, 1996); Mitsuo Hosen, *Japan's Intra-Industry Trade* (Ann Arbor, Mich.: UMI Dissertation Services, 1993); Edward E. Leamer, *Sources of Comparative Advantage* (Cambridge, Mass.: MIT Press, 1984); Marcus Noland, 'An Econometric Model of the volume of International Trade' (Washington, DC: Institute for International Economics, 1987); Marcus Noland, 'Public Policies, Private Preferences and Japan's Trade Pattern', *Review of Economics and Statistics* Vol. 79 No. 2 (May 1997); Gary R. Saxonhouse, 'The Micro- and Macroeconomics of Foreign Sales to Japan' in William R. Cline (ed.), *Trade Policy for the 1980s* (Cambridge, Mass.: MIT Press, 1983); Gary R. Saxonhouse, 'What's Wrong with Japanese Trade Structure?' *Pacific Economic Papers* No. 137 (July, 1986); Gary R. Saxonhouse, 'Economic Growth and Trade Relations: Japanese Performance in Long-Term Perspective' in Takatoshi Ito and Anne O. Krueger (eds), *Trade and Protectionism* (Chicago: University of Chicago Press for the National Bureau of Economic Research, 1993); Heizo Takenaka and Tatsuya Ishikawa, 'Is Japan Still a Closed Market?' NLI Research No. 48, 1992; Daniel Trefler, 'International Factor Price Differences: Leontief was Right!' *Journal of Political Economy* Vol. 105 No. 6 (December 1993); Shang-jin Wei, 'Intra-National versus International Trade: How Stubborn Are Nations in Global Integration?' National Bureau of Economic Research Working Paper no. 5531 (April 1996).

Table A5.7 Studies on the quantitative impact of trade barriers, part 2

Author(s)	Time period	Countries in sample	Level of aggregation	Dependent variable	Independent variables	Model	Finding
Balassa– Noland (1988)	1973–83	18	1 economy-wide sector, imports disaggregated by industrial, primary, by industrial or developing country sources	Log imports/GNP; imports/GNP	Log GNP per capita, log population, primary imports/total imports, transport costs	*Ad hoc*	Significant dummy variables for Japan
Barbone (1988)	1974–83	23	1 economy-wide sector	Industrial imports/GNP	Log GNP per capita, log population, log population squared, GNP squared	*Ad hoc*	Significant dummy variables for Japan
Lawrence (1987)	1970, 1980, 1983	13	21 sectors	Log imports/total domestic use	Log exports/total EOCD use; log production/total OECD production, distance	*Ad hoc*. Inspired by Helpman–Krugman	Generally significant dummies for Japan

Author(s)	Time period	Countries in sample	Level of aggregation	Dependent variable	Independent variables	Model	Finding
Noland (1997)	1968, 1988	30	46 sectors	Imports	Capital, 2 varieties of labor, 3 varieties of land, coal reserves, oil reserves, minerals, transport costs	*Ad hoc*. Inspired by Helpman–Krugman with endogenous correction for factor quality	Significant negative mean studentized residual for Japan
Prestowitz-Chimerine-Goldstein-Szamosszegi (1994)	1991	23	1 economy-wide sector	Imports	Population, population density, transport costs, GNP per capita, education	*Ad hoc*	Significant dummy variable for Japan
Sato (1986)	1960, 1970, 1980	15	1 economy-wide sector	Imports/total sample imports	Log population, net trade in primary/value-added in industry	*Ad hoc*	Significant dummy variable for Japan

Sources: Bela Balassa and Marcus Noland, *Japan in the World Economy* (Washington, DC: Institute for International Economics, 1988); Lucas Barbone, 'Trace Imbalances and Import Barriers' (Paris: Organization for Economic Cooperation and Development, 1988); Robert Z. Lawrence, 'Imports in Japan: Closed Markets or Closed Minds?' *Brookings Papers on Economic Activity* 1987:2; Marcus Noland, 'Public Policies, Private Preferences and Japan's Trade Pattern', *Review of Economics and Statistics* Vol.79 No.2 (May 1997); Clyde V. Prestowitz, Jr, Lawrence Chimerine, Saul Goldstein and Andrew Z. Szamosszegi, *Making the Framework Talks a Success* (Washington, DC: Economic Strategy Institute, 1994); Kazuo Sato, 'Increasing Returns to Scale and International Trade: The Case of Japan' (New Erunswick, New Jersey: Rutgers University, 1986).

6. Foreign Direct Investment in Japan: Empirical Analyses of Interactions between FDI Inflows and Trade

Masahiro Kawai and Shujiro Urata[1]

6.1 INTRODUCTION

One of the most significant developments in the world economy since the mid-1980s has been the dramatic expansion of foreign direct investment (FDI) flows. The total world FDI outflow expanded from US$57.2 billion in 1985 to US$230.6 billion in 1990 on a balance-of-payments basis (International Monetary Fund). World FDI outflows thus grew at annual compound growth rates of 32.2 per cent, while total world trade grew at about one-fourth this rate and world income at about one-fifth. FDI outflows declined in the early 1990s after reaching a peak in 1990 but started to rise again in the mid-1990s. FDI continues to play an important role in integrating national economies and globalizing economic activities.

The expansion of world FDI since the mid-1980s has depended mainly on a surge in investment flows among the major industrialized countries. The industrialized countries, particularly those of the G7, were the major investors of and hosts to FDI (see Graham and Krugman, 1993). With the exception of a small group of emerging economies, such as Mexico, Brazil and the East Asian economies, which absorbed relatively large FDI flows, the developing economies received only a limited share of world FDI.

Though this recent expansion in FDI activities is observed for both outward and inward flows for the large, industrialized countries, Japan is an exception. Japan has long been a major direct investor abroad; it was the world's largest direct investor from 1989 through 1991, though in recent years its rank has dropped. At the same time, however, Japan remains a strikingly small host country for inward FDI. The small size of FDI inflows in Japan has been noted and criticized by the United States and European countries as evidence of the closed nature of the Japanese economy. The Government of Japan has responded to such criticisms by taking measures to promote inward FDI (Japan Investment Council, 1996).

In contrast to the presence of extensive literature on Japan's FDI outflows, perhaps because of their small size, economists have not studied Japan's FDI inflows in a serious, systematic manner.[2] In this chapter we focus on foreign firms' direct investment in Japan and analyse the relationship between such investment and export–import trade. We extend the well-known gravity model of international trade to the analysis of interactions between FDI inflows and trade. Earlier work found the presence of strong, positive interactions between Japan's FDI outflows and its export–import trade, (Kawai 1997 and Kawai and Urata, 1997). Based on these earlier findings, we examine whether FDI inflows in Japan, like FDI outflows from Japan, contribute to Japan's exports and imports and whether Japan's trade encourages FDI inflows to Japan.

The chapter is organized as follows. Section 6.2 reviews recent trends in FDI inflows in Japan, paying special attention to the source economies' geographical and industry composition. Sections 6.3 and 6.4 respectively discuss the motives of foreign firms for direct investment in Japan and the patterns of procurement and sales by affiliates of foreign firms located in Japan. Section 6.5 undertakes an econometric examination of interactions between FDI inflows in Japan and Japan's exports and imports by using the 'gravity' model. Section 6.6 concludes the chapter.

6.2 RECENT TRENDS IN JAPAN'S FDI INFLOWS

6.2.1 A Rising Trend of FDI in Japan

There exist two measures of foreign direct investment inflows to Japan: balance of payments (BOP) statistics and notifications statistics. Both have merits and demerits as bases for FDI data.[3] Collected and published by the Ministry of Finance, notifications statistics indicate the intentions of foreign firms to invest in Japan. Though they do not necessarily represent realized values of net FDI inflows after taking account of investments subsequently withdrawn from the Japanese market, they do report data broken down by both country and industry. Collected and published by the Bank of Japan, BOP statistics offer a relatively limited breakdown of data by country with no breakdown of data by industry. On the other hand, because reverse flows caused by withdrawals from the Japanese market are subtracted, BOP statistics do represent the realized value of net FDI inflows.

These two measures have often revealed divergent movements since the late 1980s, particularly when BOP statistics decline sharply (Figure 6.1).

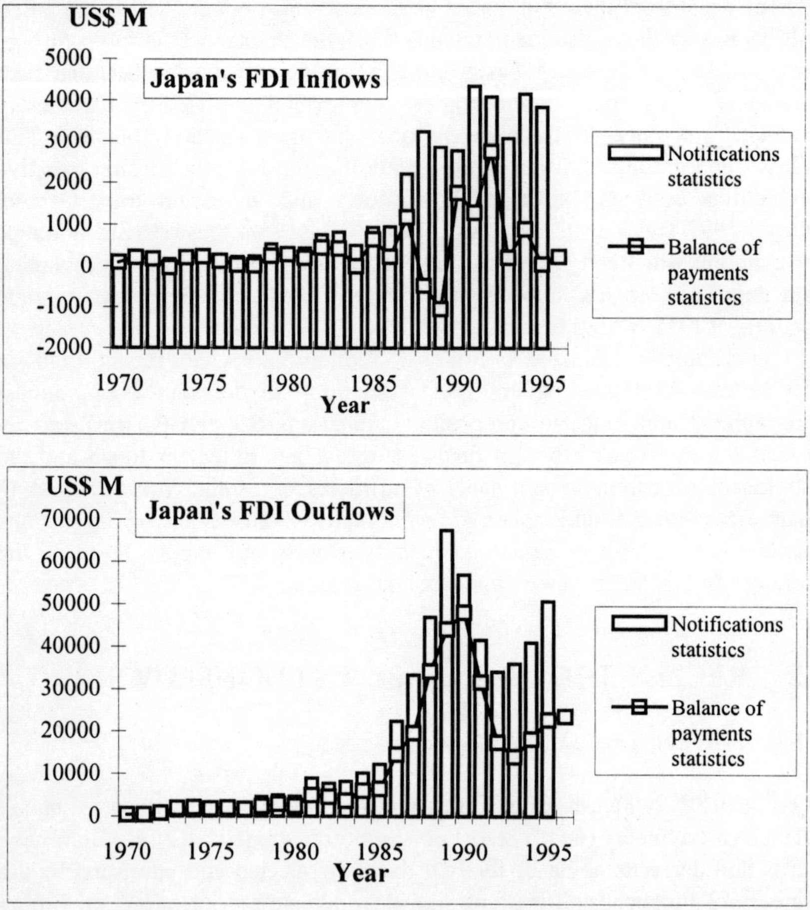

Notes: Notification of statistics are fiscal year data and balance of payments statistics are calendar year data.
Balance of payments statistics for 1991–96 are obtained by converting yen data into US dollars by using yearly average exchange rates.

Source: Ministry of Finance, *Okurasho Kokusai Kinyukyoku Nenpo* MOP International Bureau Anual Report; Bank of Japan, Balance of Payments Monthly, various issues.

Figure 6.1 Japan's foreign direct investment inflows and outflows, 1970–96

After experiencing sharp declines in 1988 and 1989,[4] the magnitude of FDI inflows in Japan on a BOP basis grew strongly in the first three years of the 1990s before it started to decline in 1993–96 (Table 6.1). FDI inflows on a notifications basis started to expand in the latter half of the 1980s, reached a peak in 1991, and have remained large for the rest of the 1990s (Figures 6.2 and 6.3).[5]

The expansion of notifications-based FDI inflows to Japan in the latter half of the 1980s was attributable mainly to a sharp yen rate appreciation and buoyant economic activities brought about by the emergence of the 'bubble' economy. The yen appreciation increased the attractiveness of importing foreign goods and services as it lowered their prices in the Japanese market. To respond to the increased demand for imports to Japan, foreign firms engaged in international businesses appear to have aggressively set up import bases in Japan.[6] Buoyant economic activities also contributed to rising inflows of notifications-based FDI in Japan by expanding business opportunities in Japan for foreign firms. We shall examine the motives of foreign firms for undertaking FDI in Japan in a later section.

Although FDI in Japan has been active recently, its magnitude is still quite small compared to the magnitude of FDI inflows in other developed countries. Various statistics attest to this observation. For example, Table 6.2 shows that the stock of inward FDI in Japan at the end of 1995 amounted to US $20 billion. This was only one-fiftieth of the corresponding figure for the United States (US$1.02 trillion).[7] The comparison becomes less lopsided when other developed countries are compared; the stock of inward FDI in Japan at the end of 1995 was one-tenth and one-fifth of the corresponding figures for the United Kingdom (US$223 billion) and Germany (US$91 billion). The limited amount of FDI in Japan can also be clearly shown when its FDI inflow is compared with either its GDP or its FDI outflow; the stock of inward FDI in Japan at the end of 1995 was only 0.4 per cent of GDP and 6.7 per cent of the stock of outward FDI from Japan. The corresponding figures for other major industrialized countries are significantly larger, indicating that Japan's FDI inflows are unusually small compared to its economic size and to those of other countries.

Various explanations are given for the limited magnitude of FDI inflows to Japan. Encarnation (1992) argues that government regulations which are intended to protect Japanese industries have discouraged FDI inflows to Japan. Mason (1992) and Lawrence (1993) find that *keiretsu* (business groupings among closely related firms) are an effective obstacle to FDI inflows to Japan because the *keiretsu* system makes it difficult for outsiders, particularly foreign firms, to develop procurement and sales networks.[8] A recent survey conducted by the Ministry of International Trade and Industry

Table 6.1 Geographical distribution of FDI inflows and stocks in Japan (balance of payments statistics), 1988–96

	Annual FDI inflows in Japan									
Source Regions	1988	1989	1990	1991	1992	1993	1994	1995	1996	FDI Stock 1996 (US$M)
Asia	-15	91	72	13	124	248	135	322	444	597
NIES	33	88	83	9	124	242	130	341	449	591
Hong Kong	n.a.	n.a.	n.a.	n.a.	n.a.	n.a.	n.a.	217	395	476
Taiwan	n.a.	n.a.	n.a.	n.a.	n.a.	n.a.	n.a.	5	28	59
Singapore	n.a.	n.a.	n.a.	n.a.	n.a.	n.a.	n.a.	4	-29	45
Korea	n.a.	n.a.	n.a.	n.a.	n.a.	n.a.	n.a.	115	55	11
ASEAN	n.a.	n.a.	n.a.	n.a.	n.a.	n.a.	n.a.	2	-11	0
China	2	0	1	-1	0	8	2	-21	0	2
India	n.a.	n.a.	n.a.	n.a.	n.a.	n.a.	n.a.	0	6	4
North America	-645	-1,529	573	647	865	539	388	-404	-899	15,953
United States	-599	-1,530	598	-89	817	510	380	292	-781	15,391
Canada	-46	1	-25	736	48	29	8	-696	-119	562
Central and South America	n.a.	n.a.	n.a.	n.a.	n.a.	n.a.	n.a.	0	-17	87
Oceania	n.a.	n.a.	n.a.	n.a.	n.a.	n.a.	n.a.	0	14	22
Australia	0	16	5	3	1	3	10	5	6	22
Western Europe	n.a.	n.a.	n.a.	n.a.	n.a.	n.a.	n.a.	33	714	8,515
European Union	100	327	1,106	630	1,329	-1,105	336	85	837	7,214
United Kingdom	-44	142	88	246	967	71	-1	113	297	2,452
Germany	48	100	152	154	56	228	44	100	580	2,181
Netherlands	n.a.	n.a.	n.a.	n.a.	n.a.	n.a.	n.a.	-197	-252	1,209
France	18	-1	46	50	168	65	41	35	13	309
Belgium-Luxembourg	n.a.	n.a.	n.a.	n.a.	n.a.	n.a.	n.a.	0	-29	162
Italy	3	2	4	3	9	1	2	4	0	0

	Annual FDI inflows in Japan									
Source Regions	1988	1989	1990	1991	1992	1993	1994	1995	1996	FDI Stock 1996 (US$M)
Switzerland	n.a.	n.a.	n.a.	n.a.	n.a.	n.a.	n.a.	-49	-124	1,278
Sweden	n.a.	n.a.	n.a.	n.a.	n.a.	n.a.	n.a.	9	152	159
	0	0	0	0	0	0	0	0	2	0
Eastern Europe, Russia, etc.										
Middle East	n.a.	n.a.	n.a.	n.a.	n.a.	n.a.	n.a.	0	-2	76
Africa	n.a.	n.a.	n.a.	n.a.	n.a.	n.a.	n.a.	0	-29	4
Other	-13	8	-73	-12	105	278	-17	0	0	0
Total	-485	-1,054	1,753	1,368	2,728	86	888	41	228	29,937

Note: The balance of payments statistics began to be reported only in terms of the Japanese yen from 1995. The flow data for 1995 and 1996 are converted into US dollars at the annual average exchange rates of 94.06 and 108.78 yen per dollar, respectively.
The stock data for 1996 are converted into US dollars at the end-of-the- period exchange rate of 116.00 yen per US dollar.
Asia refers to South East Asia for the period 1988–1994.
The European Union consists of 12 countries for the period 1988–94 and 15 countries for the period 1995–96.

Source: Bank of Japan, Balance of Payments Monthly, April issues.

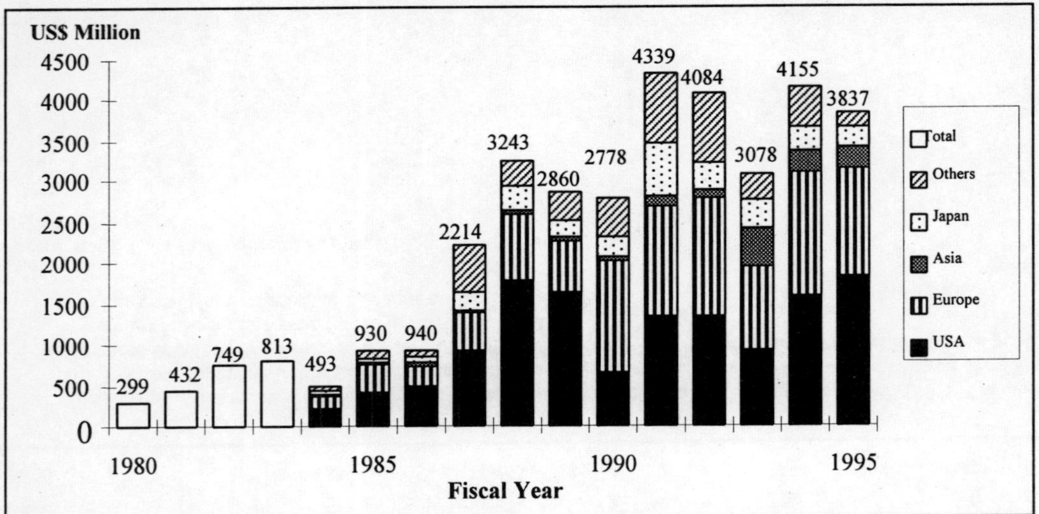

Note: Asia only includes Hong Kong for the 1984–90 period.
'Japan' indicates FDI by foreign firms located in Japan
Detailed information on geographical composition is not available for 1980–3 on a consistent basis.

Source: Ministry of Finance, *Okurasho Kokusai Kinyukyoku Nenpo, MOP International Finance Bureay Annual Report*, various issues.
Ministry of Finance, *Aaisei Kinyu Tokei Geppo, Monthly Statistics on Government Finance and Banking*, various issues.

Figure 6.2 Geographical composition of FDI inflows in Japan (Notification statistics), 1980–95

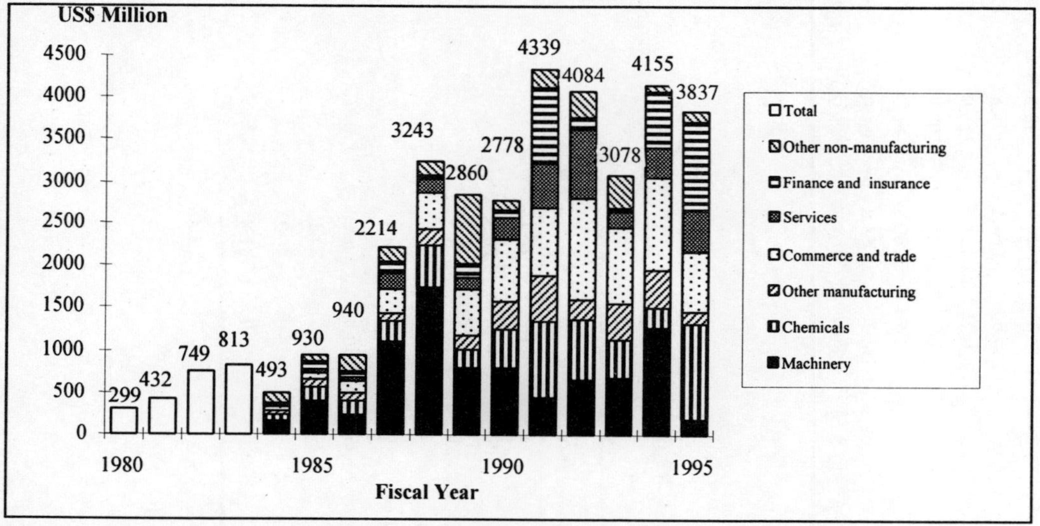

Note: Detailed information on industry composition is not available for 1980-83.

Source: Ministry of Finance, *Okurasho Kokusai Kinyukyoku Nenpo MOF International Finance Bureau Annual Report*, various issues.
Ministry of Finance, *Zaisei Kinyu Tokei Geppo Monthly Statistics on Government Finance and Banking*, various issues.

Figure 6.3 Industry composition of FDI inflows in Japan (notification statistics), 1980–95

Table 6.2 Stock of inward and outward FDI of the major industrialized countries

a. Stock of Inward FDI (Dollar Values)

(US$ Billion)

	1990	1991	1992	1993	1994	1995
United States	539.6	669.1	694.2	760.9	771.9	1019.2
United Kingdom	218.2	225.8	185.6	189.4	202.4	223.1
Japan	9.9	12.3	15.5	16.9	19.2	19.9
Germany	65.7	69.0	66.6	64.5	78.8	90.9
France	84.9	97.5	100.2	103.2	123.9	159.3
Netherlands	75.8	81.3	82.9	85.2	102.8	n.a.
Switzerland	43.4	45.0	42.6	49.5	61.7	73.3
Italy	60.0	61.6	50.7	54.5	61.0	66.0
Canada	113.0	117.5	109.1	107.5	108.9	123.1

b. Stock of Inward FDI (Relative to GDP)

(%)

1990	1991	1992	1993	1994	1995
9.1	11.3	11.1	11.6	11.1	14.1
22.2	22.2	17.6	20.0	19.8	20.2
0.3	0.4	0.4	0.4	0.4	0.4
4.4	4.0	3.4	3.4	3.8	3.8
7.1	8.1	7.6	8.3	9.3	10.4
26.7	28.0	25.8	27.3	30.8	n.a.
19.2	19.5	17.7	21.3	24.0	24.1
5.5	5.4	4.1	5.5	6.0	6.2
19.7	19.9	19.1	19.5	19.9	21.8

c. Stock of Outward FDI (Dollar Values)

(US$ Billion)

	1990	1991	1992	1993	1994	1995
United States	731.8	827.5	798.6	1027.6	1058.9	1301.1
United Kingdom	230.8	234.3	224.5	250.7	280.5	331.8
Japan	201.4	231.8	248.1	259.8	275.6	297.0
Germany	126.0	144.1	149.6	157.7	189.8	231.4
France	110.1	129.9	140.6	141.4	163.1	198.0
Netherlands	113.5	124.9	129.4	132.4	157.2	n.a.
Switzerland	65.7	75.3	73.8	91.6	112.6	142.8
Italy	57.3	67.2	71.0	81.9	91.1	109.2
Canada	78.8	88.1	84.5	86.8	93.7	104.3

d. Stock of Outward FDI (Relative to GDP)

(%)

1990	1991	1992	1993	1994	1995
12.4	14.0	12.8	15.7	15.3	17.9
23.5	23.0	21.2	26.5	27.4	30.0
6.9	6.9	6.8	6.2	6.0	5.8
8.4	8.4	7.6	8.3	9.3	9.6
9.2	10.8	10.6	11.3	12.3	12.9
40.0	43.1	40.2	42.5	47.0	n.a.
29.1	32.6	30.6	39.5	43.8	47.0
5.2	5.8	5.8	8.3	9.0	10.2
13.7	14.9	14.8	15.7	17.1	18.4

e. Stock of Inward FDI Relative to Stock of Outward FDI

(%)

	1990	1991	1992	1993	1994	1995
United States	73.7	80.9	86.9	74.0	72.9	78.3
United Kingdom	94.5	96.4	82.7	75.6	72.2	67.2
Japan	4.9	5.3	6.3	6.5	7.0	6.7
Germany	52.2	47.9	44.5	40.9	41.5	39.3
France	77.1	75.0	71.3	73.0	76.0	80.5
Netherlands	66.8	65.1	64.1	64.4	65.4	n.a.
Switzerland	66.0	59.8	57.6	54.1	54.8	51.3
Italy	104.8	91.6	71.4	66.6	66.9	60.4
Canada	143.4	133.5	129.1	123.9	116.3	118.1

f. Stock of Inward FDI/GDP Relative to the USA

(USA=100)

1990	1991	1992	1993	1994	1995
100.0	100.0	100.0	100.0	100.0	100.0
243.3	196.0	157.9	172.2	177.9	143.7
3.7	3.2	3.8	3.5	3.8	2.8
47.9	35.5	30.4	29.1	34.6	26.8
77.9	71.7	68.2	71.1	83.6	73.7
293.0	247.8	231.7	235.5	276.3	n.a.
210.5	172.4	158.9	183.8	215.4	171.7
60.1	47.3	37.3	47.7	53.8	44.1
216.0	176.0	171.9	167.5	178.9	154.9

Note: The data are based on payments statistics.

Source: International Monetary Fund, *International Financial Statistics*, May 1997.

found that the high cost of operating business in Japan was an important factor discouraging FDI in Japan. The high cost is attributable largely to high land prices and office rental rates, high wages, high materials and transportation costs, and high tax rates.[9] The survey also found that government regulations discouraged FDI inflows but that this factor was not as influential as those causing high operating costs. Other researchers point to the absence of effective markets for mergers and acquisitions (M&A) and takeovers as another factor inhibiting FDI inflows into Japan.

6.2.2 Recent Changes in the Patterns of FDI in Japan

The United States and European countries have been major sources of FDI in Japan (Table 6.1, Table 6.3 and Figure 6.2). Specifically, measured by the BOP-based stock of inward FDI, the United States and Europe respectively accounted for approximately 50 and 30 per cent of FDI in Japan at the end of 1996.[10] Until recently, the share held by Asian economies had been negligible. With rising FDI inflows from Asia in the 1990s, however, the share of Asian economies in the total stock of FDI inflows to Japan reached 2 per cent in 1996 (the BOP-based stock value) or 6 per cent over the 1991–94 period (the notifications-based cumulative value).

The industry composition of FDI in Japan has been shifting from manufacturing to non-manufacturing. Specifically, the share of manufacturing in total FDI in Japan declined from 68 per cent during 1984–88 to 46 per cent during 1989–94. Within manufacturing, the machinery and chemicals sectors account for a large proportion. Within non-manufacturing, the commerce and trade sector and the services sector have long accounted for a large proportion, with the finance and insurance sector also having become important in recent years (Figure 6.3). In terms of cumulative value of notifications-based FDI inflows over the 1991–94 period, the machinery and chemicals sectors accounted for 19 and 14 per cent of the total, respectively, while the commerce and trade sector, the services sector, and the finance and insurance sector accounted respectively for 24, 12 and 11 per cent of the total (Table 6.3).

A noticeable pattern in the FDI data is that in terms of country and industry composition a large portion of FDI in manufacturing has been undertaken by firms from developed countries. By contrast, most of the FDI undertaken by developing economies, especially those from Asia, has been in commerce and trade. One plausible explanation for this is that firms from developing Asia have invested in Japan to set up distribution networks for their trade based in Japan.[11]

Table 6.3 Geographical and industry composition of cumulative FDI inflows in Japan – cumulative values of notifications statistics over the period 1991–94

Source Regions	North America		Latin America		Asia (excl. Japan)		Middle East		Europe		Africa		Oceania		Japan		World Total	
Industries	US$ Mill	%	US$ Mill	%	US$ Mill	%	US$ Mill	%	US$ Mill	%	US$ Mill	%	US$ Mill	%	US$ Mill	%	US$ Mill	%
Manufacturing Total	2699.0	38.4	206.3	2.9	273.4	3.9	4.6	0.1	2917.7	41.5	0.1	0.0	23.9	0.3	908.6	12.9	7033.6	100.0
Food	138.9	55.4	16.5	6.6	3.7	1.5	0.1	0.0	33.8	13.5	0.0	0.0	0.5	0.2	57.4	22.9	250.9	100.0
Textiles	13.6	64.8	0.0	0.0	5.1	24.3	0.0	0.0	1.6	7.6	0.0	0.0	0.0	0.0	0.7	3.3	21.0	100.0
Chemical products	781.5	34.1	83.3	3.6	32.9	1.4	0.0	0.0	1122.8	49.0	0.0	0.0	0.0	0.0	271.0	11.8	2291.4	100.0
Petroleum	13.0	3.1	0.6	0.1	0.8	0.2	4.3	1.0	153.2	36.8	0.0	0.0	0.0	0.0	244.1	58.7	415.9	100.0
Glass and ceramics	18.2	68.4	0.7	2.6	0.3	1.1	0.1	0.4	46.6	175.2	0.0	0.0	0.0	0.0	0.7	2.6	26.6	100.0
Rubber and leather products	3.9	1.8	0.0	0.0	0.0	0.0	0.0	0.0	169.0	79.4	0.0	0.0	0.0	0.0	0.1	0.0	212.8	100.0
Metals	402.4	89.0	0.1	0.0	0.2	0.0	0.1	0.0	40.3	8.9	0.0	0.0	3.2	0.7	5.7	1.3	452.0	100.0
Machinery	1209.5	39.7	105.1	3.5	227.9	7.5	0.1	0.0	1255.7	41.3	0.0	0.0	13.1	0.4	232.5	7.6	3043.9	100.0
General machinery	99.5	29.5	0.4	0.1	2.8	0.8	0.1	0.0	157.0	46.6	0.0	0.0	13.1	3.9	64.1	19.0	336.9	100.0
Electrical machinery	1105.8	43.2	99.8	3.9	225.2	8.8	0.0	0.0	990.7	38.7	0.0	0.0	0.0	0.0	141.2	5.5	2562.6	100.0
Transport equipment	4.0	2.8	4.9	3.4	0.0	0.0	0.0	0.0	108.0	74.9	0.0	0.0	0.0	0.0	27.2	18.9	144.2	100.0
Other manufacturing	118.3	37.1	0.1	0.0	2.5	0.8	0.1	0.0	94.6	29.7	0.0	0.0	7.1	2.2	96.3	30.2	318.9	100.0
Non-manufacturing Total	3817.4	44.3	931.3	10.8	689.8	8.0	9.2	0.1	2417.8	28.0	17.9	0.2	20.8	0.2	718.8	8.3	8622.3	100.0
Commerce and trade	1444.6	36.6	196.5	5.0	450.1	11.4	6.6	0.2	1466.5	37.2	0.4	0.0	11.3	0.3	367.4	9.3	3943.2	100.0
Services	656.3	33.9	575.5	29.8	111.9	5.8	2.6	0.1	284.2	14.7	9.1	0.5	9.5	0.5	284.1	14.7	1933.3	100.0
Finance and insurance	1414.9	81.2	73.2	4.2	28.6	1.6	0.0	0.0	192.0	11.0	4.2	0.2	0.0	0.0	29.0	1.7	1742.3	100.0
Real estate	161.9	38.5	7.8	1.9	78.2	18.6	0.0	0.0	165.9	39.5	0.6	0.1	0.0	0.0	6.2	1.5	420.4	100.0
Communication	100.2	49.3	0.1	0.0	12.4	6.1	0.0	0.0	82.1	40.4	0.0	0.0	0.0	0.0	8.9	4.4	203.4	100.0
Transportation	10.6	11.1	73.5	76.7	4.4	4.6	0.0	0.0	1.0	1.0	3.6	3.8	0.0	0.0	2.7	2.8	95.8	100.0
Construction	0.6	2.2	4.3	15.9	1.4	5.2	0.1	0.4	6.4	23.6	0.0	0.0	0.0	0.0	14.3	52.8	27.1	100.0
Other non-manufacturing	27.8	10.8	0.4	0.2	2.8	1.1	0.0	0.0	219.7	85.5	0.0	0.0	0.0	0.0	6.4	2.5	257.1	100.0
Overall Total	6516.3	41.5	1137.6	7.2	963.2	6.1	13.8	0.1	4889.5	31.1	18.0	0.1	44.8	0.3	1627.4	10.4	15716.4	100.0

Notes: Acquisition of less than 10% of non-listed shares and equities are excluded beginning 1 April 1992.

Source: Ministry of Finance, *Okurasho Kokusai Kinyukyoku Nenpo MOF International Finance Bureau Annual Report* various issues.
Ministry of Finance, unpublished data.

6.3 MOTIVES BEHIND FOREIGN DIRECT INVESTMENT IN JAPAN

The previous section explained factors promoting recent FDI in Japan. This section examines motives behind foreign firms' FDI in Japan in more detail. Such motives also influence patterns of FDI–trade relationships, a major concern of this chapter.

Several questionnaire surveys on the motives of foreign firms for undertaking FDI in Japan have been conducted. The most comprehensive is a questionnaire survey by the Ministry of International Trade and Industry (MITI).[12] Table 6.4 summarizes the results of the MITI survey on motives for foreign firms undertaking FDI in Japan. The most common motive is the expansion of local sales. Four out of five foreign firms indicated local sales as one of their motives for investing in Japan. The importance of this motive for foreign firms in manufacturing may reflect their strategy of utilizing local production, rather than exporting from their home bases, as a means to penetrate the Japanese market. Other things being equal, such a strategy attempts to substitute exports with local production, thereby reducing the level of Japan's imports. In contrast, for foreign firms in commerce and trade, the importance of the local sales motive appears to reflect a strategy of setting up distribution networks for their products imported to Japan. Accordingly, an increase in such investments may promote Japan's imports.

Other important motives for foreign firms undertaking FDI in Japan include setting up bases for export expansion in Asian markets and making use of high technologies, with 34 and 25 per cent of respondents citing these respectively. These two responses are related because a large portion of Japanese exports are technology-intensive products such as electrical and transport machinery.

Significantly, the importance of the goal of setting up export bases for Asian markets has been declining over time. Among the firms that undertook FDI in 1985–87, 41 per cent indicated it as one of their motives. But the corresponding share for the firms that undertook FDI since 1991 is lower, at about 32 per cent.[13] Though declining, the share of firms undertaking FDI in Japan for the purpose of securing markets in Asia is still high. FDI in Japan by such firms is likely to stimulate exports from Japan.

Making use of high technologies is an important motive, particularly for firms in electrical machinery, chemical products and general machinery. Recognizing that Japanese firms possess high technological capabilities in these sectors, it is quite natural for foreign firms, particularly those from developing countries, to operate in Japan to exploit these capabilities. Foreign firms with more advanced technologies can utilize Japan's

Table 6.4 Motives behind foreign firms' direct investment in Japan: 1993 (percentage of total responding firms by sectors)

	Making use of			Expanding	Setting up	Taking	Other	Total
	high quality materials	high technologies	abundant financial resources	sales in local markets	bases for Asian markets	advantage of absence of competitors	motives	number of responding firms
Manufacturing Total	10.4	32.6	6.1	80.5	38.1	8.6	10.7	559
Food	0.0	15.0	10.0	80.0	30.0	5.0	0.0	20
Textiles	25.0	25.0	0.0	75.0	0.0	12.5	12.5	8
Wood, paper and printing	14.3	23.8	4.8	71.4	28.6	9.5	4.8	21
Chemical products	9.9	37.5	2.0	81.6	43.4	7.9	11.2	152
Ferrous and non-ferrous metals	0.0	31.6	5.3	78.9	42.1	15.8	0.0	19
General machinery	14.9	36.2	5.3	83.0	47.9	10.6	13.8	94
Electrical machinery	16.7	42.2	8.8	74.5	32.4	7.8	10.8	102
Transport equipment	6.9	27.6	10.3	79.3	37.9	6.9	10.3	29
Other manufacturing	4.4	21.1	8.8	85.1	33.3	7.9	12.3	114
Non-manufacturing Total	11.3	19.1	8.9	78.3	30.0	9.1	18.3	640
Commerce and trade	13.8	19.2	9.5	80.2	28.9	8.9	16.3	484
Overall Total	10.8	25.4	7.6	79.3	33.8	8.8	14.8	1199

Source: Ministry of International Trade and Industry, *Gaishikei Kigyo no Koko, Activities of Foreign Firms in Japan*, No. 28 (1995)

knowledge capital and its highly trained workforce, a product of high technologies, for their operations in Japan.

FDI by foreign firms motivated to set up bases for Asian markets or make use of high technologies in Japan is likely to stimulate Japan's exports. One can identify yet another factor related to foreign firms' operations in Japan that may lead to an increase in Japan's exports. Because Japanese consumers are considered to be highly demanding and very inquisitive, the Japanese market provides an effective market test not only for products intended for the Asian markets but also for those intended for the rest of the world. Thus, Japan can be an effective base for foreign firms interested in global businesses. Here again, successful operations by foreign firms in Japan may expand Japan's exports.

6.4 PROCUREMENT AND SALES PATTERNS OF FOREIGN FIRMS IN JAPAN

To identify the relationship between inward FDI in Japan and its trade, we now examine patterns of trade by foreign firms in Japan. The analysis is conducted at disaggregated sectoral levels, since the impact of inward FDI to Japan on its trade may vary across sectors. We begin by examining the procurement patterns of foreign firms in Japan and then turn to their sales patterns.

6.4.1 Procurement and Import Patterns

To begin with the sources of procurement for intermediate goods by foreign firms in Japan, one finds that approximately 60 per cent of total procurement is from the local market while the remaining 40 per cent comes from foreign countries (Table 6.5). It should be noted that foreign firms rely substantially more on foreign sources than do Japanese firms, which are known to source approximately 87 per cent of total procurement locally.[14] Patterns of procurement for intermediate goods by foreign firms differ substantially across sectors. The local procurement ratio, defined as the share of local procurement in total purchases, is high at above 70 per cent for food, wood, paper and printing, general machinery and electrical machinery. Local procurement for transport equipment is relatively low at 37 per cent.

Different reasons may be provided to explain the high local procurement ratios for food and wood, paper and printing on the one hand, and for general machinery and electrical machinery on the other hand. The high local procurement ratio for food and wood, paper and printing may be

Table 6.5 Procurement of foreign firms located in Japan: 1993 (percentage of total purchases)

Source Regions	Firms from World Total					Firms from the USA				
	Local		Imports			Local		Imports		
Industries	rocuremen	Total	from USA	from Asia	rom Europe	rocuremen	Total	from USA	from Asia	rom Europe
Manufacturing Total	57.1	42.9	10.4	7.0	8.8	53.2	46.8	16.3	6.7	3.3
Food	72.8	27.2	6.7	3.1	2.9	77.1	22.9	8.3	3.4	3.7
Textiles	47.7	52.3	0.0	52.3	0.7	-	-	-	-	-
Wood, paper and printing	94.3	5.7	3.8	0.2	1.7	64.3	35.7	33.4	0.0	2.3
Chemical products	51.9	48.1	16.8	1.2	27.0	57.2	42.8	26.0	1.4	11.1
Ferrous and non-ferrous metals	40.3	59.7	4.1	3.1	5.8	87.7	12.3	10.3	0.6	1.3
General machinery	72.8	27.2	10.4	1.0	15.5	81.7	18.3	16.0	0.1	2.3
Electrical machinery	73.1	26.9	18.9	3.5	2.9	73.2	26.8	19.7	3.1	2.2
Transport equipment	36.5	63.5	4.2	0.4	58.9	78.8	21.2	19.6	0.5	1.0
Other manufacturing	47.8	52.2	4.2	12.2	3.0	21.5	78.5	7.8	15.1	0.6
Non-manufacturing Total	63.2	36.8	7.3	8.9	11.5	84.9	15.1	12.6	0.8	1.1
Commerce and trade	62.5	37.5	7.1	8.8	11.7	85.2	14.8	12.4	0.7	1.0
Overall Total	59.4	40.6	9.3	7.6	9.8	64.1	35.9	15.1	4.7	2.5

Source Regions	Firms from Europe					Firms from Asia				
	Local		Imports			Local		Imports		
Industries	rocuremen	Total	from USA	from Asia	rom Europe	rocuremen	Total	from USA	from Asia	rom Europe
Manufacturing Total	62.8	37.2	2.2	5.5	18.1	45.3	54.7	0.4	47.7	6.3
Food	99.5	0.5	0.0	0.0	0.0	47.3	52.7	10.5	42.1	0.0
Textiles	57.3	42.7	0.0	41.8	0.9	33.2	66.8	0.0	66.8	0.0
Wood, paper and printing	59.4	40.6	5.4	1.8	32.7	79.1	20.9	0.0	0.0	0.0
Chemical products	44.8	55.2	3.7	1.0	49.1	10.0	90.0	3.6	0.0	86.4
Ferrous and non-ferrous metals	29.8	70.2	0.0	0.0	70.2	43.9	56.1	0.0	35.1	21.0
General machinery	58.9	41.1	1.9	2.2	37.0	87.5	12.5	0.0	8.4	0.0
Electrical machinery	72.7	27.3	7.3	7.6	12.4	54.2	45.8	0.0	45.8	0.0
Transport equipment	24.2	75.8	0.3	0.0	75.5	83.9	16.1	0.0	16.1	0.0
Other manufacturing	69.7	30.3	1.6	7.1	4.9	45.5	54.5	0.1	52.7	1.6
Non-manufacturing Total	43.2	56.8	1.5	2.2	52.4	51.5	48.5	0.4	45.8	0.4
Commerce and trade	40.0	60.0	1.6	2.5	55.2	52.9	47.1	0.5	44.6	0.4
Overall Total	57.9	42.1	2.1	4.7	26.6	50.5	49.5	0.6	46.1	1.4

Source: Ministry of International Trade and Industry, *Gaishikei Kigyo no Koko, Activities of Foreign Firms in Japan*, No. 28 (1995).

explained by the high cost of importing and transporting materials necessary for the production of these products. Production of food requires fresh materials, which are expensive to import. In addition, various restrictions such as sanitary requirements make the importation of some food materials impractical. The high cost of transporting materials, such as paper, appears to lead to the high local procurement ratio for wood, paper and printing.

The high local procurement ratio for general machinery and electrical machinery is mainly attributable to the presence of competitive parts suppliers. The relatively loose supplier network in these machinery sectors appears to have contributed to high local procurement ratios by foreign manufacturers. In contrast, foreign firms in transport equipment, particularly those from Europe, rely relatively heavily on imports, particularly from Europe, for the supply of intermediate goods. A possible explanation for this is that they do not maintain effective supplier networks in Japan or that they prefer intermediate inputs produced in their home countries. The low local procurement ratio for transport equipment is essentially attributable to European firms' propensity to import almost all parts and components from Europe.

Local procurement ratios also vary across foreign firms from different geographical origins. In the overall total, US firms have the highest local procurement ratio, followed by European firms. Asian firms have the lowest local procurement ratio.[15] It is interesting to observe that foreign firms tend to source a significant proportion of intermediate goods imports from their respective originating regions, most likely from their home economies. This tendency is most pronounced for Asian firms and least noticeable for US firms. Essentially, US firms are so globalized that they tend to diversify import sources to minimize the cost of production from a global perspective.

6.4.2 Sales and Export Patterns

Turning to the sales patterns of foreign firms in Japan, one finds that on average 12 per cent of their sales are exported from Japan (Table 6.6). The export ratio, defined as the share of exports in total sales, for foreign firms in Japan is smaller than the corresponding ratio of 17 per cent for Japanese firms in Japan.[16]

The average share masks variations in the export ratios of foreign firms in different industries and from different geographical origins. For the export ratios across sectors, both general machinery and electrical machinery show relatively high ratios exceeding 20 per cent, while the corresponding ratios for other manufacturing sectors are significantly lower. This finding is consistent with our earlier observation that one of the important motives of foreign firms for undertaking FDI in Japan is to make

Table 6.6 Sales of foreign firms located in Japan: 1993 (percentage of total sales)

Source Regions	Firms from World Total					Firms from the USA				
	Local		Exports			Local		Exports		
Industries	**Sales**	**Total**	**to USA**	**to Asia**	**to Europe**	**Sales**	**Total**	**to USA**	**to Asia**	**to Europe**
Manufacturing Total	89.8	10.2	4.4	3.2	1.9	87.4	12.6	6.6	3.0	1.9
Food	98.9	1.1	0.0	0.4	0.7	98.7	1.3	0.0	0.5	0.8
Textiles	95.9	4.1	0.0	4.1	0.0	-	-	-	-	-
Wood, paper and printing	98.4	1.6	0.0	1.5	0.2	90.2	9.8	0.0	8.6	1.2
Chemical products	93.7	6.3	0.7	2.9	2.4	95.0	5.0	0.9	3.4	0.4
Ferrous and non-ferrous metals	90.1	9.9	3.3	6.3	0.2	92.1	7.9	3.5	1.7	2.2
General machinery	75.8	24.2	9.2	8.6	1.7	69.5	30.5	12.7	9.6	1.7
Electrical machinery	77.1	22.9	13.1	3.9	4.4	77.1	22.9	13.8	3.4	4.1
Transport equipment	95.4	4.6	2.1	2.2	0.1	85.6	14.4	8.7	4.9	0.6
Other manufacturing	96.8	3.2	0.7	2.0	0.3	97.6	2.4	1.0	1.0	0.1
Non-manufacturing Total	84.7	15.3	2.8	8.6	1.7	88.7	11.3	4.5	3.2	0.5
Commerce and trade	85.7	14.3	2.4	8.8	0.9	89.5	10.5	4.0	3.0	0.2
Overall Total	88.2	11.8	3.9	4.9	1.8	87.8	12.2	6.0	3.1	1.5

Source Regions	Firms from Europe					Firms from Asia				
	Local	Exports				Local	Exports			
Industries	**Sales**	**Total**	**to USA**	**to Asia**	**to Europe**	**Sales**	**Total**	**to USA**	**to Asia**	**to Europe**
Manufacturing Total	94.8	5.2	1.1	1.7	2.2	68.6	31.4	0.2	30.9	0.3
Food	100.0	0.0	0.0	0.0	0.0	100.0	0.0	0.0	0.0	0.0
Textiles	99.1	0.9	0.0	0.9	0.0	79.4	20.6	0.0	20.6	0.0
Wood, paper and printing	95.9	4.1	0.0	3.8	0.0	-	-	-	-	-
Chemical products	91.7	8.3	0.5	2.0	5.5	97.5	2.5	1.5	0.0	1.1
Ferrous and non-ferrous metals	72.7	27.3	20.2	7.1	0.0	81.0	19.0	2.2	16.8	0.0
General machinery	92.0	8.0	0.4	5.8	1.7	99.9	0.1	0.0	0.0	0.0
Electrical machinery	75.0	25.0	6.0	10.6	7.7	95.3	4.7	0.0	4.7	0.0
Transport equipment	99.8	0.2	0.0	0.0	0.0	36.8	63.2	0.0	63.2	0.0
Other manufacturing	98.6	1.4	0.5	0.3	0.5	59.0	41.0	0.0	40.8	0.2
Non-manufacturing Total	88.2	11.8	1.1	3.3	5.9	56.9	43.1	0.5	42.0	0.3
Commerce and trade	91.5	8.5	0.8	3.3	3.5	55.1	44.9	0.5	43.8	0.3
Overall Total	93.2	6.8	1.1	2.1	3.2	59.5	40.5	0.4	39.5	0.3

Source: Ministry of International Trade and Industry, *Gaishikei Kigyo no Koko, Activities of Foreign Firms in Japan*, No.28 (1995).

use of high technologies in Japan. Essentially, foreign firms in the general and electrical machinery sectors exploit Japan's high technological capabilities to improve their international competitiveness in the global market, leading to high export ratios.

The export ratio also differs notably across foreign firms from different geographical regions. The ratio is the highest for firms from Asia at 40 per cent, while the corresponding ratio is significantly lower for firms from the United States (12 per cent) and from Europe (7 per cent). It is noteworthy that almost all exports by firms from Asia are directed to Asia, probably to their home markets. Their export ratio is particularly high for the transport equipment, commerce and trade, and other manufacturing sectors. The high export ratio for transport equipment appears to be due to the lack of competitive parts suppliers in their home markets; Asian firms in transport equipment may rely on their affiliates in Japan for the supply of parts and components. Firms from the United States and Europe tend to direct about half of their exports from Japan to their respective home regions; this tendency is particularly pronounced for US firms in the general and electrical machinery sectors and for European firms in the ferrous and non-ferrous metals sector. In other sectors, however, they direct most exports to third markets. This suggests the presence of a strong linkage between a firm's FDI in Japan and its exports.

6.5 ECONOMETRIC ANALYSES OF FDI INFLOW–TRADE INTERACTIONS

6.5.1 The Gravity Model

This section examines econometrically the extent of linkages between Japan's FDI inflows and its trade at aggregated levels. The findings in the previous sections suggested the presence of such linkages. The objective of the empirical analysis in this section is to test the hypothesis of FDI–trade interactions by extending the 'gravity model'.

The standard gravity model of international trade relates bilateral trade flows to the levels of economic activity in the exporting and importing countries and to the distance between them.[17] We extend this framework to examine whether Japan's FDI inflows and its trade are interrelated. In particular, we ask whether Japan's trade is affected by FDI inflows in Japan, and vice versa. Earlier work by Kawai (1997) and Kawai and Urata (1997) found the presence of strong, two-way interactions between Japan's FDI *outflows* and its trade; they positively affect each other. In this section we focus on the interactions between Japan's FDI *inflows* and trade by controlling for the positive effects of Japan's FDI outflows on trade. For this purpose, we run two types of regression equations separately, one for Japan's *trade flows* and the other for Japan's FDI *inflows*, and include both FDI inflows and outflows in the first equation and the value of trade in the second equation as respective explanatory variables.

6.5.2 The Trade Equation

The first regression equation we shall estimate is for trade. The dependent variable in the trade equation is *TRADE* (exports, imports, or exports plus imports), in natural-log form, between Japan and its trading partner in a given calendar year. We do not have a large sample because not many countries invest directly in Japan and detailed country breakdown data, on a notifications basis, are available only from fiscal year 1991. Though country-cum-industry breakdown data (notifications statistics) are also available, we do not utilize such data here because of the smallness of the sample size.

The two most important explanatory variables are, first, the economic sizes of Japan and the trading partner (*GNP* expressed in US dollars) and, second, the geographical distance between Tokyo and the capital or major city of each trading partner (*DISTANCE* expressed in kilometres).[18] Other explanatory variables used are per capita income (*GNP/POP*), three regional dummy variables (*APEC*, *EAEC* and *OILEXPORTER*), and, most importantly, the FDI inflow and outflow variables (*FDIINFLOW* and *FDIOUTFLOW*). The basic gravity equation to be estimated is:

$$\begin{aligned}\log(TRADE_{ij}) = {} & a_0 + a_1[\log(GNP_i) + \log(GNP_j)] + a_2[\log(GNP_i/POP_i) \\ & + \log(GNP_j/POP_j)] + a_3\log(DISTANCE_{ij}) + a_4APEC_i \\ & + a_5EAEC_i + a_6OILEXPORTER_i + a_7\log[FDIOUTFLOW_{ij}(-1)] \\ & + a_8\log[FDIINFLOW_{ij}(-1)] + u_{ij}. \qquad (6.1)\end{aligned}$$

Here, a subscript *j* refers to Japan and *i* refers to an individual trading partner (i = 1, 2, ..., n). The regional dummy variable *APEC* is expected to capture how much of Japan's active trade with APEC members (Asian NIEs, ASEAN Four, China, Australia, New Zealand, United States, Canada, Mexico and Chile) may be attributable to a special regional effect. The regional dummy variable *EAEC* (Asian NIEs, ASEAN Four, and China) is included to examine if and to what extent Japan's trade is influenced by a special regional factor associated with East Asia. The *OILEXPORTER* dummy represents a bias related to Japan's trade with oil-exporting countries. The FDI variables included on the right-hand side of the equation are Japan's FDI outflows to, and FDI inflows from, trade partner *i* in the previous year. The FDIs used are the figures for the previous year, rather than for the current year, to ensure that they are exogenous in the TRADE equation.[19]

The pooled OLS (ordinary least squares) regression results, covering 1991–94, are reported in Table 6.7. The table summarizes the results when the dependent variable *TRADE* is represented by *EXPORT*, *IMPORT* and *EXPORT+IMPORT* (exports, imports, and the sum of exports and imports, respectively). Results of these three types of regression equations are reported for each; that is, the equations with *FDIOUTFLOW* only, *FDIINFLOW* only, and both *FDIOUTFLOW* and *FDIINFLOW* as explanatory variables. The results shown in Table 6.7 largely confirm earlier findings in the literature: *GNP* has statistically significant, positive effects on trade, the *APEC*, *EAEC* and *OILEXPORTER* dummies have in most cases statistically significant, positive effects, and *FDIOUTFLOW* has statistically significant, positive effects. The only deviations in results from the earlier findings are that the positive coefficient on *GNP/POP* is not always statistically significant and that *DISTANCE* does not exert a statistically significant, negative impact on trade flows.

Our new finding in this estimation is that the coefficient on *FDIINFLOW* is always positive and often statistically significant, despite being smaller in size than the coefficient on *FDIOUTFLOW*. This indicates that FDI inflows do have a trade-creation effect, although one which is smaller than the effect of FDI outflows. An interesting contrast is also observed between the export and import equations. The *FDIINFLOW* coefficient in the export equation is always statistically significant, while the coefficient in the import equation is not with the *FDIOUTFLOW* variable included on the right-hand side. The *FDIINFLOW* coefficient in the import equation is statistically significantly positive only when *FDIOUTFLOW* is excluded from the equation but that statistical significance is lost once *FDIOUTFLOW* is included.[20] In addition, the size of the *FDIINFLOW* coefficient in the export equation is larger than that in the import equation; an increase in FDI inflows would lead to an improvement in Japan's trade balance. The estimated coefficient on *FDIINFLOW* in the export-plus-import equation largely mimics that of the export equation; that is, countries investing more in Japan tend to trade more with Japan.

An additional test is conducted to examine whether FDI inflows in the manufacturing industry and those in the commerce and trade sector exert differential effects on *TRADE* (Table 6.8). The number of observations is now less than in the previous regression because of the smaller sample size due to the limited availability of disaggregated FDI variables and the shorter sample period, 1992–94. The results for the export equation, reported in Table 6.8, give support to the view that FDI inflows in manufacturing stimulate Japan's exports while FDI inflows in commerce

Table 6.7 Gravity model of Japan's trade: a pooled sample over 1991–94

Dependent variables	*EXPORT*			*IMPORT*			*EXPORT+IMPORT*		
Explanatory variables	(1)	(2)	(3)	(4)	(5)	(6)	(7)	(8)	(9)
CONSTANT	–8.145**	–6.698**	–5.321**	–13.232**	–13.017**	–12.189**	–8.594**	–7.297**	–6.044**
	(2.041)	(2.244)	(2.018)	(2.651)	(2.832)	(2.046)	(1.924)	(2.111)	(1.914)
log(*GNPi*)+log(*GNPj*)	0.426**	0.452**	0.385**	0.685**	0.710**	0.670**	0.466**	0.490**	0.429**
	(0.043)	(0.045)	(0.041)	(0.056)	(0.056)	(0.057)	(0.041)	(0.042)	(0.039)
log(*GNPi/POPi*)+log(*GNPj/POPj*)	0.148**	0.055	0.059	0.127**	0.091	0.094	0.148**	0.064	0.067
	(0.045)	(0.053)	(0.047)	(0.059)	(0.067)	(0.065)	(0.043)	(0.050)	(0.045)
log(*DISTANCE*)	0.090	0.098	0.098	–0.140	–0.137	–0.137	0.076	0.083	0.084
	(0.178)	(0.186)	(0.166)	(0.230)	(0.235)	(0.230)	(0.167)	(0.175)	(0.158)
APEC	1.196**	0.874**	0.641**	1.335**	1.499**	1.359**	0.843**	1.113**	0.902**
	(0.303)	(0.188)	(0.172)	(0.238)	(0.237)	(0.238)	(0.173)	(0.177)	(0.163)
EAEC	0.576**	1.096**	1.060**	0.275	0.246	0.225	0.893**	0.803**	0.770**
	(0.183)	(0.320)	(0.286)	(0.393)	(0.403)	(0.395)	(0.286)	(0.301)	(0.271)
OILEXPORTER	0.468*	0.474*	0.574**	2.039**	2.019**	2.078**	1.174**	1.179**	1.270**
	(0.235)	(0.247)	(0.221)	(0.305)	(0.311)	(0.306)	(0.221)	(0.232)	(0.210)
log[*FDIOUTFLOW*(–1)]	0.123**	–	0.101**	0.069**	–	0.061**	0.112**	–	0.092**
	(0.018)		(0.017)	(0.023)		(0.024)	(0.017)		(0.016)

Dependent variables		EXPORT			IMPORT			EXPORT+IMPORT	
Explanatory variables	(1)	(2)	(3)	(4)	(5)	(6)	(7)	(8)	(9)
log[*FDIINFLOW*(−1)]	–	0.101** (0.018)	0.073** (0.017)	–	0.044* (0.022)	0.027 (0.023)	–	0.092** (0.017)	0.066** (0.016)
R–squared Adjusted	0.832	0.815	0.853	0.819	0.812	0.820	0.858	0.844	0.874
Sum of Squared Errors	0.6635	0.6961	0.6215	0.8615	0.8782	0.8603	0.6255	0.6547	0.5894
Number of Countries (Pooled Sample)	138	138	138	138	138	138	138	138	138

Notes: Numbers in parentheses are the estimated standard errors of the coefficients.
A single asterisk (*) indicates statistical significance at the 10% level (2–tailed test).
Double asterisks (**) indicate statistical significance at the 5% level (2–tailed test).

Table 6.8 The role of FDI Inflows in manufacturing and commerce and trade in the gravity model of Japan's trade: a pooled sample over 1992–94

Dependent Variable	EXPORT		IMPORT		EXPORT+IMPORT	
Explanatory Variables	(1)	(2)	(3)	(4)	(5)	(6)
CONSTANT	-5.056**	-2.321	-7.977**	-7.218**	-4.236*	-1.821
	(2.560)	(2.631)	(3.149)	(3.383)	(2.298)	(2.383)
log(*GNPi*)+log(*GNPj*)	0.389**	0.343**	0.662**	0.641**	0.433**	0.387**
	(0.052)	(0.054)	(0.064)	(0.069)	(0.047)	(0.049)
log(*GNPi/POPi*)+log(*GNPj/POPj*)	0.065	0.046	0.016	0.021	0.035	0.024
	(0.057)	(0.054)	(0.070)	(0.070)	(0.051)	(0.049)
log(*DISTANCE*)	0.046	-0.061	-0.403	-0.429*	-0.056	-0.142
	(0.200)	(0.199)	(0.245)	(0.255)	(0.179)	(0.180)
APEC	0.590**	0.601**	1.503**	1.507**	0.651**	0.955**
	(0.210)	(0.204)	(0.258)	(0.262)	(0.294)	(0.184)
EAEC	1.104**	0.999**	-0.149	-0.183	0.651**	0.557*
	(0.328)	(0.318)	(0.403)	(0.409)	(0.294)	(0.288)
OILEXPORTER	0.387	0.486*	1.652**	1.684**	0.945**	1.031**
	(0.263)	(0.255)	(0.323)	(0.328)	(0.236)	(0.231)
log[*FDIOUTFLOW*(-1)]	0.095**	0.103*	0.035	0.043*	0.075**	0.084**
	(0.020)	(0.019)	(0.025)	(0.024)	(0.018)	(0.017)

Dependent Variable	EXPORT		IMPORT		EXPORT+IMPORT	
Explanatory Variables	(1)	(2)	(3)	(4)	(5)	(6)
log[*FDIINFLOW* (-1)]	0.076**	-	0.052*	-	0.081**	-
	(0.022)		(0.027)		(0.020)	
log[*FDIINFLOW_MANUFACTURE* (-1)]	-	0.059**	-	0.019	-	0.051**
		(0.019)		(0.025)		(0.018)
log[*FDIINFLOW_COMM&TRADE* (-1)]	-	0.028	-	0.028	-	0.038
		(0.027)		(0.034)		(0.024)
R-squared Adjusted	0.844	0.854	0.835	0.832	0.876	0.882
Sum of Squared Errors	0.6205	0.5987	0.7632	0.7696	0.5570	0.5421
Number of Countries (Pooled Sample)	105	105	105	105	105	105

Notes: The dependent variable is log(*EXPORT*), log(*IMPORT*), or log (*EXPORT+IMPORT*).

The explanatory variables log[*FDIIFLOW_MANUFACTURE* (-1)] and log[*FDIINFLOW_COMM&TRADE* (-1)] are natural logs of FDI inflows in Japan's manufacturing industry and in the commerce and trade sector of non-manufacturing, respectively, in the previous year.

Numbers in parentheses are the estimated standard errors of the coefficients.

A single asterisk (*) indicates statistical significance at the 10% level (2-tailed test).

Double asterisks (**) indicate statistical significance at the 5% level (2-tailed test).

and trade do not. This indicates that foreign manufacturing firms in Japan tend to export their products to their home countries, while foreign firms in commerce and trade do not. The results for the import equation do not support the view that FDI inflows, once disaggregated into manufacturing and commerce and trade, stimulate Japan's imports. However, one must be cautious about interpreting this result, which is somewhat different from those presented in Table 6.7.[21]

6.5.3 FDI Inflow Equation

The next equation to be estimated is the FDI inflow equation. The explanatory variables used are similar to those which appear in the trade equation. The only difference is that, instead of the FDI variable, the *TRADE* variable is now included on the right-hand side of the equation:

$$\log(FDIINFLOW_{ij}) = b_0 + b_1[\log(GNP_i) + \log(GNP_j)] + b_2[\log(GNP_i/POP_i) + \log(GNP_j/POP_j)] + b_3\log(DISTANCE_{ij}) + b_4APEC_i + b_5EAEC_i + b_6OILEXPORTER_i + b_7\log[TRADE_{ij}(-1)] + v_{ij} \quad (6.2)$$

The dependent variable *FDIINFLOW* is Japan's FDI inflow from country i in the current year and the *TRADE* variable included on the right-hand side is Japan's bilateral trade with country *i* in the previous year. For *TRADE*, three alternative measures are used: Japan's exports to country *i* (*EXPORT*), its imports from country *i* (*IMPORT*), and the sum of exports and imports (*EXPORT+IMPORT*). The FDI inflow equation is undoubtedly very simple, but it does allow us to test some of the central elements of the 'gravity' approach.

The regression results for FDI inflows are summarized in Table 6.9, which allows comparison with the results from the FDI outflow equation and those from the sum of FDI outflows and inflows. Again, three types of regressions are run for each, by using *EXPORT*, *IMPORT*, and *EXPORT+IMPORT* as explanatory variables. Similarly to the previous work by Kawai (1997) and Kawai and Urata (1997), the estimated coefficients on *GNP*, *GNP/POP*, and *DISTANCE* do not always produce results predicted by the gravity model for trade. Concerning regional dummy variables, *OILEXPORTER* has a negative sign in the FDI inflow as well as FDI outflow equations; oil-exporting countries are neither direct investors in Japan nor recipients of direct investment from Japan. The coefficients on *APEC* and *EAEC* are not estimated to be statistically significantly positive in the FDI inflow equation, reflecting the fact that Europe, not part of *APEC*, is an equally large investor in Japan.

Table 6.9 Gravity model of Japan's FDI inflows and outflows: a pooled sample over 1991–94

Dependent Variable	FDIINFLOW			FDIOUTFLOW			FDIINFLOW+FDIOUTFLOW		
Explanatory Variables	(1)	(2)	(3)	(4)	(5)	(6)	(7)	(8)	(9)
CONSTANT	-14.969	-31.622**	-14.133	-6.835	-14.221	-2.767	-7.987	-13.500	-3.964
	(9.876)	(11.684)	(10.309)	(9.573)	(10.921)	(9.613)	(7.449)	(8.556)	(7.374)
log(GNPi)+log(GNPj)	-0.393	0.424	-0.450	-0.279	0.099	-0.494*	-0.147	0.137	-0.357*
	(0.266)	(0.329)	(0.291)	(0.258)	(0.308)	(0.271)	(0.201)	(0.241)	(0.208)
log(GNPi/POPi)+log(GNPj/POPj)	0.752**	1.115**	0.763**	-0.223	0.052	-0.265	-0.042	0.180	-0.086
	(0.215)	(0.240)	(0.221)	(0.208)	(0.224)	(0.206)	(0.162)	(0.176)	(0.158)
log(DISTANCE)	-0.741	-0.644	-0.811	0.468	0.604	0.385	0.225	0.340	0.154
	(0.807)	(0.929)	(0.827)	(0.782)	(0.868)	(0.771)	(0.609)	(0.680)	(0.592)
APEC	-1.796**	-0.958	-2.482**	-0.010	-0.045	-0.981	-0.107	-0.191	-0.968
	(0.858)	(1.065)	(0.929)	(0.831)	(0.995)	(0.866)	(0.647)	(0.780)	(0.664)
EAEC	-1.765	0.803	-1.098	-0.666	1.682	-0.249	-0.584	1.341	-0.290
	(1.434)	(1.587)	(1.450)	(1.390)	(1.483)	(1.352)	(1.082)	(1.162)	(1.037)
OILEXPORTER	-2.285**	-2.694*	-3.976**	-1.748*	-3.287**	-3.722**	-0.946	-2.290**	-2.638**
	(1.069)	(1.390)	(1.166)	(1.036)	(1.299)	(1.087)	(0.806)	(1.018)	(0.834)
log[EXPORT(-1)]	2.399**	-	-	2.374**	-	-	1.959**	-	-
	(0.347)			(0.337)			(0.262)		

Dependent Variable		FDIINFLOW			FDIOUTFLOW			FDIINFLOW+FDIOUTFLOW	
Explanatory Variables	(1)	(2)	(3)	(4)	(5)	(6)	(7)	(8)	(9)
log[IMPORT(-1)]	-	0.688**	-	-	1.250**	-	-	1.068**	-
		(0.335)			(0.313)			(0.245)	
log[EXPORT(-1)+IMPORT(-1)]	-	-	2.402**	-	-	2.650**	-	-	2.243**
			(0.384)			(0.358)			(0.274)
R-squared Adjusted	0.584	0.449	0.563	0.523	0.412	0.536	0.589	0.488	0.612
Sum of Squared Errors	3.0166	3.4708	3.0912	2.9238	3.2442	2.8825	2.2752	2.5416	2.2111
Number of Countries (Pooled Sample)	138	138	138	138	138	138	138	138	138

Note: 1. The dependent variable is log(FDIINFLOW), log(FDIOUTFLOW), or log (FDIINFLOW+FDIOUTFLOW).

2. Numbers in parentheses are the estimated standard errors of the coefficients.

3. A single asterisk (*) indicates statistical significance at the 10% level (2-tailed test).
Double asterisks (**) indicate statistical significance at the 5% level (2-tailed test).

The most important coefficient is that for *TRADE*, which captures the effect of trade on FDI inflows and outflows; the coefficient is always positive and statistically significant in all the equations. This finding indicates that a larger bilateral trade flow, defined by exports, imports or the sum of exports and imports, does induce greater FDI inflows in Japan as well as greater FDI outflows from Japan.

6.6 CONCLUDING REMARKS

This chapter has discovered the existence of two-way interactions between FDI inflows in Japan and Japan's trade. FDI inflows and trade affect each other. This is so even when the effects of Japan's FDI outflows on its trade are controlled for in the trade equation. Our findings suggest that FDI inflows in Japan are driven by market incentives. They also suggest that an expansion of FDI inflows in Japan strengthens trade linkages between Japan and FDI source economies and that the increased trade linkages further promote FDI inflows in Japan.

Promotion of Japan's FDI inflows clearly benefits both the Japanese and foreign economies because it enhances efficiency of resource allocation and expands Japan's trade with the rest of the world. It also deepens integration of the Japanese economy with the global community. Since government regulations are one obstacle to FDI in Japan, the Government of Japan must pursue further deregulation to encourage more entry of foreign firms in the domestic market.

Further investigation is needed to examine the extent of interactions between FDI inflows and trade using more disaggregated, sectoral data because different sectors are expected to exhibit different patterns of interactions. For this purpose more data observations must be accumulated for a satisfactory econometric study.

NOTES

1. This is a revised version of the paper presented to the conference on 'Japan in the International Economy and Structural Adjustment in Japan', which was sponsored by the Centre for Japanese Economic Studies, Macquarie University and held in Sydney, Australia on 22–23 August 1996. The authors are thankful to the conference participants for helpful comments and discussions. David Leheny and Andrew Robertson have provided editorial assistance.
2. Encarnation (1992), Mason (1992), Lawrence (1993) and Wakasugi (1995) are among the few exceptions.
3. There are several problems with each type of statistics. First, the notifications statistics (a) indicate the intentions of foreign firms to invest in Japan and do not necessarily represent realized values, (b) do not net out FDI withdrawn from the Japanese market through

liquidation of the assets, (c) report 'Japan' as a source (or investing) country when foreign firms located in Japan conduct additional FDI, and (d) do not include reinvested earnings as part of FDI, which are available only from BOP statistics beginning in 1996. Second, the BOP statistics (e) do not give detailed time series data, broken down by source countries, and (f) do not report country-cum-industry breakdown data, which are available only from notifications statistics.

4. Net FDI inflows in 1988 and 1989 were negative, reflecting the fact that foreign firms sold their assets at the time when the asset prices in Japan soared due to the 'bubbles'.
5. The notifications statistics of FDI inflows after 1992 may underestimate the actual value, because starting in fiscal year 1992 foreign investments that acquire less than 10 per cent of unlisted companies are excluded from the statistics.
6. As will be shown below, firms engaged in commerce and trade account for a significant part of Japanese inward FDI.
7. The FDI stock data used here, which are taken from the IMF's *International Financial Statistics*, are based on balance of payments statistics.
8. It should be noted that contrasting empirical observations have been made by Horaguchi (1995) and Nakamura, Fukao and Shibuya (1995). Horaguchi found that *keiretsu* did not reduce FDI inflows significantly and Nakamura, Fukao and Shibuya found that past regulations on FDI inflows by the Japanese Government did not have a significant, adverse influence on FDI inflows.
9. Ministry of International Trade and Industry (1995a).
10. Measured by the cumulative value of notifications-based FDI inflows over the 1991-94 period, the United States and Europe account for 40 and 30 per cent (Table 6.3).
11. This was indeed a strategy adopted by Japanese firms when they expanded their business activities abroad. See Yamawaki (1991) for the case of Japanese firms in the United States.
12. MITI conducts a survey of the activities of foreign firms in Japan every year. The survey results are published under the title, *Gaishikei Kigyo no Doko* (*Activities of Foreign Firms*). In the 1993 survey, a questionnaire was sent to 3006 foreign firms operating in Japan, 1351 of which responded. JETRO (Japan External Trade Organization) also conducts a questionnaire survey, but its coverage is significantly smaller and it is not conducted on a regular basis.
13. Ministry of International Trade and Industry (1995a).
14. Ministry of International Trade and Industry (1995b).
15. In manufacturing, European firms have the highest local procurement ratio on average, except for ferrous and non-ferrous metals and transport equipment where the local procurement ratio is low. US firms have the second highest ratio.
16. Ministry of International Trade and Industry (1995b).
17. See Drysdale and Garnaut (1982) and Deardorff (1984) for a survey of the gravity approach. Although the gravity model is often criticized for the lack of solid theoretical foundations, several studies have shown that theoretical support exists for the model. Anderson (1979) demonstrated that gravity equations can be derived from the properties of expenditure systems under the assumptions of cross-country similarities in preferences for traded goods, in trade tax structures, and in transport structures. Deardorff (1995) demonstrated that the use of gravity equations can be justified by standard trade theories such as the Heckscher–Ohlin model.

    Kawai (1997) examined the FDI–trade interactions using aggregated data for Japan's FDI outflows and trade and Kawai and Urata (1997) tested the relationship by using disaggregated manufacturing data. This chapter extends the approach taken by these authors by focusing on interactions between Japan's FDI inflows and its trade.
18. This is the essence of the 'gravity model', named for the analogy with the law of gravitational attraction between masses. The *DISTANCE* variable is taken from Gary L. Fizpatrick and Marilyn J. Modlin, *Direct-Line Distances: International Edition* (Metuchen, NJ and London: The Scarecrow Press, 1986).
19. It should also be noted that *TRADE* is a calendar year variable ending in December of the current year while *FDIOUTFLOW* and *FDIINFLOW* are fiscal year variables ending in

March of the following year. The *TRADE* variable is obtained from IMF, *Direction of Trade*; the FDI variables are from the Ministry of Finance's published and unpublished data; *GNP* and *POP* variables are taken from World Bank, *World Tables*, IMF, *International Financial Statistics*, and ADB, *Key Indicators of Developing Asian and Pacific Countries*.

20. This suggests the presence of multicollinearity between *FDIOUTFLOW* and *FDIINFLOW*.
21. Specifically, the coefficient on *FDIOUTFLOW* is estimated to be statistically significantly positive regardless of the specification of the import equation (Table 6.7), while the estimated coefficient is positive without being statistically significant when *FDIINFLOW* is included in the equation (Table 6.8). The statistical significance of the estimated coefficients on *FDIINFLOW* differs depending on specification. With *FDIINFLOW* included as an aggregate FDI variable in the import equation, its coefficient is estimated to be statistically significantly positive, while with *FDIINFLOW* divided into manufacturing and commerce and trade, their coefficients are estimated to be statistically insignificant.

REFERENCES

Anderson, J.E. (1979), 'A Theoretical Foundation for the Gravity Equation'. *American Economic Review*, **69**, March, 106–16.

Deardorff, A.V. (1984), 'Testing Trade Theories and Predicting Trade Flows', in Ronald W. Jones and Peter B. Kenen (eds), *Handbook of International Economics*, **1** Amsterdam: North-Holland, 467–517.

Deardorff, A.V. (1995), 'Determinants of Bilateral Trade: Does Gravity Work in a Neoclassical World?' Research Forum on International Economics Discussion Paper no.382, 7 November, School of Public Policy, University of Michigan.

Drysdale, P. and Garnaut, R. (1982), 'Trade Intensities and the Analysis of Bilateral Trade Flows in a Many-Country World: A Survey', *Hitotsubashi Journal of Economics*, **22**, February, 62–84.

Encarnation, D.J. (1992), *Rivals Beyond Trade,* New York: Cornell University Press.

Graham, E.M. and Krugman, P.R. (1993), 'The Surge in Foreign Direct Investment in the 1980s', in Kenneth A. Froot (ed.), *Foreign Direct Investment,* Chicago: University of Chicago Press, pp. 13–33.

Horaguchi, H. (1995), '*Tainichi Chokusetsu Toshi*' (Inward Foreign Direct Investment in Japan), in Masu Uekusa (ed.), *Nihon no Sangyo Soshiki* (*Industrial Organization in Japan*), Tokyo: Yuhikaku.

Japan Investment Council, Economic Planning Agency (1996), *Yearbook of the Japan Investment Council* (*Provisional Translation*), 2, April.

Kawai, M. (1997), 'Japan's Trade and Investment in East Asia', in David Robertson (ed), *East Asian Trade after the Uruguay Round,* Cambridge: Cambridge University Press, pp. 209–223.

Kawai, M. and Urata, S.(1997) 'Are Trade and Direct Investment Substitutes or Complements?: An Analysis of the Japanese Manufacturing Industry', in Hiro Lee and David W. Roland-Holst (eds), *Economic Development and Cooperation in the Pacific Basin: Trade, Investment, and Environmental Issues*, Cambridge: Cambridge University Press, forthcoming 1997. (Discussion Paper Series No. F-50, October 1995, Institute of Social Science, University of Tokyo).

Lawrence, R.Z. (1993), 'Japan's Low Levels of Inward Investment: The Role of Inhibitions on Acquisitions', in Kenneth A. Froot (ed.), *Foreign Direct Investment* Chicago: University of Chicago Press.

Mason, M. (1992), *American Multinationals and Japan: The Political Economy of Japanese Capital Controls, 1899–1980,* Cambridge: Harvard University Press.

Ministry of International Trade and Industry (1995a), *Gaishikei Kigyo no Doko* (*Activities of Foreign Firms in Japan*) No. 28.

Ministry of International Trade and Industry (1995b) *Wagakuni Kigyo no Kaigai Jigyo Katsudo* (*Overseas Activities of Japanese Firms*), No. 24.

Nakamura, Y., Fukao, K. and Shibuya, M. (1995), *Tainichi Chokusetsu Toshi* (*Inward Foreign Direct Investment in Japan*), Discussion Paper no. 95-DIH-63, MITI Research Institute.

Wakasugi, R. (1995), 'On the Causes of Low Levels of FDI in Japan', in. Edward K.Y. Chen and Peter Drysdale (eds), *Corporate Links and Foreign Direct Investment in Asia and the Pacific,* Sydney: HarperEducational.

Yamawaki, H. (1991), 'Exports and Foreign Distributional Activities: Evidence on Japanese Firms in the United States', *Review of Economics and Statistics*, **73**, May, 294–300.

7. Japanese Foreign Direct Investment: The Role of Technology and *Keiretsu*

Colin R. McKenzie[1]

7.1 INTRODUCTION

The purpose of this chapter is to analyse empirically two decisions of the Japanese firm: first, whether or not to produce overseas; and second, when overseas production is decided on, the determinants of the ratio of the amount of labour used in the overseas operation to the amount of labour used in Japan. One focus of the analysis is the extent to which membership of either a vertical *keiretsu* or a horizontal *keiretsu* affects each of these two decisions. A second focus is the extent to which the stock of technology within the firm affects each of these decisions.

Japan's recent experience with foreign direct investment has been attracting attention for various reasons. With respect to inward foreign investment, interest has focused on the extremely low level of inward foreign investment into Japan and the reasons for this (see Yoshitomi and Graham, 1996). For example, Lawrence (1993) has noted that quitters tend to be associated with low levels of inward foreign investment, while Weinstein (1996) has suggested that domestic regulation may be important. On the other hand, Japan's outward foreign direct investment has increased dramatically recently. According to the Bank of Japan's *Balance of Payments Monthly,* Japan's stock of overseas foreign direct investment has increased 3.5 times over the period 1987 to 1994. Various reasons have been suggested for this explosion of foreign direct investment at the macro level, including continuing Japanese current account surpluses, overseas protectionism, and valuation effects from changing stock prices and the yen exchange rate (see, for example, Froot, 1991).

Complementing this macroeconomic perspective is a good deal of work using firm (or industry) level data attempting to determine the factors influencing the Japanese firms' foreign behaviour (for example, Kimura,

1989; Horaguchi, 1992; Fukao *et al*, 1994a, b; Trevino and Daniels, 1994; and Wakasugi, 1994). An examination of the data in Toyo Keizai (1995) indicates that the overseas activities of Japanese firms include sales, advertising and service operations; production operations; research and development (R&D) operations (relatively small in number); and financial operations. The factors influencing each of these operations are likely to differ. In the existing empirical analyses of the foreign investment behaviour of Japanese firms, the firm's foreign behaviour includes: the decision of whether or not to invest overseas (Kogut and Chang, 1991 and Belderbos and Sleuwaegen, 1993); the decision of whether or not to produce overseas (Hennart and Park, 1992 and Fukao *et al*, 1994a); the ratio of foreign to domestic production or value-added (Wakasugi, 1994 and Fukao *et al*, 1994b); and the ratio of foreign to domestic labour used (Fukao *et al.*, 1994a). Quite a few of these papers focus only on firms in the electric machinery industry (Kimura, 1989; Kogut and Chang, 1991; Belderbos and Sleuwaegen, 1993; Fukao *et al.*, 1994a, b and Wakasugi, 1994). With the exception of Fukao *et al.* (1994a), which uses data up to 1992, data in all the other studies are for the 1980s or 1990 at the latest.

In contrast, this chapter contains a *cross-section* analysis using firm level data based on a survey conducted by the Toyo Keizai Shinposha in October 1994 (see Toyo Keizai, 1995). Although the analysis is limited to companies listed on the first board of the Tokyo Stock Exchange, companies involved in machinery manufacturing (general machinery, electrical machinery and precision instruments) and transport machinery are analysed. One of the reasons for choosing a broader spectrum of industries than earlier papers is to avoid the concern about the lack of generality of the results if the sample is restricted to electric machinery.

While both company size and the stock of knowledge are found to be important determinants of the decision whether or not to manufacture abroad in either a developed or developing country, this decision does not appear to be strongly influenced by whether or not the company is a member of either a vertical *keiretsu* or a horizontal *keiretsu*. The ratio of labour used overseas to the ratio of labour used domestically does not appear to be strongly affected by the stock of knowledge (see Fukao *et al.,* 1994a). For developing countries, membership of either a vertical or horizontal *keiretsu* appears to have the impact of reducing the proportion of labour used overseas. For developed countries, membership of either a vertical or horizontal *keiretsu* does not appear to have a strong impact on the proportion of labour used overseas.

The chapter is structured as follows. Section 7.2 discusses the factors influencing the decision whether or not to produce overseas, and, if production overseas is decided on, how much labour to use overseas relative to that used in Japan. Details of the data used are provided in Section 7.3. Results of probit estimation for the decision of whether or not to produce overseas are presented in Section 7.4. Given a decision to produce overseas, results explaining the ratio of the amount of labour used overseas to the amount of labour used in Japan are presented in Section 7.5. Section 7.6 contains some concluding comments.

7.2 DETERMINANTS OF OVERSEAS BEHAVIOUR

There are many ways of assessing the extent to which a firm is involved in foreign activities, for example, the number of countries in which a firm operates and the firm's foreign to total sales ratio (see the discussion in Nguyen and Cosset, 1995 for example).

In this chapter, following Fukao *et al.* (1994a), two particular decisions of the firm are analysed: the decision whether or not to produce abroad; and if a decision is made to produce abroad, how much foreign labour to use relative to how much domestic labour is used. Since this chapter is a cross-section analysis of individual firm behaviour, the determinants of overseas behaviour discussed focus on individual company characteristics. Although relative wage differences, exchange rate effects and trade barriers have been suggested as important influences on foreign investment decisions, they will not show up in a cross-section analysis. This chapter does not deny the importance of these factors but seeks to add to the list of relevant variables.

It is important to make a distinction between the impact that a particular variable will have on: (a) the probability that a firm will be a foreign investor (or producer); and (b) given that the firm has decided to be a foreign investor (or producer), the extent of its overseas activities, for example, the share of production carried out overseas or the proportion of labour used overseas (see Blomstrom and Lipsey, 1986 for a discussion of this point within the context of firm size).

7.2.1 The Decision to Produce Abroad

One important modelling question to be faced in this type of cross-section analysis is what exactly is the firm decision being modelled. Here, it is assumed that in *every* period, firms not already producing overseas consider whether they should produce overseas and firms already producing overseas consider whether they should stop producing overseas. There are two reasons why the actual decision to produce overseas is more complex than just a decision to produce outside Japan: first, a country of production must be chosen; and, second, what is going to be produced domestically and what is going to be produced overseas must be decided (these products may be the same or different). While data concerning the country of production and, to some extent, items being produced overseas are available in Toyo Keizai (1995), for simplicity, foreign countries are divided into either developed or developing countries and production is assumed to be of a homogeneous good.

The model which describes the decision of whether or not to produce abroad in the cross section of observed firms is assumed to be as follows:

$$O_i = a_1 + a_2 Z_i + a_3 S_i + a_4 I_i + a_5 V_i + a_6 H_i + u_i \tag{7.1}$$

where O_i is a zero–one variable taking the value 0 if the *i*th firm does not produce overseas and the value 1 if the *i*th firm does produce overseas; Z_i is the stock of technology of the *i*th firm; S_i is the size of the *i*th firm; I_i is a variable to take account of the industry in which the *i*th firm operates; V_i is a variable that indicates whether the *i*th firm is a member of a vertical *keiretsu*; H_i is a variable that indicates whether the *i*th firm is a member of a horizontal *keiretsu*; and u_i is an error term. The discussion that follows suggests why these variables may be important in explaining the overseas production decision and the expected sign of their associated parameter.

The stock of technology possessed by a firm, Z_i, has often been suggested as a factor that significantly influences the firm's decision whether or not to produce overseas (see, for example, Helpman, 1984 and Dunning, 1996). The public-good nature of technology within a firm is often stressed. In this case, access to the technology held by the parent firm can provide its foreign affiliates with an advantage over local firms (or more accurately provide something to compensate for the disadvantages arising from the firm operating in an unfamiliar, foreign environment). Why does the level of technology matter? Fukao *et al.* (1994a) provide a rigorous model with which to determine the sign of the impact of the level of technology within the firm on the decision whether or not to produce overseas. They suggest that it is important to distinguish the decision to produce in developing countries from the decision to produce in developed countries.

Assume that labour, capital and technology are the inputs into the production process both at home and abroad, and the stock of technology is common to both production processes. A change in the stock of technology within the firm will therefore affect the optimal level of production at home and abroad (assuming foreign production) and as a result the total profits from both operations. Let Π^M $(W_J, W_F, R_J, R_F, H, Z)$ be the firm's profit function when it produces a homogeneous good, both at home and abroad, under monopolistic competition conditions (so the price of the good in each country is a choice variable), with W and R being the wage rate and cost of capital, respectively; the subscripts J and F refer to Japan and the foreign country, respectively; H is the fixed costs associated with going overseas; and Z is the firm's stock of knowledge. Let Π^J (W_J,R_J,H,Z) be the firm's profit function when it produces only at home, again assuming monopolistic competition. When Π^M (.) $>^J$(.), it is assumed the firm produces at home and overseas. When $\Pi^M(.) < \Pi^J(.)$, the firm is assumed to produce at home only. Since both ^{M} and ^{J} are not observed simultaneously, it is natural to apply a probit/logit style model to analyse this decision.

For a developing country, it is typical to assume $W_J/R_J > W_F/R_F$. In this case, Fukao *et al.* (1994a) find that since there are two opposing effects, it is not possible to determine whether the level of a firm's technology has a positive or negative influence on its decision to produce overseas. First, a firm with a small stock of knowledge tends to be labour intensive (when the degree of substitution between labour and knowledge is higher than the degree of substitution between capital and knowledge). This provides an incentive to produce overseas. Second, a firm with a small stock of knowledge is likely to have a high marginal cost and a low level of optimal output, which is likely to restrain the company from going overseas. As a result, the sign of a_2 is indeterminate. For developed countries (where it is assumed that $W_J/R_J < W_F/R_F$), Fukao *et al.* (1994a) find that there is a critical stock of technology. Firms with stocks of technology higher (lower) than this critical level will (will not) produce overseas, that is, $a_2 > 0$. In their empirical study, Fukao *et al.* (1994a) find that increases in the stock of technology raise the probability of producing overseas in both developing and developed countries.

Horst (1972) suggests two reasons why the size of the firm, S_i, is likely to affect whether or not a firm operates overseas. First, he argues that larger firms are likely to be better credit risks and so have an easier time financing the fixed costs associated with an overseas investment. Second, Horst suggests that smaller firms are likely to be more risk-averse. If overseas investment is a risky activity then it is more likely to be undertaken by larger, less risk-averse firms. This suggests that $a_3 > 0$. Belderbos and Sleuwaegen (1993) find significant and positive size effects on the decision of Japanese firms to invest in Europe, America and South East Asia. Surprisingly, Fukao *et al.* (1994a) do not include a size variable in their analysis of the decision to produce abroad.

There are three reasons for taking account of industry differences, I_i. The first is that there are likely to be differences in the production functions used (or technology adopted) across industries. The second is that the foreign trade barriers (tariffs and so on) that goods face differ significantly across goods and industries. Finally, the extent of R&D spillovers may differ across industries. These types of industry effects have been found to be statistically significant in Belderbos and Sleuwaegen (1993) and Fukao *et al.* (1994a).

There are now several studies that examine the impact of horizontal *keiretsu* on various aspects of the Japanese economy, for example, Japan's trade patterns (Fung, 1991 and Lawrence, 1991) and the Japanese firm's investment behaviour (Hoshi *et al.*, 1990, 1991). If the suggestion of Hoshi *et al.* (1991) that liquidity constraints are less important for the investment decisions of companies that are members of corporate groups is correct and this also applies to investment decisions abroad, then it may be that overseas production by companies that are members of corporate groups is more likely. This suggests that the coefficient of H_i in (1), a_6, is likely to be positive. Main bank monitoring that reduces the informational asymmetries between the firm and its lenders is suggested as the reason for these reduced liquidity constraints. Monitoring the overseas activities of companies is likely to be more difficult than monitoring their domestic activities but it may be the case that monitoring by the main bank in the corporate group may also reduce the informational asymmetries in the case of foreign investments as well. Notwithstanding this argument, earlier studies looking at the impact of *keiretsu* find no strong effect of *keiretsu* membership on the decision whether or not to produce overseas (Hennart and Park, 1992 and Belderbos and Sleuwaegen, 1993).

The important role of subcontracting relationships (manufacturer–supplier relationships) in Japan's automobile and electric machinery has been highlighted recently (see, for example, Asanuma, 1989 and Asanuma and Kikutani, 1990). If the manufacturer–supplier relationships are critical to the apparent comparative advantage enjoyed by these Japanese industries and these relationships are to be maintained, this suggests that factors influencing the decision whether or not to produce overseas for companies in a manufacturer–supplier relationship may be slightly different from those for companies not involved in a manufacturer–supplier relationship. In addition, Suzuki (1993) has reported significant positive R&D spillover effects within and among vertical *keiretsu* groups in the electrical machinery industry. This might suggest that for a company that is a member of a vertical *keiretsu*, its stock of technology is augmented positively by the stock of technology within its *keiretsu* group (and other vertical *keiretsu*). That is, membership of a vertical *keiretsu* implies a higher true stock of technology than a company has when considered on its own. Combining this idea with the earlier arguments in Fukao *et al.* (1994a) suggests that membership of vertical *keiretsu* might increase the probability of production in developed countries (a_5>0), while for developing countries the effect might be either positive or negative (the sign of a_5 is indeterminate).

7.2.2 Labour Usage

Given that a decision has been made to produce overseas, what affects the usage of labour overseas, L_F, compared to the usage of labour within Japan, L_J? The following model is used to analyse this decision:

$$(L_F/ L_J)_i = b_1 + b_2 Z_i + b_3 I_i + b_4 Vi + b_5 H_i + e_i \tag{7.2}$$

where e_i is a disturbance term. The discussion that follows in this subsection suggests why these variables may be important in explaining the labour usage ratio.

Similar to the model discussed in Section 7.2.1 (the impact of the stock of technology on the decision whether to produce overseas), the factor demand functions when the firm chooses to produce overseas as well as domestically will be of the form:

$$L_F = g\,(W_J, W_F, R_J, R_F, Z) \tag{7.3}$$
$$L_J = g\,(W_J, W_F, R_J, R_F, Z) \tag{7.4}$$

so that

$$L_F / L_J = h(W_J, W_F, R_J, R_F, Z). \tag{7.5}$$

Fukao *et al.* (1994a) suggest that the response of L_F/L_J to changes in technology is likely to differ when overseas production is in an advanced country and when it is in a developing one. When a firm is producing in a developed country, Fukao *et al.* (1994a) suggest that an increase in Z is likely to cause L_F/L_J to increase ($b_2 > 0$) whereas in a developing country the effect is likely to be to reduce L_F/L_J ($b_2 < 0$).

For the same reasons as in Section 7.2.1, when viewed across industries, foreign trade barriers and differences in R&D spillover effects are likely to influence L_F/L_J.

Essentially for the reasons discussed in Section 7.2.1, Fukao *et al.* (1994b) suggest that main bank monitoring or membership of a horizontal *keiretsu* is likely to imply a larger proportion of overseas production (although they tend to observe the reverse). However, their argument, although made in the context of the proportion of overseas production, really relates to the likelihood of producing overseas. Given a decision to produce overseas, membership of a horizontal *keiretsu* presumably influences capital usage both domestically and overseas (and as a result may later affect capital–labour usage ratios). It is unfortunately not clear whether membership necessarily implies a higher proportion of overseas production (or a higher proportion of labour usage overseas). That is, the sign of b_5 is indeterminate.

Following the Suzuki (1993) spillover suggestion, membership of a vertical *keiretsu* might imply a higher true stock of technology than is given by the firm's own stock.

Combining this with the argument about how the stock of technology affects the ratio of labour used abroad to labour used domestically suggests that membership of a vertical *keiretsu* might increase this ratio for developed countries ($b_4>0$) and reduce the ratio for developing countries ($b_4<0$).

7.3 DATA

Every year the Toyo Keizai Shinposha conducts a survey of the foreign activities of listed and unlisted Japanese firms. Toyo Keizai (1995) contains the results of this survey performed in October 1994 on about 4800 listed and unlisted Japanese companies. Based on company responses, Toyo Keizai (1995) lists for each company details of their overseas affiliates. In the best case, the details include country of operation, principal shareholders and their shareholdings, establishment date, capital, number of employees, the number of employees dispatched from Japan, the value of sales, and the activities of the affiliates. When data are missing they are most likely to be sales, followed by capital and then the number of employees. The principal types of activities of overseas affiliates in the machinery and transport industries are production, marketing and servicing. An extremely small number of companies have overseas affiliates engaged in financing and research and development.

A company was treated as producing overseas in a developed (developing) country if it had at least one affiliate in a developed (developing) country whose purpose was stated to be production (or production and sales). Following Fukao *et al.* (1994a, 1994b), countries were divided into developed and developing countries based on World Bank definitions. Countries listed as high-income countries by the World Bank (1994, pp. 251, 252) with the exception of Taiwan and China are treated as developed countries. Countries listed as low- or middle-income countries by the World Bank (1994) (together with Taiwan and China) are treated as developing countries. It should be noted that according to this division both Singapore and Hong Kong are classified as developed countries, and Greece and Portugal are classified as developing countries.

Although the overseas affiliates are not always truly subsidiaries, the Japanese shareholder is referred to as the parent company for the sake of convenience. Parent shareholdings in the overseas affiliates range from relatively small amounts to 100 per cent ownership. There are at least two ways to compute the labour usage in the foreign affiliate. We could ignore the size of the parent shareholding and just add up the amount of labour in each affiliate. Or we could choose to weight the labour usage according to the parent company's shareholding (including indirect shareholdings).

More concretely, if there are two foreign affiliates using amounts of labour L_1 and L_2 and the proportion of outstanding shares held by the Japanese company are a_1 and a_2 ($0< a_i \leq 1$), then the amount of foreign labour can be calculated as $L_1 + L_2$ or $a_1L_1 + a_2L_2$. Both measures of foreign labour are used in the empirical investigation in Section 7.5.

Data on the value of research and development expenditure for each company from 1987 to 1994 were obtained from the annual spring issues of the English edition of the Toyo Keizai's *Japan Company Handbook: First Section.* Those companies for which a full set of data on R&D expenditure from 1987 to 1994 are not available are still included if at least the last four years (1991–94) of data on R&D expenditure are available. To compute the stock of technical knowledge, Z_i, the nominal values of R&D expenditure are first converted to real values using the value of the wholesale price index for each year. The stock of technical knowledge in 1994 is computed from these time series on real R&D expenditures using the perpetual inventory method (see Goto *et al.*, 1986). The Science and Technology Agency (1985, p. 46) indicates that there are large differences in the useful life of a patent during which time revenues are generated across the industries being examined here (four years in the case of precision machinery to nearly fourteen years in the case of general machinery). These different patent periods are used to compute rates of technological obsolescence for the perpetual inventory method that differ across industry. Finally, a measure of R&D intensity is obtained by dividing the stock measure by the domestic value-added of the company. A potential alternative source of data on firm R&D expenditure is the Japan Development Bank's corporate database. However, it should be noted that research and development expenditure is reported as zero for many companies listed there!

Industry dummy variables, I_i, were created according to the industry of the parent company. The industry of the parent was determined by using the industrial classification for the item that was the number one sales earner for the company in the year to March 1994. Three-digit industrial classifications provided by the Management and Coordination Agency (1986) were used in making this classification. Industries were grouped as follows:

General Machinery: Codes 291–299 (includes machinery for agriculture, metal manufacturing, construction and general industrial uses).
Electrical Machinery: Codes 300–309 (includes machinery for electricity generation and transmission, communications and data processing, and electronic appliances).

Motor Vehicles: Code 311 (includes motor vehicles and motor vehicle parts and accessories).
Precision Machinery: Codes 320–327 (includes surveying, optical and medical instruments).
All Other: Codes: 312–319 (includes shipbuilding, aircraft and other transport equipment).

Zero–one industry dummy variables were created for the first four industry groups so that the All Other group is the base group for comparison.

A zero–one dummy variable, H_i, was created to capture membership of a horizontal *keiretsu* where the variable took the value one if the company was a member of the Presidents' Club of one of the six traditional enterprise groups, Mitsui, Mitsubishi, Sumitomo, Fuyo, Sanwa and Daiichi-Kango, and zero otherwise. For this purpose, lists of members of the Presidents' Club contained in the Toyo Keizai's *Kigyo Keiretsu Soran* were used. This is not the only possible way to define membership in a horizontal *keiretsu*. It is perhaps the narrowest definition.

A zero–one dummy variable, V_i, was created to capture membership in a vertical *keiretsu* where the variable took the value one if the company was a member of the following groups: Hitachi, Toshiba, NEC, Fujitsu, Matsushita, Nissan, Toyota and Honda, and zero otherwise. For this purpose, lists of members of these groups contained in the Toyo Keizai's *Kigyo Keiretsu Soran* were used.

Company size, S_i, was measured by the domestic sales of the company. Data on the number of employees and sales in Japan as of March 1994 were taken from Japan Development Bank's corporate data bank.

The Appendix contains a list of the 223 companies that were used to analyse the decision whether to produce overseas. Information on the labour usage of the overseas affiliates is available less often. As a result, when analysing labour choices, some companies had to be excluded (see Appendix). That exclusion depended on whether the analysis was for labour in developed or developing countries.

7.4 DETERMINANTS OF THE DECISION TO PRODUCE OVERSEAS

Of the 223 companies for which a complete set of data is available, 53 companies engage in no overseas production, 19 companies engage in production only in developed countries, 31 companies engage in production only in developing countries, while the remaining 120 companies engage in production in both developing and developed countries. In all the probit models discussed, the dependent variable, O_i, takes the value one when the firm produces abroad in the appropriate region and zero when it does not. All estimations in this section and the next section were performed using LIMDEP 6.0 (see Greene, 1991).

Table 7.1 contains estimates of probit models for firms choosing whether or not to manufacture in developing countries. An increase in R&D intensity tends to increase the likelihood that the firm will produce in a developing country although it is significant at the 10 per cent level in only three of the four cases. An increase in firm size also has the effect of increasing the likelihood that the firm will produce overseas and this effect is significant at the 5 per cent level in three of the four cases. The dummy variables for the vertical *keiretsu* and the horizontal *keiretsu*, whether included jointly or separately, suggest that *keiretsu* membership tends to increase the likelihood of manufacturing in developing countries. However, the dummy variables are not strongly significant.

The *F*-test refers to the test statistic for the test of the null hypothesis that all the coefficients (excluding the constant) are zero. 'Correct 0s' and 'Correct ls' refer to the number of zeros and ones in the sample correctly predicted by the model, respectively.

Table 7.2 contains estimates of probit models for firms choosing whether or not to manufacture in developed countries. As in the case of developing countries, an increase in R&D intensity tends to increase the likelihood that the firm will produce in a developed country and this variable is significant at the 5 per cent level in all four cases. An increase in firm size also has the effect of increasing the likelihood that the firm will produce overseas and this effect is significant at the 1 per cent level in all four cases. Although the dummy variables for the vertical *keiretsu* and the horizontal *keiretsu*, whether included jointly or separately, are statistically insignificant, membership of a vertical *keiretsu* tends to lead to a slightly lower probability of manufacturing overseas while membership of a horizontal *keiretsu* tends to lead to a slightly higher probability of manufacturing overseas.

Tables 7.3 and 7.4 provide similar analyses when the developing countries are restricted to those in Asia and the developed countries are restricted to those in Europe and North America, respectively. The results are more or less the same as those in Tables 7.1 and 7.2, respectively.

In summary, these probit models provide no strong evidence that membership of either a vertical or horizontal *keiretsu* alters the likelihood that a firm produces overseas in either a developed or developing country.

Table 7.1 ***Probit analysis of firms choosing whether or not to manufacture in developing countries***

	(1.1)	(1.2)	(1.3)	(1.4)
Constant	-1.018	-1.115	-1.015	-1.104
	(2.73)	(2.87)	(2.72)	(2.86)
General Machinery	0.514	0.588	0.519	0.569
	(1.31)	(1.45)	(1.32)	(1.42)
Electric Machinery	1.258	1.304	1.227	1.323
	(3.24)	(3.23)	(3.14)	(3.31)
Motor Vehicles	1.119	1.110	0.965	1.260
	(2.65)	(2.46)	(2.19)	(2.89)
Precision Machinery	1.049	1.071	1.068	1.038
	(1.85)	(1.85)	(1.88)	(1.80)
R&D Intensity	4.698	4.826	4.312	5.244
	(1.78)	(1.81)	(1.62)	(1.97)
Size	0.0229	0.0155	0.0217	0.0173
	(2.86)	(1.83)	(2.73)	(2.00)
Vertical *Keiretsu*		0.445	0.398	
		(1.50)	(1.35)	
Horizontal *Keiretsu*		0.834		0.767
		(1.69)		(1.58)
Sample Size	223	223	223	223
Log-Likelihood	-114.82	-112.27	-113.88	-113.43
F-Test	50.89	56.00	52.77	53.68
Correct 0s	32/72	33172	32172	31/72
Correct ls	130/151	132/151	131/151	131/151

Note: Figures in parentheses are the absolute values of the asymptotic *t*-statistics.

Table 7.2 Probit analysis of firms choosing whether or not to manufacture in developed countries

	(2.1)	(2.2)	(2.3)	(2.4)
Constant	-1.753	-1.807	-1.754	-1.807
	(3.84)	(3.90)	(3.84)	(3.90)
General Machinery	1.148	1.173	1.145	1.175
	(2.50)	(2.53)	(2.49)	(2.54)
Electric Machinery	1.396	1.431	1.401	1.428
	(3.11)	(3.14)	(3.11)	(3.13)
Motor Vehicles	1.627	1.729	1.655	1.710
	(3.38)	(3.46)	(3.36)	(3.49)
Precision Machinery	1.940	1.918	1.935	1.921
	(3.01)	(2.93)	(2.99)	(2.93)
R&D Intensity	5.482	5.903	5.570	5.848
	(2.00)	(2.12)	(2.02)	(2.12)
Size	0.0365	0.0335	0.0370	0.0330
	(3.45)	(2.92)	(3.41)	(2.96)
Vertical *Keiretsu*		-0.0530	-0.778	
		(0.19)	(0.28)	
Horizontal *Keiretsu*		0.557		0.563
		(1.20)		(1.21)
Sample Size	223	223	223	223
Log-Likelihood	-115.68	-114.88	-115.64	-114.91
F-Test	64.07	65.66	64.15	65.62
Correct 0s	46/84	46/84	46/84	46/84
Correct ls	114/139	114/139	114/139	114/139

Note: As for Table 7.1.

Table 7.3 *Probit analysis of firms choosing whether or not to manufacture in Asian developing countries*

	(3.1)	(3.2)	(3.3)	(3.4)
Constant	-1.015	-1.131	-1.019	-1.109
	(2.80)	(3.00)	(2.81)	(2.95)
General Machinery	0.514	0.604	0.525	0.577
	(1.34)	(1.52)	(1.36)	(1.47)
Electric Machinery	1.306	1.368	1.283	1.376
	(3.44)	(3.48)	(3.37)	(3.53)
Motor Vehicles	0.905	0.915	0.759	1.056
	(2.26)	(2.11)	(1.81)	(2.53)
Precision Machinery	1.091	1.138	1.116	1.095
	(1.95)	(2.00)	(2.00)	(1.93)
R&D Intensity	4.916	5.027	4.555	5.435
	(1.88)	(1.91)	(1.73)	(2.08)
Size	0.0151	0.0094	0.0143	0.0103
	(2.22)	(1.40)	(2.15)	(1.46)
Vertical *Keiretsu*		0.401	0.360	
		(1.41)	(1.28)	
Horizontal *Keiretsu*		0.738		0.683
		(1.63)		(1.52)
Sample Size	223	223	223	223
Log-Likelihood	-119.89	-117.61	-119.06	-118.64
F-Test	47.65	52.22	49.32	50.16
Correct 0s	35/77	38/77	38/77	38/77
Correct ls	123/146	125/146	123/146	124/146

Note: As for Table 7.1.

Table 7.4 Probit analysis of firms choosing whether or not to manufacture in developed countries (North America and Europe)

	(4.1)	(4.2)	(4.3)	(4.4)
Constant	-2.123	-2.253	-2.125	-2.249
	(4.24)	(4.29)	(4.24)	(4.28)
General Machinery	1.101	1.193	1.103	1.188
	(2.16)	(2.26)	(2.17)	(2.25)
Electric Machinery	1.417	1.505	1.415	1.507
	(2.86)	(2.91)	(2.86)	(2.92)
Motor Vehicles	0.872	1.023	0.855	1.050
	(1.74)	(1.90)	(1.67)	(1.99)
Precision Machinery	2.002	2.037	2.006	2.030
	(3.06)	(3.02)	(3.06)	(3.01)
R&D Intensity	6.093	6.537	6.050	6.610
	(2.33)	(2.46)	(2.30)	(2.51)
Size	0.0263	0.0220	0.0262	0.0222
	(3.64)	(2.84)	(3.63)	(2.86)
Vertical *Keiretsu*		0.0673	0.0374	
		(0.26)	(0.14)	
Horizontal *Keiretsu*		0.644		0.637
		(1.56)		(1.55)
Sample Size	223	223	223	223
Log-Likelihood	-119.42	-118.14	-119.41	-118.18
F-Test	68.68	71.24	68.70	71.17
Correct 0s	100/121	97/121	99/121	98/121
Correct ls	57/102	57/102	57/102	58/102

Note: As for Table 7.1.

7.5 DETERMINANTS OF LABOUR USAGE

Since labour usage in the foreign country is only observed if the decision is made to produce overseas, the possibility of sample selection bias arising in an analysis of the determinants of the foreign labour to domestic labour ratio needs to be taken into account when estimating an appropriate model. In addition, this has an important impact on how the marginal effect of regressors on the dependent variable in the observed sample should be calculated.

Following Greene (1990, p. 742) we write the model for determining whether to produce overseas or not as

$$z_t = \boldsymbol{c}'\boldsymbol{w}_t + u_t,\ u_t \sim N(0,1), \quad (7.6)$$

where z_t is not observed but $z_t > 0$ means that overseas production occurs and $z_t < 0$ means overseas production does not occur, $\boldsymbol{w}_t$ is a vector of explanatory variables, $\boldsymbol{c}$ is a vector of parameters, and u_t is a disturbance term. The dependent variable in Equation (7.6) can be viewed as the difference in profit when production occurs both domestically and overseas and when it occurs only domestically, $\Pi^M(.)\Pi^J(.)$ in the notation of Section 7.2.1. Rewrite the model determining the ratio of labour usage (Equation 7.2) as

$$y_t = \boldsymbol{b}'\boldsymbol{x}_t + e_t, \quad (7.7)$$

where y_t is only observed when $Z_t > 0$, $\boldsymbol{x}_t$ is a vector of explanatory variables, $\boldsymbol{b}$ is a vector of parameters, and e_t is a disturbance term.

A commonly used method to estimate this model is to use a variation of Heckman's two-step method which relies on y_t satisfying Equation (7.8) if y_t is actually observed.

$$y_t = \boldsymbol{b}\,\boldsymbol{x}_t + dh(a_t) + n_t\,, \quad (7.8)$$

This assumes n_t has zero mean but is heteroscedastic, $h(a_t) = f(a_t)/F(a_t)$ and $f(.)$ and $F(.)$ are the probability density and the cumulative distribution functions for the normal distribution, respectively, and $a_t = \boldsymbol{c}'\boldsymbol{w}_t$ (see Greene, 1990). Equation (7.8) is estimated by ordinary least squares with $a_t = \boldsymbol{c}'\boldsymbol{w}_t$ replaced by $a_t^* = \boldsymbol{c}^{*\prime}\boldsymbol{w}_t$ ($\boldsymbol{c}^*$ is the probit estimate of $\boldsymbol{c}$ in (7.6)) but the standard errors need to be correctly computed to take account of the heteroscedasticity and serial correlation in the disturbance.

The results from applying Heckman's two-step method to the ratio of labour used overseas to labour used domestically for developing and developed countries are given in Tables 7.5 and 7.6, respectively. The measures of foreign labour used here are based on the parent company's shareholding in the affiliate. The dependent variable in these models is

Table 7.5 Model explaining the ratio of labour used in developing countries to labour used in Japan (weighted)

	Sample selection				
	Probit	(5.1)	(5.2)	(5.3)	(5.4)
Constant	-1.000	0.131	0.443	0.169	0.339
	(2.67)	(0.56)	(1.63)	(0.73)	(1.26)
General Machinery	0.504	0.052	-0.058	0.028	-0.011
	(1.28)	(0.39)	(0.42)	(0.21)	(0.08)
Electric Machinery	1.175	0.313	0.161	0.299	0.208
	(3.00)	(2.19)	(1.01)	(2.12)	-0.058
Motor Vehicles	1.088	0.038	-0.071	0.079	-0.086
	(2.57)	(0.24)	(0.41)	(0.50)	(0.49)
Precision Machinery	0.968	0.247	0.097	0.226	0.150
	(1.66)	(1.38)	(0.51)	(1.28)	(0.79)
R&D Intensity	4.111	-1.089	-1.281	-1.033	-1.292
	(1.52)	(1.10)	(1.26)	(1.06)	(1.27)
Size	0.0231				
	(2.83)				
Vertical *Keiretsu*			-0.190	-0.157	
			(2.25)	(2.10)	
Horizontal *Keiretsu*			-0.208		-0.163
			(2.55)		(1.77)
Lambda		-0.024	-0.219	-0.027	-0.173
		(0.12)	(1.01)	(0.14)	(0.80)
Sample Size	201	129	129	129	129
Log-Likelihood	-110.54				
R^2		0.152	0.213	0.180	0.173
F-Test	41.19				
Correct 0s	34/72				
Correct ls	109/129				

Note: As for Table 7.1.

Table 7.6 Model explaining the ratio of labour used in developed countries to labour used in Japan (weighted)

	Sample selection				
	Probit	(6.1)	(6.2)	(6.3)	(6.4)
Constant	-1.739	0.017	0.084	0.0155	0.075
	(3.79)	(0.17)	(0.72)	(0.15)	(0.63)
General Machinery	1.079	0.094	0.073	0.100	0.071
	(2.35)	(1.19)	(0.89)	(1.28)	(0.86)
Electric Machinery	1.285	0.176	0.160	0.186	0.154
	(2.85)	(2.36)	(2.07)	(2.51)	(1.96)
Motor Vehicles	1.572	0.101	0.089	0.131	0.063
	(3.26)	(1.25)	(0.98)	(1.60)	(0.70)
Precision Machinery	1.828	0.159	0.130	0.167	0.128
	(2.75)	(1.63)	(1.28)	(1.72)	(1.25)
R&D Intensity	5.577	-0.018	-0.077	0.015	-0.097
	(1.99)	(0.04)	(0.15)	(0.03)	(0.19)
Size	0.0356				
	(3.35)				
Vertical *Keiretsu*			-0.070	-0.065	
			(1.66)	(1.55)	
Horizontal *Keiretsu*			-0.055	-0.046	
			(1.06)		(0.89)
Lambda		0.035	-0.006	0.035	0.103
		(0.49)	(0.08)	(0.49)	(0.01)
Sample Size	200	116	116	116	116
Log-Likelihood	-109.71				
R^2		0.076	0.103	0.094	0.082
F-Test	52.70				
Correct 0s	53/84				
Correct ls	89/116				

Note: As for Table 7.1.

In $(1 + L_F / L_J)$ and the variable labelled LAMBDA corresponds to $h(a_t)$ in Equation (7.8). Since the available samples in Table 7.5 and 7.6 differ slightly from those used in Tables 7.1–7.4, the probit model (excluding the *keiretsu* dummy variables) used for determining the sample selection is re-estimated and the results presented for completeness.

As can be seen from Table 7.5, for developing countries, estimates of the parameter associated with R&D intensity are consistently negative which is what Fukao *et al.* (1994a) found but in no case are they statistically significant (see Fukao *et al.*, 1994a). For developed countries, estimates of the parameter associated with R&D intensity in Table 7.6 are negative in three of the four cases whereas Fukao *et al.* (1994a) find a positive effect but again the effects are not statistically significant.

Fukao *et al.* (1994a) use the signs of these parameter estimates to verify the consistency of their theoretical model's predictions and the empirical results. Such a comparison, however, ignores the impact of the sample selection term in the calculation of the marginal impact of R&D intensity on the labour ratio when production occurs overseas.

For a variable x_{kt} that appears both in $\boldsymbol{x}_t$ in (7.8) with associated parameter b_k and in $\boldsymbol{w}_t$ in (7.6) with associated parameter c_k, the full effect of a change in the variable is

$$\delta E[y_t/z_t > 0]/\delta x_{kt} = b_k - c_k\, dg(a_t) \tag{7.9}$$

where $g(a_t) = h(a_t)^2 + a_t\, h(a_t)$ (see Greene, 1990, p. 743). It is possible that the signs of $\delta E[y_t/z_t > 0]/\delta x_{kt}$ and b_k will differ. Calculating the marginal effects of R&D intensity using (7.9) for probit equations (5.1)–(5.4) found in Table 7.5 at the means of the variables gives estimates of –0.026, 0.28, 0.027 and 0.224, respectively. In all four cases, the sign of the marginal effect is positive and the reverse of the estimate of the parameter associated with R&D intensity. This is contrary to the theoretical prediction of Fukao *et al.* (1994a). Calculating the marginal effects of R&D intensity for probit equations (6.1)–(6.4) found in Table 7.6 at the means of the variables gives estimates of 0.0006, 0.0005, 0.0005 and –0.0001 respectively. There is a sign reversal in only one case. Hence, only probit equations (6.2) and (6.3) provide an estimate with a sign that is consistent with Fukao *et al.*'s (1994a) theoretical prediction. Although it is possible to calculate standard errors for these marginal effects, this has not been attempted. Given the insignificance of the estimates of the parameters associated with R&D intensity and the sample selection term in Tables 7.5 and 7.6, it seems likely that these effects are not significantly different from zero.

An examination of the impacts of membership in a vertical or horizontal *keiretsu* indicates that in both the developing and developed countries cases, membership tends to be associated with a lower foreign labour ratio. The impact of membership of a vertical *keiretsu* for the developing countries case is consistent with the predictions in Section 7.2.2 but for the developed countries case it is the opposite of what was predicted. These *keiretsu* membership variables are not statistically significant in the case of developed countries but are statistically significant for developing countries (at the 1 per cent level when both are included). One point of concern about the models for the developed countries is the low R^2 s.

Tables 7.7 and 7.8 report results corresponding to Tables 7.5 and 7.6, respectively, when the amount of foreign labour used is calculated as the unweighted sum of all labour in foreign production affiliates regardless of the parent company's shareholding. There are no qualitative differences in the results for labour in developing countries as reported in Table 7.7. For the developed country case in Table 7.8, there are two important differences. First, the sign of the parameter on R&D intensity is reversed in two of the four cases although the variable is still statistically insignificant in all cases. Second, the significance of the dummy variable for the vertical *keiretsu* has increased. Company size and advertising intensity were also included as explanatory variables in these models but they were generally insignificant. Some attempts were made at redefining the industry dummy variables more narrowly (particularly subdividing the electric machinery industry into sub-groups) but these modifications did not lead to any major change in the estimated results.

Table 7.7 Model explaining the ratio of labour used in developing countries to labour used in Japan (unweighted)

	Sample selection			
	(7.1)	(7.2)	(7.3)	(7.4)
Constant	0.172	0.152	0.215	0.396
	(0.69)	(1.78)	(0.88)	(1.39)
General Machinery	0.061	–0.060	0.033	–0.007
	(0.43)	(0.41)	(0.24)	(0.05)
Electric Machinery	0.352	0.186	0.336	0.239
	(2.32)	(1.11)	(2.25)	(1.42)
Motor Vehicles	0.081	–0.035	0.127	–0.052
	(0.49)	(0.19)	(0.77)	(0.28)
Precision Machinery	0.252	0.089	0.229	0.148
	(1.33)	(0.44)	(1.22)	(0.73)
R&D Intensity	–1.155	–1.360	–1.092	–1.373
	(1.10)	(1.26)	(1.06)	(1.27)
Vertical *Keiretsu*		–0.213	–0.177	
		(2.70)	(2.24)	
Horizontal *Keiretsu*		–0.225		–0.175
		(2.31)		(1.79)
Lambda	–0.020	–0.232	–0.024	–0.181
	(0.10)	(1.01)	(0.12)	(0.78)
Sample Size	129	129	129	129
R^2	0.154	0.219	0.185	0.175

Note: Figures in parentheses are the absolute values of the asymptotic *t*-statistics.

Table 7:8 Model explaining the ratio of labour used in developed countries to labour used in Japan (unweighted)

	Sample selection			
	(8.1)	(8.2)	(8.3)	(8.4)
Constant	0.033	0.122	0.031	0.108
	(0.29)	(0.90)	(0.27)	(0.79)
General Machinery	0.094	0.067	0.102	0.064
	(1.03)	(0.72)	(1.14)	(0.68)
Electric Machinery	0.161	0.140	0.174	0.131
	(1.85)	(1.57)	(2.03)	(1.45)
Motor Vehicles	0.123	0.110	0.166	0.075
	(1.32)	(1.06)	(1.75)	(0.72)
Precision Machinery	0.147	0.109	0.159	0.106
	(1.29)	(0.93)	(1.40)	(0.89)
R&D Intensity	0.100	0.024	0.146	–0.004
	(0.17)	(0.04)	(0.25)	(0.01)
Vertical *Keiretsu*		–0.097	–0.091	
		(2.00)	(1.88)	
Horizontal *Keiretsu*		–0.073		–0.060
		(1.21)		(0.99)
Lambda	0.042	–0.013	0.041	–0.003
	(0.50)	(0.13)	(0.50)	(0.03)
Sample Size	116	116	116	116
R^2	0.039	0.079	0.067	0.047

Note: As for Table 7.7.

7.6 CONCLUSION

The stock of technology is found to be positively related to the likelihood of producing overseas for both production in developing and developed countries. However, the stock of technology is not a significant explanatory variable of the ratio of foreign labour to domestic labour for either developing or developed countries. This latter finding contrasts with Fukao *et al.* (1994a) for the same ratio and Fukao *et al.* (1994b) for the ratio of foreign value-added to domestic value-added.

Membership in a vertical or horizontal *keiretsu* does not appear to influence the likelihood that a company produces overseas in either a developing or a developed country. Membership in a vertical and a horizontal *keiretsu* appears to reduce significantly the relative use of labour in developing countries but not in developed countries. Of course, these results may be sensitive to the specification of the equation estimated and to the definition of membership in a *keiretsu*.

One unsatisfactory feature of the analysis of the decision whether or not to produce overseas is to treat the decisions to produce in developed countries and developing countries separately. An attempt was made to estimate a multinominal logit model allowing for four possible outcomes: no overseas production, overseas production only in developing countries, overseas production only in developed countries, and overseas production in both developed and developing countries. The results of this analysis were very discouraging as the model really only separated observations into two groups: the no overseas production outcome and the overseas production in both developed and developing countries outcome.

NOTE

1 The author wishes to thank Masahiro Kawai and participants at the conference on 'Japan in the International Economy and Structural Adjustment in Japan' held at Macquarie University for their helpful and constructive comments on an earlier version of this chapter, and Satoko Rolland for her excellent research assistance. He also wishes to acknowledge the financial assistance of Macquarie University and the Asset Management Service Industry Fund, Osaka School of International Public Policy, Osaka University.

REFERENCES

Asanuma, B. (1989), 'Manufacturer–Supplier Relationships in Japan and the Concept of Relation-Specific Skill', *Journal of the Japanese and International Economies,* **3**, 1–30.

Asanuma, B. and Kikutani, T. (1990), 'Risk Absorption in Japanese Subcontracting:

A Microeconometric Study of the Automobile Industry', *Journal of the Japanese and International Economies,* **6**: 1–29.

Belderbos, R.A. and Sleuwaegen, L. (1993), 'Japanese Firms and the Decision to Invest Abroad: Business Groups, Regional Core Networks and Corporate Development', mimeo, Erasmus University.

Blomstrom, M. and Lipsey, R.E. (1986), 'Firm Size and Foreign Direct Investment', NBER Working Paper No. 2092.

Dunning, J.H. (1996), 'Explaining Foreign Direct Investment in Japan: Some Theoretical Insights', chapter 2 in M. Yoshitomi, and E.M. Graham (eds), *Foreign Direct Investment in Japan*, Cheltenham: Edward Elgar.

Froot, K.A. (1991), 'Japan's Foreign Direct Investment', NBER Working Paper No. 3737.

Fukao, K., Izawa, T., Kuninori, M. and Nakakita, T. (1994a), 'R&D Investment and Overseas Production: An Empirical Analysis of Japan's Electric Machinery Industry Based on Corporate Data', *Monetary and Economic Studies,* **12**, 2: 1–60.

Fukao, K., Izawa, T., Kuninori, M. and Nakakita, T. (1994b), 'Taigai chokusetsu toshi no kettei yoin: waga kuni denki sangyo kigyo no paneru deta ni yoru jissho bunseki, (The Determinants of Outward Direct Foreign Investment: An Empirical Analysis Using Panel Data on Firms in Japan's Electric Machinery Industry), *Keizai Kenkyu*, **45**, 3: 261–278.

Fung, K.C. (1991), 'Characteristics of Japanese Industrial Groups and Their Potential Impact on U.S.–Japanese Trade', in R.E. Baldwin (ed.), *Empirical Studies of Commercial Policy*, Chigaco: University of Chicago Press.

Goto, A., Honjo, N., Suzuki, K. and Takinosawa, M. (1986), 'Kenkyu kaihatsu to gijutsu shinpo no keizai bunseki, (An Economic Analysis of R&D and Technical Progress), *Keizai Bunseki*, 103, Economic Planning Agency, Tokyo.

Greene, W.H. (1990), *Econometric Analysis*, New York: Macmillan.

Greene, W.H. (1991), *LIMDEP: User's Manual and Reference Guide Version 6.0,* Econometric Software, Bellport, NY.

Helpman, E. (1984), 'A Simple Theory of International Trade with Multinational Corporations', *Journal of Political Economy*, 92, 451 -471.

Hennart, J. and Park, Y. (1992), 'Location, Governance, and Strategic Determinants of Japanese Manufacturing Investment in the United States', *Strategic Management Journal*, **15**: 419–36.

Horaguchi, H. (1992), *Nihon kigyo no kaigai chokusetsu toshi: ajia he no shinshutsu to tettai* (Japanese Firms' Foreign Direct Investment: Entry and Exit from Asia), Tokyo: Tokyo University Press.

Horst, T. (1972), 'Firm and Industry Determinants of the Decision to Invest Abroad: An Empirical Study', *Review of Economics and Statistics,* **54**: 258–66.

Hoshi, T., Kashyap, A. and Scharfstein, D. (1990), 'The Role of Banks in Reducing the Costs of Financial Distress in Japan', *Journal of Financial Economics,* **27**,1: 67–88.

Hoshi, T., Kashyap, A. and Scharfstein, D. (1991), 'Corporate Structure, Liquidity, and Investment: Evidence from Japanese Industrial Groups', *Quarterly Journal of Economics*, 106,1: 33–60.

Kimura, Y. (1989), 'Firm-Specific Strategic Advantages and Foreign Direct Investment Behaviour of Firms: The Case of Japanese Semi-conductor Firms',

Journal of International Business Studies, **20**: 296–314.
Kogut, B. and Chang, S.J. (1991), 'Technological Capabilities and Japanese Foreign Direct Investment in the United States', *Review of Economics and Statistics*, **73**, 3: 401–13.
Lawrence, R.Z. (1991), 'Efficient or Exclusionist? The Import Behaviour of Japanese Corporate Groups', *Brookings Papers on Economic Activity*, **1**: 311–31.
Lawrence, R.Z. (1993), 'Japan's Low Levels of Inward Investments: The Role of Inhibitions on Acquisitions', chapter 4 in K.A. Froot (ed.), *Foreign Direct Investment*, Chicago: University of Chicago Press.
Management and Coordination Agency (Statistical Standards Department, Statistics Bureau) (1986), *Standard Industrial Classification for Japan*, Tokyo: National Federation of Statistics Associations.
Nguyen, T.H. and Cosset, J.C. (1995), 'The Measurement of the Degree of Foreign Involvement', *Applied Economics*, **27**: 343–51.
Science and Technology Agency (1985), *Showa 60 nenpan kagaku gijutsu hakusho* 'White Paper on Science and Technology', Science and Technology Agency, Tokyo.
Suzuki, K. (1993), 'R&D Spillovers and Technology Transfer Among and Within Vertical Keiretsu Groups: Evidence from the Japanese Electrical Machinery Industry', *International Journal of Industrial Organization*, **11**: 573–91.
Toyo Keizai (1995), *Kaigai shinshutsu kigyo soran '95: kaishabetsu hen* (*The 1995 Compendium of Multinational Firms: Edition Bv Firms*), Toyo Keizai Shinposha, Tokyo.
Trevino, L.J. and Daniels, J.D. (1994), 'An Empirical Assessment of the Preconditions of Japanese Manufacturing Foreign Direct Investment in the United States', *Weltwirtschaftliches Archiv*, **130**: 576–99.
Wakasugi, R. (1994), 'On the Determinants of Overseas Production: An Empirical Study of Japanese FDI', paper presented at a Ministry of International Trade and Industry Conference entitled 'Payments Imbalance and the Japanese Industry', Tokyo.
Weinstein, D.E. (1996), 'Foreign Direct Investment and Keiretsu: Rethinking US and Japanese Policy', paper presented at a joint conference sponsored by Columbia and Osaka Universities entitled 'Microeconomic Reform and Deregulation in Japan' held at Columbia University.
World Bank (1994), *World Development Report 1994: Infrastructure for Development*, New York: Oxford University Press.
Yoshitomi, M. and Graham, E.M. (eds) (1996), *Foreign Direct Investment in Japan*, Cheltenham: Edward Elgar.

APPENDIX: COMPANIES INCLUDED IN THE ANALYSIS

The following companies are the subject of analysis in the probit analysis of the decision whether to produce overseas or not:

Hitachi, Toshiba, Mitsubishi Electric, Fuji Electric, Yaskawa Electric, Shinko

Electric, Meidensha, Nippon Electric Industry, Origin Electric, Hitachi Koki, Matsushita Refrigeration, Makita, Matsushita Seiko, TEC, Shibaura Engineering Works, Takaoka Electric Mfg, Daihen, Aichi Electric, Nissin Electric, Osaki Electric, Omron, NEC, Fujitsu, Oki Electric Industry, Iwatsu Electric, Nitsuko, Denki Kogyo, Sanken Electric, Toyo Communication Equipment, Tamura Electric Works, Nippon Signal, Kyosan Electric Mfg, Nohmi Bosai, Hochiki, Japan Radio, Matsushita Electric Industrial, Sharp, Anritsu, Fujitsu General, Kokusai Electric, Sony, Tokin, TDK, Teikoku Tsushin Kogyo, Kenwood, Mitsumi Electric, Tamura, Ikegami Tsushinki, Pioneer Electronic, Matsushita Communication Industrial, Kyushu Matsushita Electric, Nippon Columbia, Victor Co. of Japan, Clarion, SMK, Toko, TEAC, Hosiden, Hirose Electric, Japan Aviation Electronics Industry, Shintom, Hitachi Maxell, Furuno Electric, Yokogawa Electric, Shindengen Electric Mfg, Nihon kohden, Chino, Horiba, Advantest, Tabai Espec, Sawafuji Electric, Toko Electric, Ushio, Japan Storage Battery, Yuasa, Shin-Kobe Electric Machinery, Furukawa Battery, Kinseki, JEOL, Casio Computer, Amada Metrecs, Daishinku, Rohm, Mitsui High-Tec, Graphtec, Nippon Conlux, Kyocera, Sumitomo Special Metals, Futaba, Nitto Denko, Hokuriku Electric Industry, Tokai Rika, Nippon Chemi-Con, KOA, Mitsui Engineering & Shipbuilding, Hitachi Zosen, Sasebo Heavy Industries, Mitsubishi Heavy Industries, Kawasaki Heavy Industries, Ishikawajima Harima Heavy Industries, Namura Shipbuilding, Sanoyas Hishino Meisho, Fuji Car Mfg, Nippon Yusoki, Kinki Sharyo, Tokyu Car, Nabco, Nissan Motor, Komatsu Zenoah, Hino Motors, Nissan Diesel Motor, Mitsubishi Motors, Nissan Shatai, ShinMaywa Industries, Komatsu Forklift, Topy Industries, Toyo Radiator, Akebono Brake Industry, NOK, Futaba Industrial, Kayaba Industry, Ichikoh Industries, Calsonic, Pacific Industrial, Tochigi Fuji Industrial, Aisin Seiki, Mazda Motor, Daihatsu Motor, Aichi Machine Industry, Honda Motor, Suzuki Motor, Fuji Heavy Industries, Yamaha Motor, Showa, Unisia Jecs, Koito Mfg, Mitsuba Electric Mfg, Kansei, Araya Industrial, Japan Aircraft Mfg, Shimadzu, JMS, Star Micronics, Sokkia, Tokimec, Aichi Tokei Denki, Kimmon Mfg, Tokyo Seimitsu, Nikon, Topcon, Olympus Optical, Dainippon Screen Mfg, Hoya, Asahi Optical, Ricoh, Minolta, Copal, Sankyo Seiki Mfg, Citizen Watch, Rhythm Watch, Miura, Niigata Engineering, Takuma, Zexel, Tsugami, Okuma, Toshiba Machine, Hitachi Seiki, Amada Sonoike, Amada Wasino, Amada, Aida Engineering, Fuji Machine Mfg, Dijet Industrial, Toshiba Tungaloy, Asahi Diamond Industrial, Mori Seiki, Toyoda Automatic Loom Works, Howa Machinery, OKK, Toyoda Machine Works, Ishikawa Seisakusho, Teijin Seiki, O-M, Okuma & Howa Machinery, Enshu, Nihon Spindle Mfg, SMC, Komatsu, Hitachi Construction Machinery, Kitagawa Iron Works, Kubota, Toyo Engineering, Mitsubishi Kakoki, Tsukishima Kikai, Sintokogio, Aichi, Komori, Ebara, Ishii Iron Works, Torishima Pump Mfg, Chiyoda, Daikin Industries, Organo, Toyo Kanetsu, Kurita Water Industries, Tsubakimoto Chain, Daido Kogyo, Toyo Umpanki, Nikkiso, Kimura Chemical Plants, Iwata Air Compressor Mfg, Daifuku, Tadano, Fujitec, CKD, Amano, JUKI, Janome Sewing Machine, Max, Nippon Piston Ring, Riken and Eagle Industry.

Due to missing data on the amount of labour used in production overseas, the following 23 companies are excluded in the analysis of the amount of labour used in advanced countries:

Hitachi, Hitachi Koki, Fujitsu, Sanken Electric, Japan Radio, Matsushita Electric Industrial, Anritsu, Sony, Tokin, Kyushu Matsushita Electric, Victor Co. of Japan, Hitachi Maxell, Amada Metrecs, Nabco, Nissan Motor, Honda Motor, Olympus Optical, Hoya, Ricoh, Minolta, Asahi Diamond Industrial, Komatsu and Riken.

Due to missing data on the amount of labour used in production overseas, the following 22 companies are excluded in the analysis of the amount of labour used in developing countries:

Shinko Electric, Hitachi Koki, Fujitsu, Toyo Communication Equipment, Matsushita Electric Industrial, Anritsu, Sony, Victor Co. of Japan, Clarion, Shintom, Hitachi Maxell, Nihon Kohden, Casio Computer, Nippon Conlux, Kyocera, Honda Motor, Suzuki Motor, Olympus Optical, Hoya, Ricoh, Asahi Diamond Industrial and Eagle Industry.

PART THREE:

The Financial Sector

8. Monetary Policy in Japan, Germany and the United States: Does One Size Fit All?

Menzie Chinn and Michael Dooley[1]

8.1 INTRODUCTION

Recent empirical studies of monetary policies in the United States and Germany suggest that overnight interest rates are the dominant monetary policy tool and that a simple reaction function provides an adequate description of the relationship between the policy tool and deviations in inflation and employment from target levels. This result seems inconsistent with the US Federal Reserve's and German Bundesbank's description of policies in several respects. While the Federal Reserve in recent years has explicitly targeted the overnight 'federal funds' interest rate, the Bundesbank apparently targets a broad monetary aggregate, central bank money. Moreover, the Bundesbank, in commenting on policy objectives, places primary emphasis on price stability, while the Federal Reserve characterizes its policy goals over the business cycle as fighting both inflation and recessions. Finally, the United States and Germany differ in important respects in terms of economic structure including labour markets, openness to international trade and capital movements and in the structure of their financial systems. These differences would in general suggest different specifications both for the interaction of interest rates and other variables and for policy reaction functions for the Federal Reserve and the Bundesbank.

In this chapter we study postwar evidence for Japan to see if the basic ideas that seem to be useful for Germany and the United States can be extended to Japan. Apparent differences in policy procedures and objectives between Japan and other industrial countries have been a recurrent theme in the literature on monetary policy in Japan. For example, there is considerable support for the view that the Bank of Japan regards the exchange rate as a policy goal (Hutchison 1988; Glick and Hutchison, 1994). Moreover, the structure of financial markets and the nature of the transmission mechanism also appear to be quite dissimilar in Japan as compared to other industrial countries. The relatively late and gradual decontrol of interest rates in Japan is frequently cited as a factor that has made quantitative control of credit aggregates an important policy tool. Hamada and Hayashi, for example, observe that 'Many economists at the Bank of Japan thought they could control the money supply through the control of bank loans' (Hamada and Hayashi, 1985: 93). Research reported in Chinn and Dooley (1996) suggests that the transmission mechanism in Japan seems atypical of industrial countries. In particular, time series evidence for Japan suggests that a credit view of the transmission mechanism might be relevant for Japan.

Our motivation is partly to see if recent work by Taylor (1993) for the United States and Clarida and Gertler (1996) for Germany stands up to another data set. We think this is important because, as is pointed out by these authors, statistical identification of interactions among macroeconomic variables involves very difficult statistical problems. There may be even less agreement concerning the right way to identify policy goals in a sensible statistical manner. In our view the fact that a simple specification 'works' for central banks that are as different as the Federal Reserve and the Bundesbank suggests that this might be a very useful specification.

Any set of restrictions that produces 'sensible' parameter estimates for a policy reaction function is suspect in that the researcher has wide discretion in adjusting the restrictions in order to justify preconceived ideas about how the economy and the central bank interact. In this chapter we propose an 'out-of-sample' test of a set of restrictions on a vector autoregression proposed by Clarida and Gertler (1996). If these restrictions really are economically meaningful they *might* also produce sensible results for Japan. If they are not meaningful the chance that they might produce sensible results for Japan is remote.

Our interpretation of the evidence that simple policy reaction functions fit apparently different central banks is that although the central bank's *description* of its policy rule might vary considerably across countries and for a given country over time, the realities of decision making about monetary policy force central banks in industrial countries to behave in similar ways. If so, it might be possible to quantify policy rules as responses of overnight interest rates to gaps between targets and outcomes for inflation and output.

Several monetary economists, both critics of and participants in central banking, have argued that it is easier to modify the description of monetary policy than the substance. Ito (1989) examined the behaviour of the Bank of Japan and concluded that 'the Bank of Japan did not practice what monetarism preached ... In particular, when there is an unexpected jump in money supply, the base is adjusted to a new level (bygones are bygones) and a further accommodation in growth is allowed in new "forecasts".

We do not claim that this policy rule is likely to be effective. Stuart (1996) argues that there is too much uncertainty about output gaps and inflation forecasts to make the policy rule studied here a 'good' guide for policy. We interpret this as a modern version of a very old search for an alternative to a discretionary monetary policy. For example, in arguing that the Bank of England should be restrained by reestablishing convertibility of sterling into gold, that is cash payments, the authors of the Bullion Report of 1810 observed:

> The suspension of Cash payments has had the effect of committing into the hands of the Directors of the Bank of England, to be exercised by their sole discretion, the important charge of supplying the Country with that quantity of circulating medium which is exactly proportioned to the wants and occasions of the Public. In the judgment of the Committee, that is a trust, which it is unreasonable to expect that the Directors of the Bank of England should ever be able to discharge. The most detailed knowledge of the actual trade of the Country, combined with the profound science in all the principles of Money and Circulation, would not enable any man or set of men to adjust, and keep always adjusted, the right proportion of circulating medium in a country to the wants of trade.

While the Bank of England was again subjected to the discipline of the gold standard in 1821, we doubt that central banks of industrial countries have adopted any of the alternative monetary policy rules that have been suggested since the demise of the Bretton Woods system of fixed exchange rates in 1973. The data do suggest that the different central banks follow subtly different versions of the same rule.[2]

8.2 HISTORICAL CONTEXT

We introduce the hypothesis with an informal description of the political economy of monetary policy. Our rationalization of the 'one policy rule fits all' hypothesis is that central banks have moved away from explaining policy actions in terms of interest rates but have not moved away from interest rates as policy tools. Moreover, the weights that central bankers assign to policy goals, inflation or exchange rates, versus activity, in public are influenced by the political game played against the rest of the government and private interest groups.

Two historical episodes are important in understanding the postwar evolution of the description but perhaps not the substance of monetary policies in industrial countries. The first is the process through which central banks have gained some independence from Treasury departments and

Finance ministries. In the United States, for example, the Federal Reserve–Treasury 'accord' of 1951 permitted the Federal Reserve greater freedom in setting interest rates in order to stabilize the economy. Prior to this date the main objective of monetary policy was to keep interest rates low in order to minimize debt service costs of the national debt accumulated during the war. The 'accord' partially freed monetary policy for stabilization policy but it is easy to forget that the Federal Reserve remained under considerable pressure to avoid *rapid changes* in short-term interest rates.

The generally accepted argument was that uncertainty about the time derivative of short rates would induce a risk premium in the yield curve because variability in short rates would be transmitted to long rates, thereby generating capital gains and losses for dealers that were obliged to hold inventories of government securities. Since the Treasury viewed long-term debt as the preferred financing technique, a stable money market was thought to be essential to the ability of the Treasury to roll over the national debt at reasonable cost.

In a period of increasing inflationary expectations a constraint on the time derivative of the overnight interest rate can be as destructive as a constraint on the level of the rate for a countercyclical monetary policy. Clearly if inflationary expectations increase faster than the overnight interest rate, real interest rates fall, money growth rises, and policy becomes procyclical. The fundamental technical problem is the fact that a nominal interest rate target can be procyclical if the central bank limits the size and frequency of changes in the rate. In the 1970s in the United States many observers argued that the Fed was too timid in raising its nominal interest rate target in the face of rising inflationary expectations. Thus a rising nominal interest rate target was a falling real interest rate target. Monetary aggregates were supposed not to share this flaw and *in order to monitor and change the behaviour of the central bank* it became popular to argue that monetary aggregates were 'better' policy tools.

In the United States, for example, the Federal Reserve is required to explain itself to Congress twice a year and is required to couch this explanation in terms of monetary aggregates. It does so even though under Alan Greenspan the Fed has repeatedly stated that short-term interest rates rather than monetary aggregates are its policy tool. The Fed has consistently stated that its policy is to be both an inflation fighter and a recession fighter. In Germany the Bundesbank also states its policy in terms of a monetary aggregate and always emphasizes controlling inflation as its primary objective. Yet if we believe the evidence presented by Taylor and Clarida and Gertler, both central banks respond in similar ways to changes in economic conditions.

Our conjecture is that different public relations versions of the policy rule are better explained by the need for the central bank to explain its policies to other power bases within the government and the private sector. The executive and legislative branches demand explanations and the central bank provides them. But the basic policy depends on the economic structure of the economy. An intriguing possibility is that the private sector's expectations about policies are independent of the political story. It follows that monetary policy is the same in all similar economies.

In our view the campaign for the use of monetary aggregates instead of interest rates was mostly an argument about relaxing the constraint on changes in interest rates as policy. Thus the Federal Reserve under Paul Volker found monetary aggregates a convenient justification for increasing the variability of their interest rate targets in an era of increasingly volatile inflationary expectations. This interpretation suggests that policy can be adequately described by interest rates even if the central bank sells the policy as an effort to control the growth of monetary aggregates. James Pierce, a senior staff member at the Federal Reserve during the Volker era, observed (after leaving the Fed), 'Perhaps the Fed had not really embraced monetarism. It may have found that focusing on money growth was a convenient means of absolving itself from responsibility for record-high interest rates that occurred' (Pierce, 1984). Ito (1989: 24) observes:

> An oral tradition among experts on monetary policy suggests a similar story in Japan. The Bank of Japan was politically defeated in 1972 and was forced to lower the discount rate against its will. ... Therefore having money supply established as a 'target' the Bank now has a contingent weapon in order to implement a necessary tightening (or interest rate hike) when it is needed.

If an interest rate target has serious political disadvantages, why use it? One answer would be that impulses in the interest rate have predictable effects on the economy. Bernanke and Blinder (1992) argue for the United States that the federal funds rate is by far the dominant policy variable in generating future changes in macroeconomic variables. The monetary authority would naturally want to choose the variable that is predictably related to policy goals. Another possibility is that the main advantage of an overnight interest target *within* the central bank is that it is the one variable that clearly can be controlled and monitored.

In the central banks of industrial countries a committee or council has to agree on policy actions. While the committee may be dominated by an individual, the members still have to agree on some policy target that can be communicated to subordinates that actually conduct open market operations. The directive to maintain an overnight interest rate at a certain level or within a certain range is clear and easily monitored.

Alternative directives are much less transparent. The instruction to adjust a monetary or credit aggregate is subject to a large number of qualifications related to discount window borrowing, reserve requirements on different classes of bank liabilities, float, treasury balances and so forth. Our guess is that central banks always, at a minimum, supplement their policy directives with a range of overnight interest rates that are expected to be consistent with other policy variables. McCallum (1993) has argued that the monetary base is free of this problem and has simulated a base target regime for Japan but to date only the Swiss National Bank seems to have adopted a monetary base operating target.

As argued in detail below, a natural way to define an array of policy variables is that they be contemporaneously determined over the policy period. Given this identification, the central bank's target for one policy variable is also an implied target for all the contemporaneously determined variables.

8.3 IDENTIFYING THE BANK OF JAPAN'S POLICY REACTION FUNCTION

Clarida and Gertler (1996) provide an interesting identification strategy for monetary policy. First they argue that in a simple vector autoregression representation all past values of variables are determinants of current policies. In contrast, contemporaneous variables are naturally separated into those that are jointly determined with the assumed policy tool of short-term interest rates, such as exchange rates, and long-term interest rates, and those which are independent of the policy tool such as economic activity and prices. The set of jointly determined variables is, of course, not independent. In principle, the central bank could choose any such variable as the policy tool and simply solve for values for all the other contemporaneously determined variables. In practice, central banks apparently believe that a short-term interest rate is the preferred variable to control. Figure 8.1 depicts several short-term interest rates, including the money market rate used in our analysis.

The basic problem is that central banks are to some extent driven by economic variables and at the same time changes in the policy instruments influence a subset of contemporaneously determined variables. Although the dynamics of this process are difficult to disentangle, there is a general consensus on how to approach the problem. The standard methodology for doing so entails use of some semi-structural modelling approach, such as a structural VAR. Recent examples of this literature, in the US context, include Blanchard (1989), Gali (1992), Walsh (1993), and Bernanke and Mihov (1995). A recent application to the Japanese case is Kasa and Popper (1995).

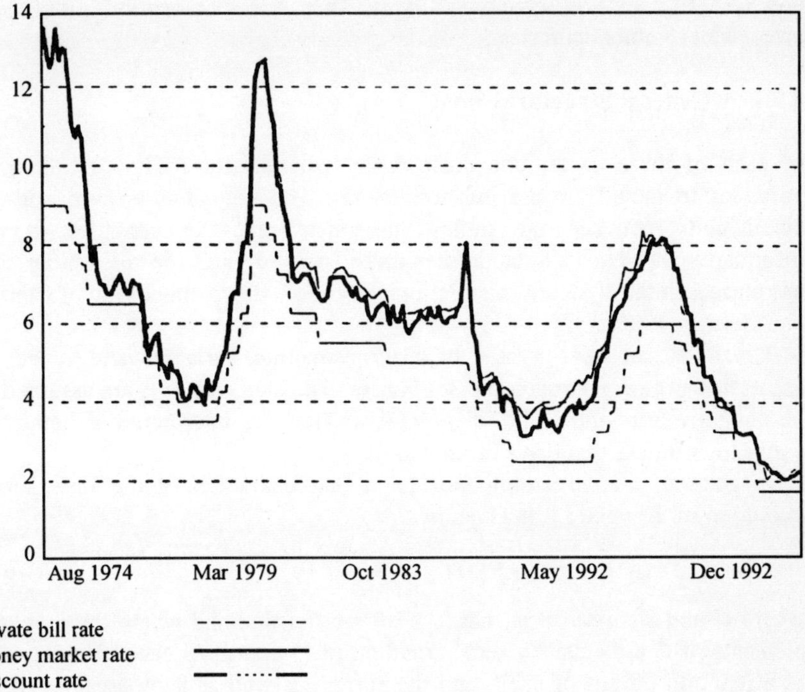

Figure 8.1 Short-term interest rate

The Clarida and Gertler approach to the problem adopted in this chapter is to place some restrictions on the influence that innovations (forecast errors) for some variables have on the observed forecast errors of others. The first set of exclusion restrictions divides variables into those that are predetermined in the time period (a month) and those that are determined along with the policy variable. Predetermined variables include retail sales, the consumer price level, world commodity prices and the US interest rate. Contemporaneous policy variables include the short-term interest rate, the exchange rate and the money supply.

A virtue of this approach to identifying an economic system is that the nature of the restrictions is fairly transparent. Nevertheless, it is clear that a good deal of art has gone into this set of restrictions. We can get a feel for the plausibility of the restrictions by examining the impulse reaction functions to innovations in each of the variables. In a way, the specification test is simply a comparison of what we think is reasonable with what the data suggest, subject to the restrictions described above. If the whole exercise suffers from the objection that some set of restrictions will force the data to confess to any preconception of how economies work, then the specification should not travel well to other countries.

8.3.1 A General Structural VAR

In each of these cases, one must make two decisions. The first is what variables to include in the information set. The second is how to address simultaneity between the policy instrument and the variables in the information set. How one addresses these issues defines the restrictions that are placed on the VAR. In this section, we follow the methodology of Clarida and Gertler (1996).

Let y_t be an $m \times 1$ vector of macroeconomic variables and e_t be an associated vector of structural disturbances. The elements of e_t are assumed to be mutually orthogonal i.i.d. disturbances. They are interpreted as being the exogenous shocks that drive the economy.

A general, non-structural expression that characterizes the time series evolution of the vector y_t is given by:

$$\mathbf{y}_t = \mathbf{C}\mathbf{y}_t + \sum_{i=1}^{\infty} \mathbf{A}_i \mathbf{y}_{t-i} \qquad (8.1)$$

where C and A_i are $m \times m$ matrices of coefficients, and where the diagonal elements of C are equal to zero. Equation (8.1) expresses each element of y_t as a function of lags of itself, and the current as well as lagged values of all the other variables in the system.

The key issue is to restrict certain elements of the C matrix to be zero; this in effect sets certain *contemporaneous* effects to zero. Once one estimates the C matrix, one can calculate the underlying 'exogenous' shocks to the economy (the e_ts); then using these e_ts and a transformation of the C matrix, one can trace out the impact of each of these shocks on the economy. In particular, one obtains a reaction function for each policy element of y_t.

In practice, the coefficients are estimated by working with the forecast errors from a reduced-form VAR incorporating the restrictions, u_t. To see this, consider rewriting (8.1):

$$y_t = \sum_{i=1}^{\infty} B_i y_{t-i} + u_t \qquad (8.2)$$

where

$$B_i = (1 - C)^{-1} Ai \quad \text{and} \quad u_t = (1 - C)^{-1} e_t$$

Then the optimal forecast of Y_t (based on the variables in the VAR) is given by (8.2). The forecast error is:

$$u_t \equiv y_t - E_{t-1}y_t$$

Then estimating:

$$\boldsymbol{u}_t = \boldsymbol{C}\boldsymbol{u}_t + \boldsymbol{e}_t \tag{8.3}$$

8.3.2 Defining the Policy and Information Variables

We take as the policy variables the same ones as Clarida and Gertler (1996): the direct policy instrument (the overnight interest rate), as well as any other variable that is indirectly influenced by the central bank within the period. This includes the money stock and the exchange rate.

The non-policy variables are those that, by assumption, do not respond within the period to the policy variables. These domestic non-policy variables are industrial production, retail sales and prices (CPI). Foreign influences are represented by commodity prices and the US Federal Funds rate. We diverge from the Clarida–Gertler model by including a variable representing bank credit. This addition is justified by the apparent behaviour of the Bank of Japan, as discussed above.

The causal ordering adopted for the non-policy variable block is uncontroversial: commodity prices (*cp*), industrial production (*ip*), retail sales (*ret*), bank credit (*bc*), prices (CPI), and the US Fed Funds rate (*ff*). The placement of the first two variables is clearly standard. The location of the subsequent variables is debatable, but the results are not sensitive to the particular ordering of these variables.

Within the policy variable block of the short-term interest rate (*rs*), real money stock (*m*) and the real exchange rate (*er*), the identification scheme is as follows. Money demand and supply are given as:

$$u^m = \alpha u_1^{ret} + \alpha_2 u^{rs} + e^m \tag{8.4}$$

$$u^{rs} = \beta_1 u^{cp} + \beta_2 u^m + \beta_3 u^{er} + e^{rs} \tag{8.5}$$

(suppressing the time subscripts).

The exchange rate is assumed to respond to all the structural and non-structural shocks, so there are no restrictions placed on this variable's behaviour.

This identification scheme differs slightly from Clarida–Gertler, in that money demand (Equation 8.4) depends upon retail sales, instead of industrial production. The main reason for this specification is empirical: inclusion of industrial production as a proxy for income yields an incorrectly signed income elasticity. Hence we use retail sales, which presumably proxies more accurately for transactions demand for money (it also has the correct sign when included in the regression).

Equation (8.5) is the key equation, as it represents how the Bank of Japan reacts to various exogenous shocks and through which channels. The Bank of Japan is assumed to react directly only to commodity price and exchange rate forecast surprises. It only indirectly reacts to the US Federal Funds rate, and other non-policy variables, through the exchange rate.

8.3.3 Data, Sample Period and Specification

The data frequency is monthly. When relying upon identification schemes that impose zero restrictions on some contemporaneous effects, it is crucial to use the highest-frequency data available, and monthly data are the best choice, as a consequence. All the important non-policy variables are available (while, for instance, industrial production is not available at higher frequency).

The data are drawn from the International Monetary Fund's *International Financial Statistics* database (July 1996 CD-ROM) and extend from 1974:08 to 1994:12. Further details are provided in the Appendix.

The interest rate is the overnight repo rate. The money supply is broad money (narrow money plus quasi money) deflated by the Japanese CPI. The exchange rate is the yen/dollar rate adjusted by the Japanese and US CPI. The commodity price variable is the world commodity price index (based on US$ prices), converted into yen equivalent using the exchange rate, and deflated by the Japanese CPI. The industrial production and retail sales are real indices. The bank credit variable is total credit extended to the private sector. The price variable is the Japanese CPI. Several of the key variables are depicted in Figures 8.2 and 8.3.

We estimate the nine-variable VAR entering all the variables (except interest rates) as first differences of the logged variables. Two cointegrating vectors are also included as error correction terms:

$(m - ip)$
$(ret - ip)$

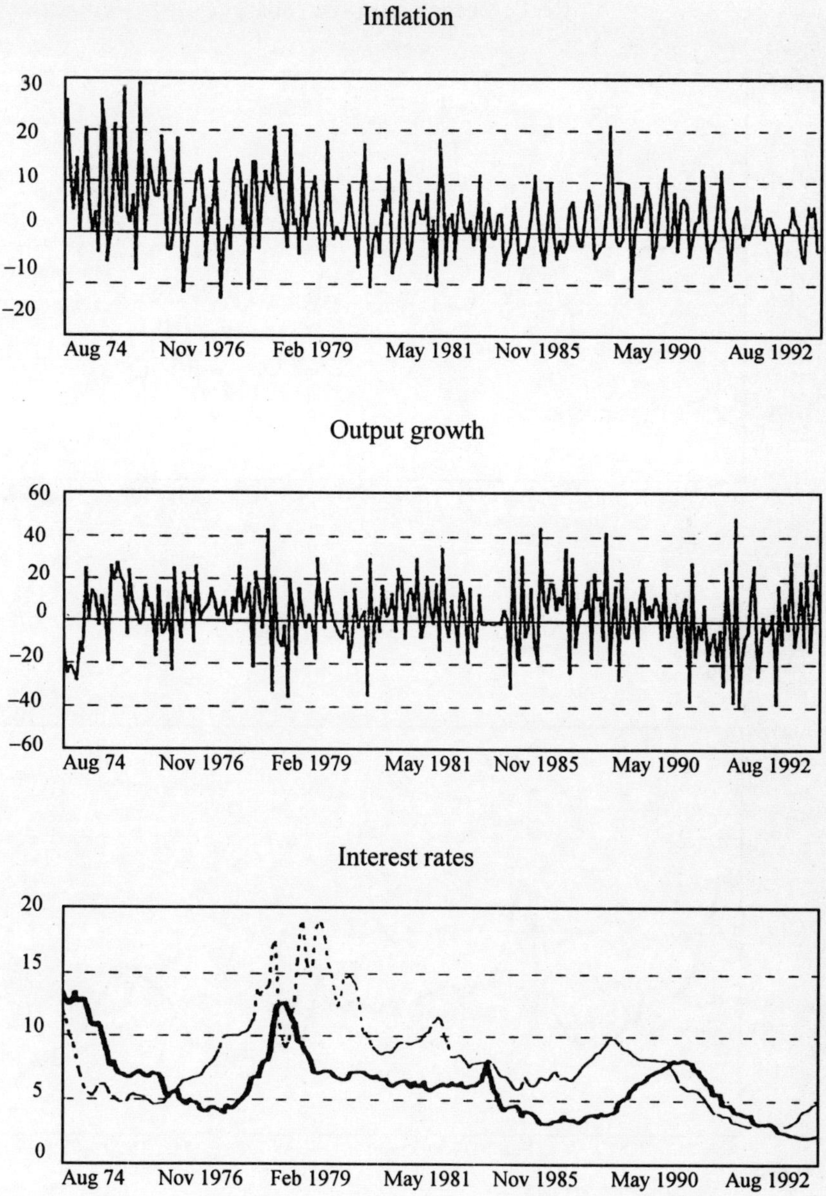

Figure 8.2 Inflation, output growth and interest rates

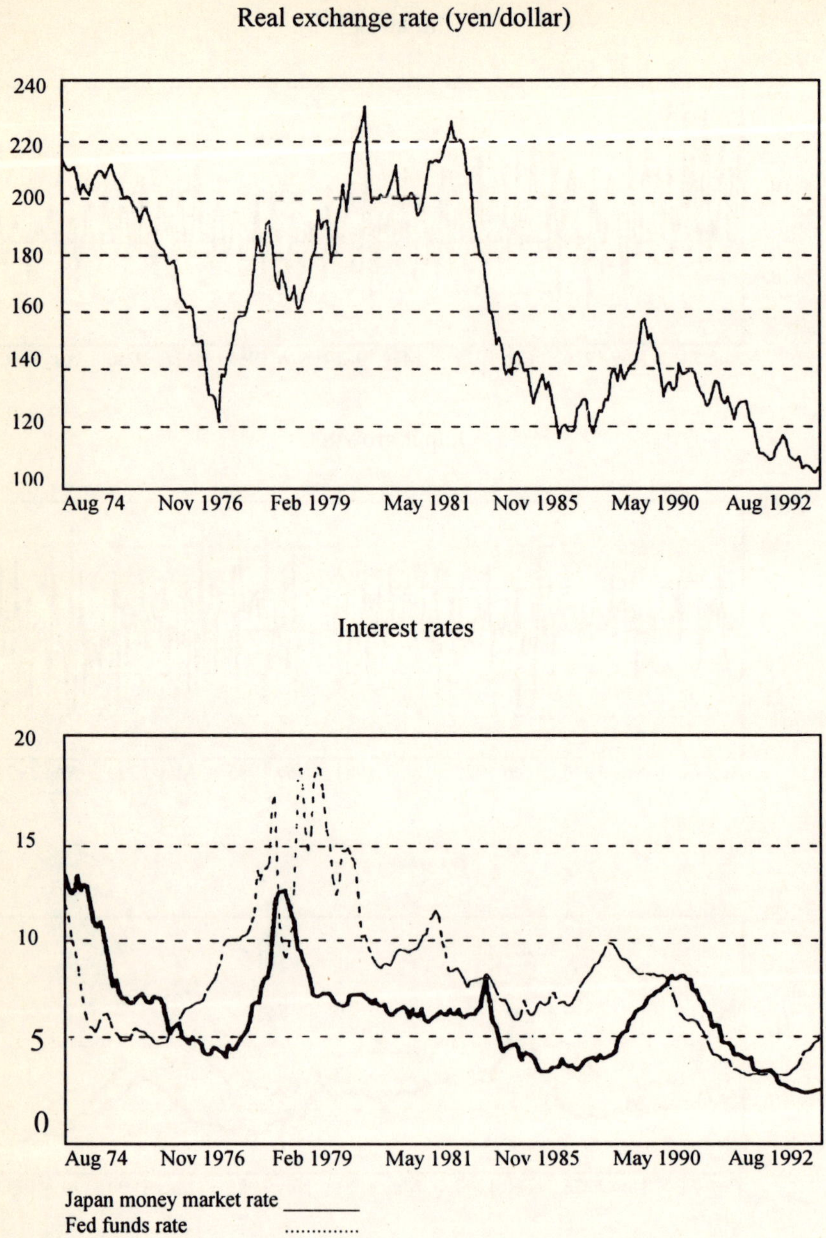

Figure 8.3 Exchange rates and interest rates

so that the specification is technically a vector error correction model (VECM).

These long-run restrictions are theoretically plausible. They impose stationary long-run velocity (after allowing for a deterministic trend) and a long run relationship between sales and income. They are also empirically justifiable, since cointegration tests reject the no cointegration null hypothesis.

Hence the VAR is ordered as:

$$(\Delta cp, \Delta ip, \Delta ret, \Delta bc, \Delta p, ffr, rs, \Delta m, \Delta er \mid (m - ip), (ret - ip)$$

where the | separates the error correction terms, which are treated as exogenous.

We include lags of up to 12 months to account for the seasonality in Japanese data. However, for the sake of parsimony, we include only lags 1–3, 6 and 12.

8.3.4 Empirical Results

In Table 8.1, the results of the key regressions are reported. Consider the first regression. This states that innovations in money demand respond positively to innovations in retail sales, a proxy for transactions demand, and negatively to interest rate shocks. This accords remarkably well with theory, although none of the coefficients is statistically significant.

Next consider the exchange rate equation. Most of the coefficients are not statistically significant. However, those that are significant conform to theory; a positive innovation in the Japanese short-term interest rate appreciates the yen, while one in the US Federal Funds rate depreciates it.

The Bank of Japan's behaviour is summarized in the second equation. It states that the Bank of Japan responds to a positive commodity price shock by allowing the short-term interest rate to rise. A 1 per cent innovation in commodity prices induces a 3 basis point increase in interest rates. On the other hand, there is no apparent response to money demand shocks. This implies that shocks to money demand are fully accommodated in order to smooth interest rates. An exchange rate shock also has some effect, according to the point estimate. The monetary authority increases interest rates in response to an exchange rate innovation. The estimate is not, however, statistically significant. The weakness of these results may reflect the fact that the Bank of Japan does not react strongly within the month to innovations in the other variables and rather focuses more on lagged information. This is Clarida and Gertler's interpretation of similar results for the Bundesbank.

Table 8.1 Structural VAR estimates from over-identified model

$u^{m} =$	$0.00265\ u^{ret} -$	$0.3025\ u^{rs} + e^{m}$			
	(0.041)	(2.2984)			
$u^{rs} =$	$0.00033\ u^{com} +$	$0.0008\ u^{m} +$	$0.0024\ u^{er} + e^{rs}$		
	(0.0008	(0.0036)	(0.0031)		
$u^{er} =$	$-\ 0.0332\ u^{com} -$	$0.0333\ u^{ip} +$	$0.1900\ u^{ret} -$	$0.1717\ u^{cp} +$	$0.3292\ u^{dc}$
	(0.1040)	(0.2044)	(0.1701)	(0.6505)	(0.4415)
	$-\ 44.9251\ u^{rs} +$	$12.1830\ u^{ffr} -$	$0.0846\ u^{m} + e^{er}$		
	(9.3268)	4.1076)	(0.3547)		

Notes:
The sample is 1974:08 – 1994:12. Estimation is done by instrumental variables. For the u^{rs} equation the instruments are u^{com}, u^{ip}, u^{ret}, u^{cp}, u^{dc}. For the u^{m} equation, the instruments are u^{com}, u^{ip}, u^{ret}, u^{cp}, u^{dc}. For the u^{m} equation, the instruments are u^{com}, u^{ip}, u^{ret}, u^{cp}, u^{dc}, e^{rs}, e^{m}. Standard errors in parentheses.

One would like to know if the estimates implicit in these regressions are consistent with our views of the propagation mechanism. In Figures 8.4a–i, impulse response functions are shown for a variety of shocks. The variance decomposition for the interest rate is presented in Table 8.2.

Table 8.2 Variance decomposition for the nominal interest rate

Sample 1974:08 – 1994:12

Horizon	e^{com}	e^{ip}	e^{cpl}	e^{ret}	e^{dc}	e^{ffr}	e^{m}	e^{rs}	e^{er}
6	2.98	3.28	0.71	0.89	0.66	7.48	0.10	81.76	2.10
12	7.15	2.67	0.96	0.63	0.94	23.28	0.47	57.64	6.23
24	13.83	2.38	2.66	0.73	1.64	42.16	1.59	29.52	5.44
48	11.26	5.01	5.58	1.75	1.52	50.08	4.77	16.81	3.19

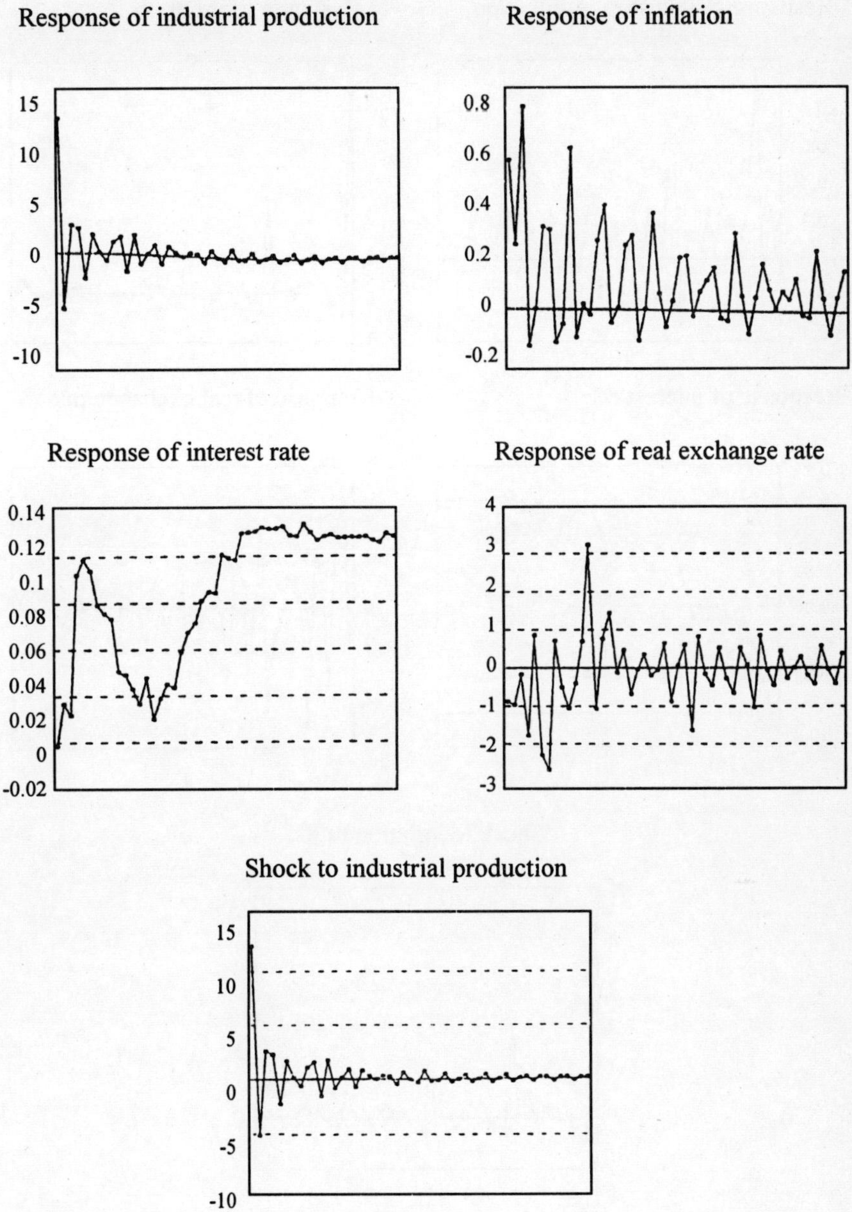

Figure 8.4a Impulse response to IP shock

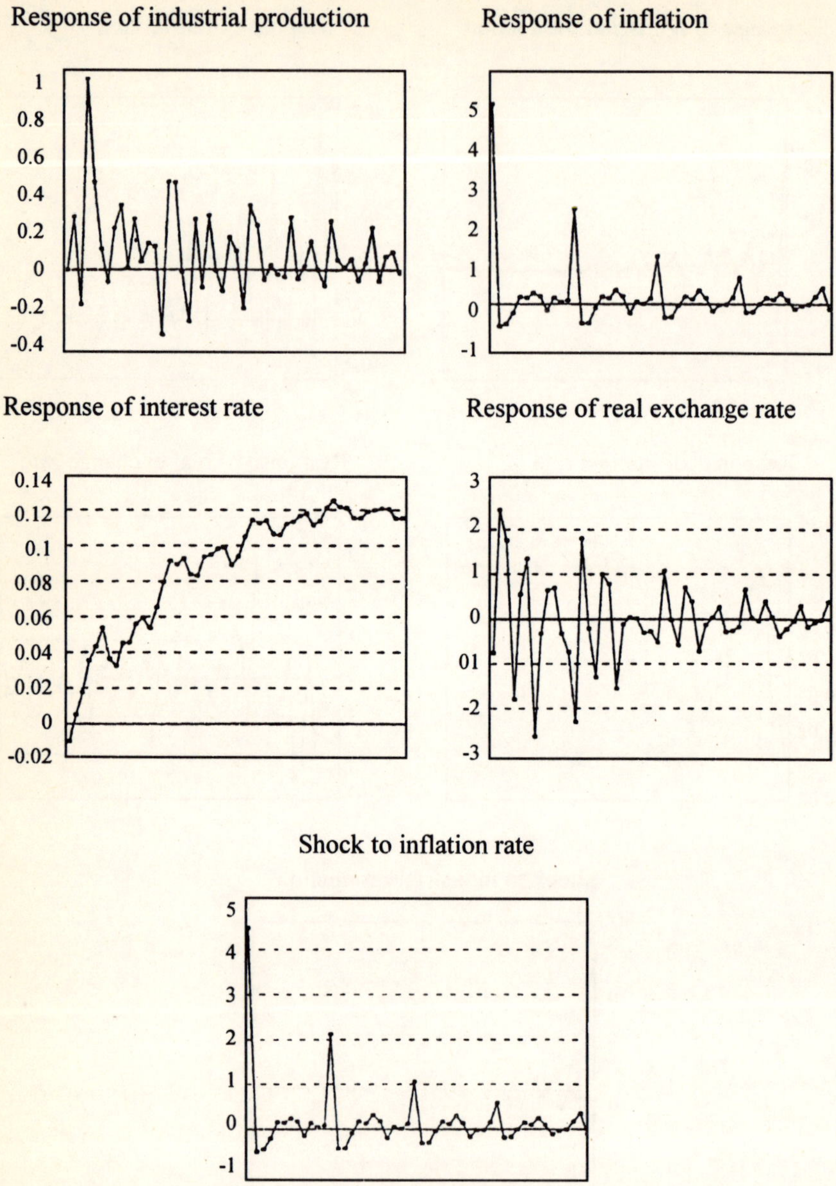

Figure 8.4b Impulse response to inflation shock

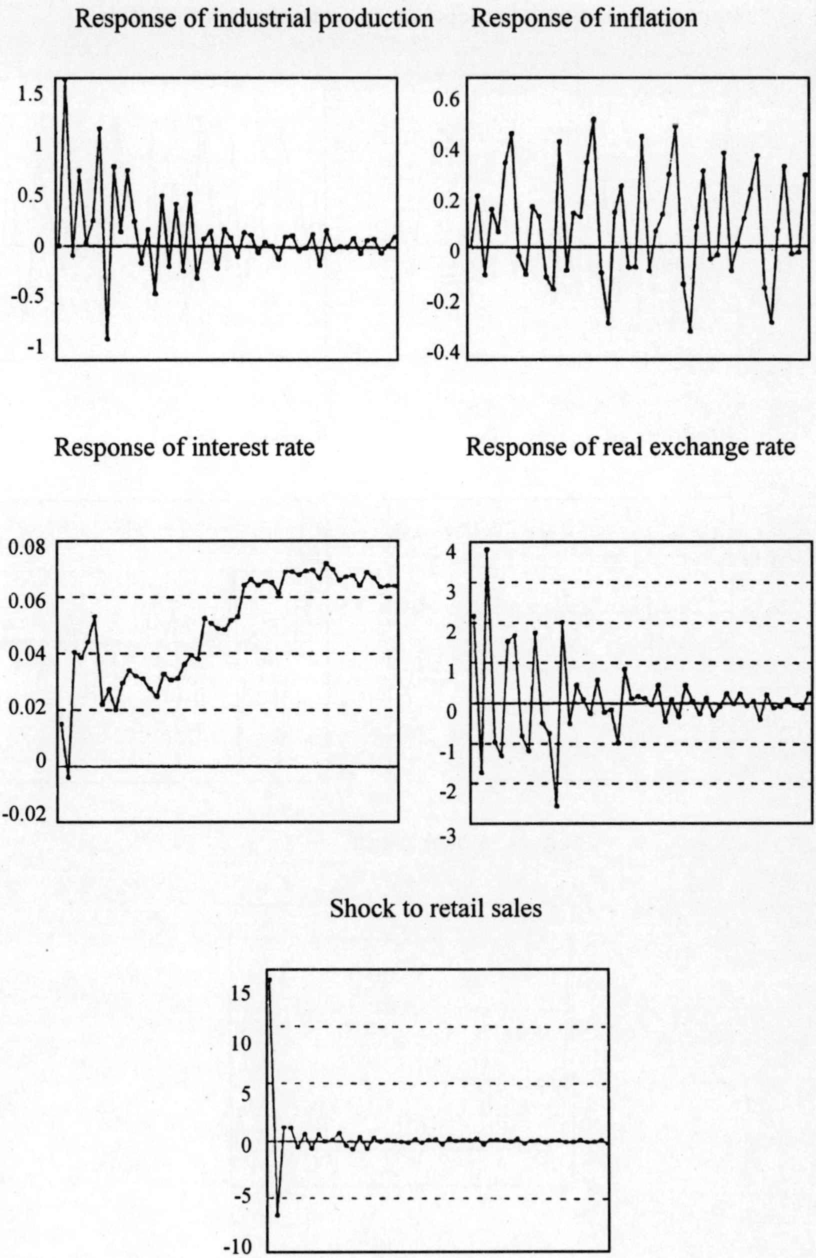

Figure 8.4c Impulse response to retail shock

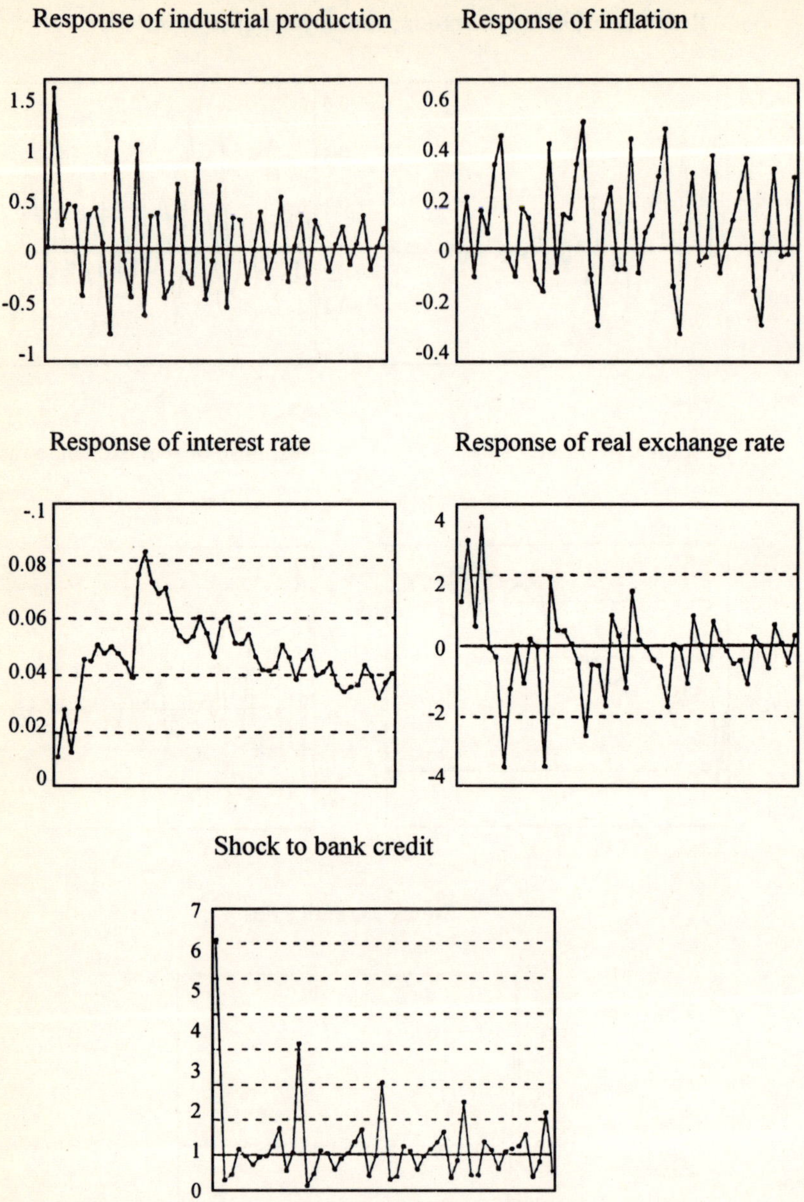

Figure 8.4d Impulse response to domestic credit shock

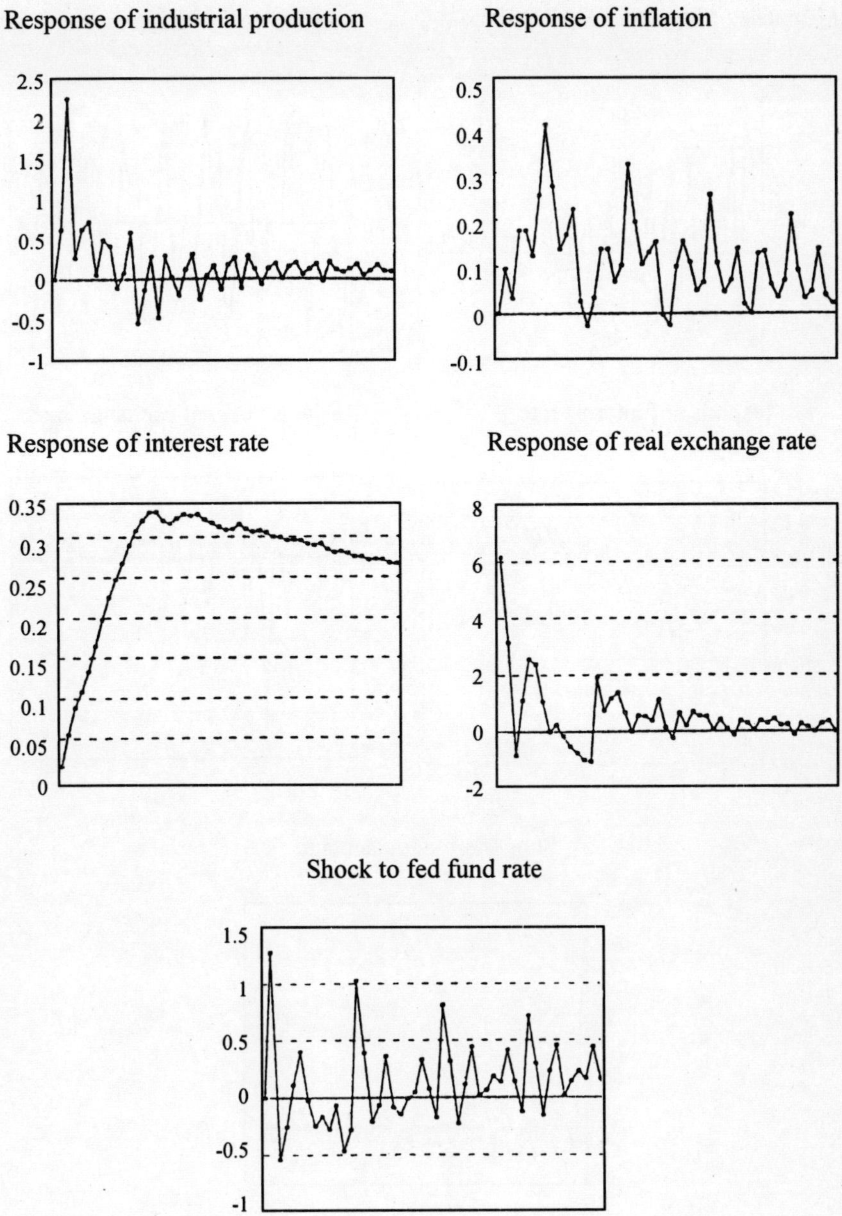

Figure 8.4e Impulse response to Fed Fund shock

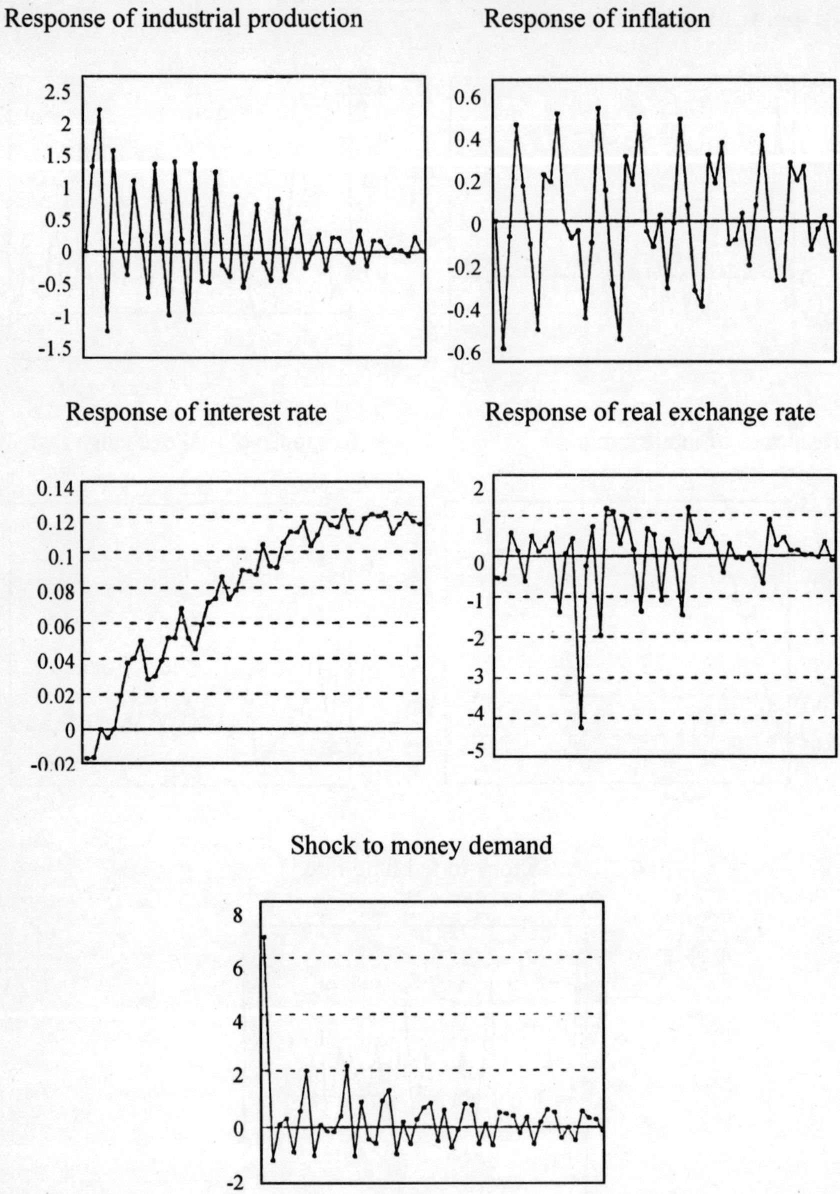

Figure 8.4f Impulse response to money shock

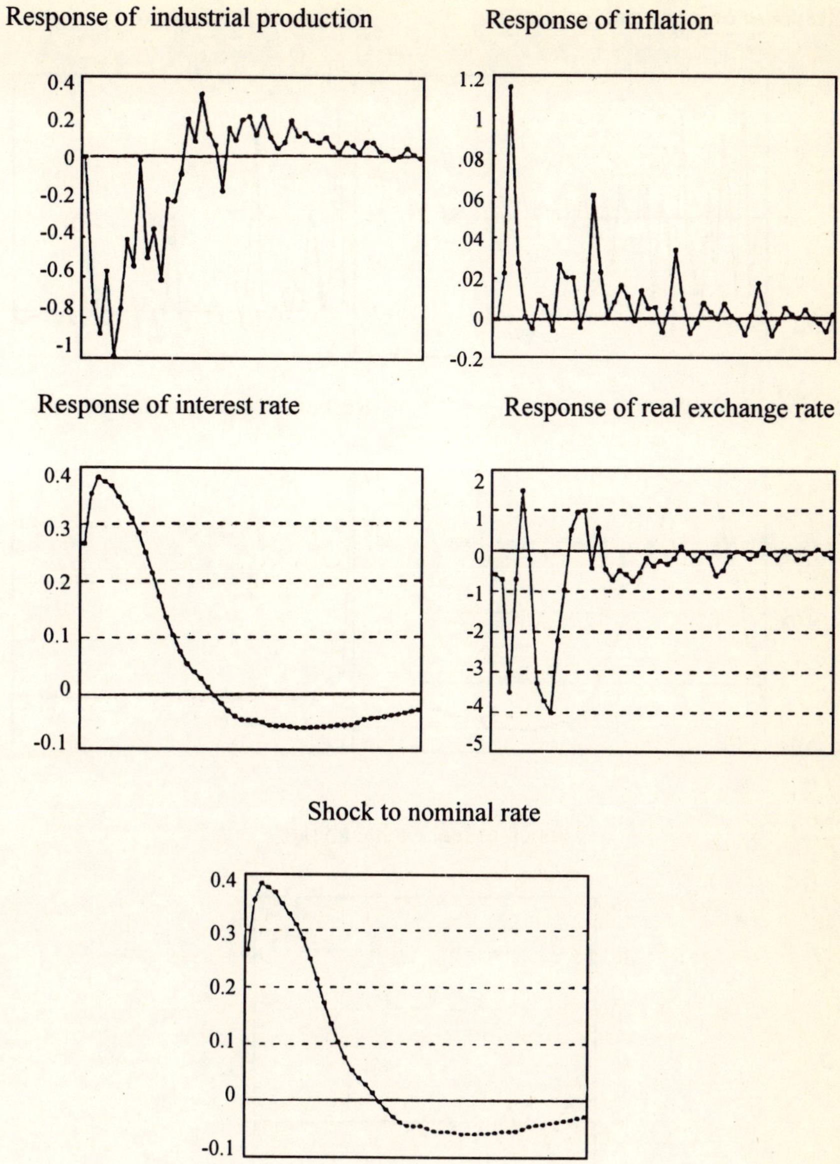

Figure 8.4g Impulse response to nominal rate shock

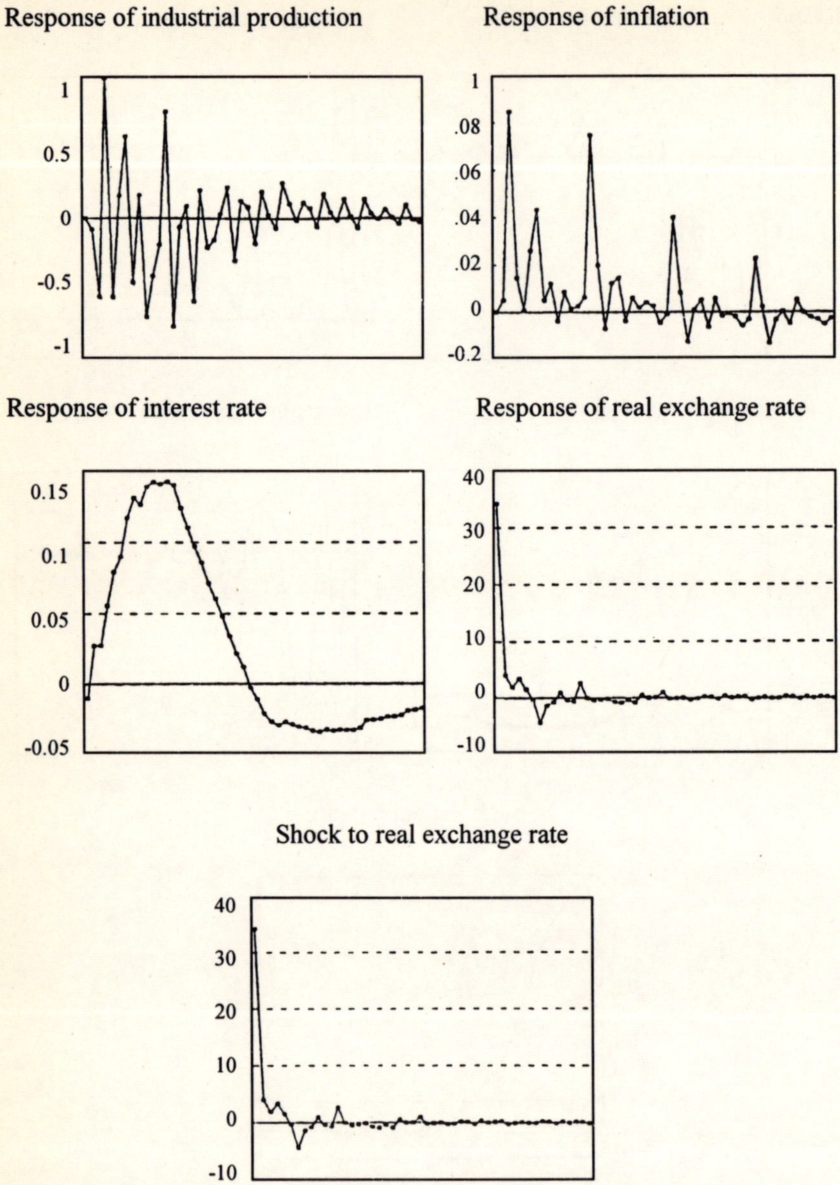

Figure 8.4h Impulse response to real exchange rate shock

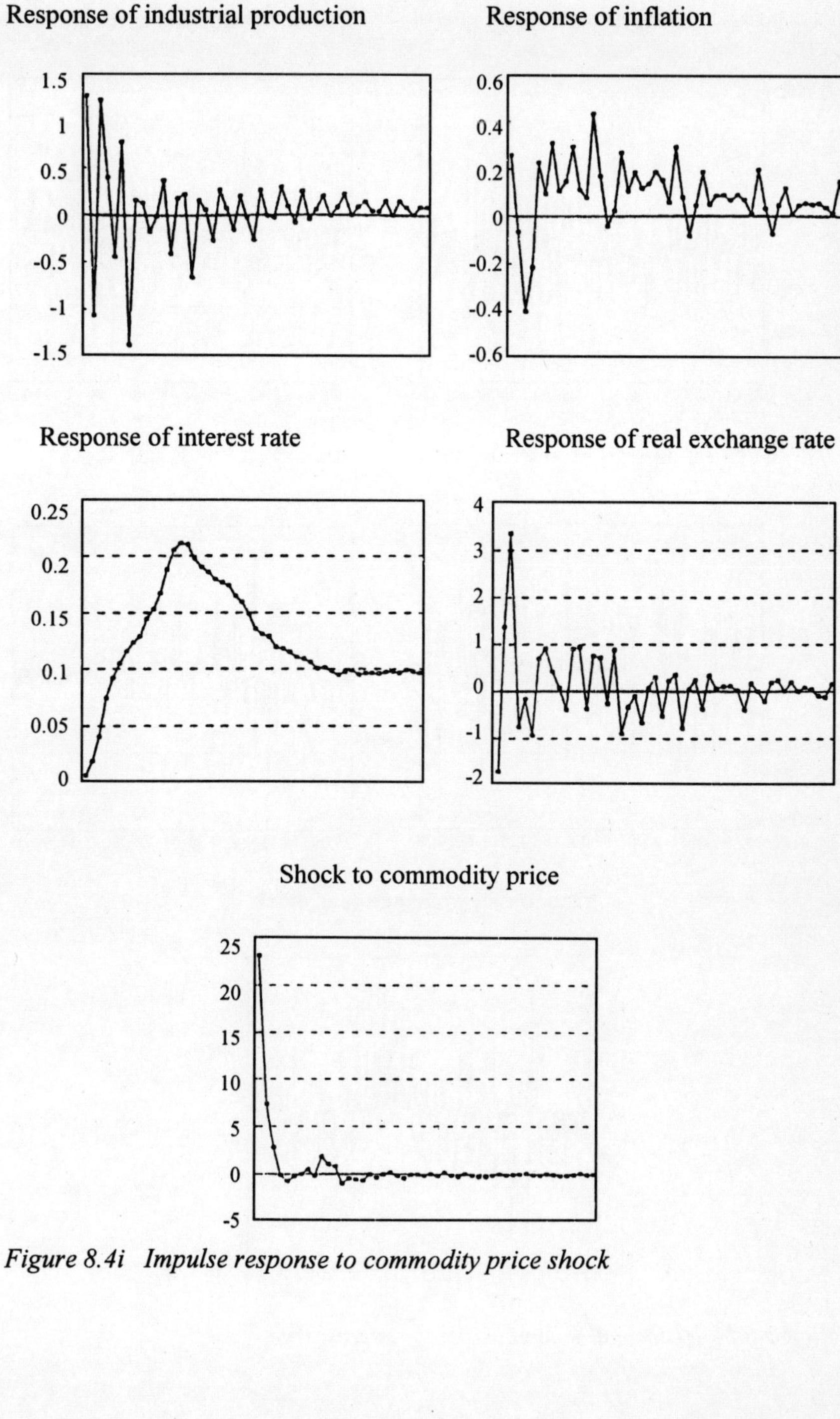

Figure 8.4i Impulse response to commodity price shock

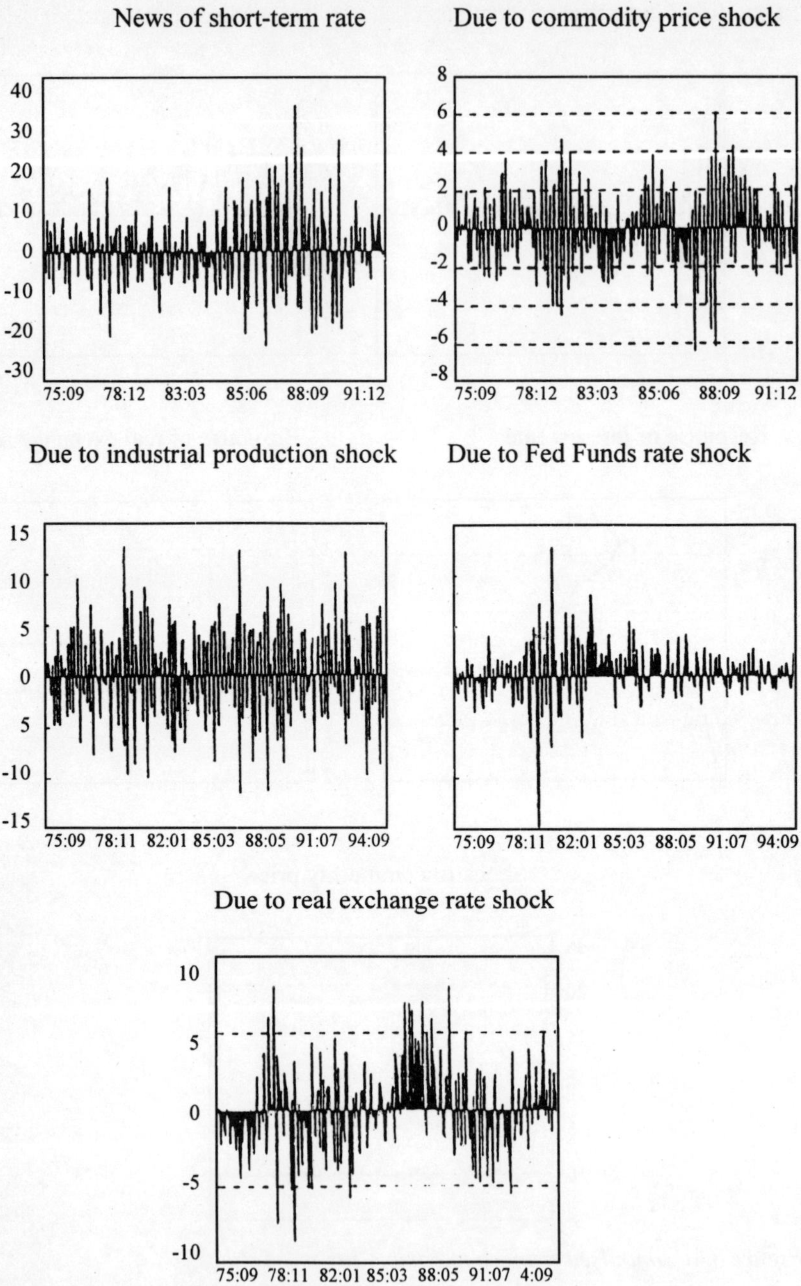

Figure 8.5 Historical decomposition of interest rate

The graphs indicate that, for instance, the response of the interest rate to an industrial production shock makes sense – it rises over time. Interest rates also rise in response to an inflation shock. A US Federal Funds shock also raises Japanese short-term interest rates, while depreciating the yen.

Notice that the responses of key variables to a shock in the short-term interest rate make sense: industrial production drops, and the exchange rate appreciates. The finding that inflation rises immediately after the interest rate shock is counter-intuitive, but is a common finding, for both the US and Germany. A historical decomposition of the short-term rate is presented in Figure 8.5.

8.4 A MORE STRUCTURAL INTERPRETATION OF BANK OF JAPAN POLICY: OUTPUT AND INFLATION TARGETS

The reaction function derived in Section 8.3 above is rich in its implications. It provides, for instance, the reaction of the unforecastable component of the policy instrument to a shock in, for instance, commodity prices. However, it is difficult to compare the estimated reaction function to objectives that a typical observer would think important – such as inflation and output, and perhaps other variables. Hence, in this section, we express the short-term interest rate as a function of expected deviations from target output and target inflation.

While this approach is seemingly quite different from that put forward in the previous section, in fact the two are consistent, in the sense that the 'expected' values of inflation and output, as well as the estimated target output and inflation rates, are derived from the VECM of the previous section. This means that the modelling of expectations and long-run equilibria is not purely *ad hoc*.

8.4.1 The Reaction Function

Let rs_t be the nominal repo rate, rs_t^o be the Bank of Japan's target for this interest rate, and rrs_t be the *ex ante* real interest rate, such that

$$rrs_t \equiv rs_t + \pi_{t-j}^{k}$$

$$\pi_{t-j}^{k} \equiv p_{t-j+k} - p_{t-j}$$

π_{t-j}^{k} is the inflation rate from period $t-j$ to $t-j+k$. Then express the Bank of Japan's interest rate target function as:

$$rs_t^0 = E_t\left(\pi_{t-j}^k\right) + rrs^* + \gamma^p\left[E_t\left(\pi_{t-j}^k\right) - \pi^{*k}\right] + \gamma^{ip}\left[E_t\left(ip_t - ip_t^*\right)\right] \tag{8.5}$$

The * superscripts denote target values, and the expectations operator, E_t, is conditional on the information set (defined in Section 8.3) available at time t.

Equation (8.5) indicates that the Bank of Japan targets the nominal interest rate as a function of the expected inflation 'gap' and the expected output 'gap'. When these deviations are zero (so that the target inflation rate and output level are achieved), then the targeted interest rate equals the sum of the expected inflation rate and the target real interest rate.

It is assumed that the Bank of Japan cannot exactly set the short-term interest rate at its target level; hence the actual interest rate is described by a partial adjustment mechanism, such that it is a weighted average of the target rate, and lagged actual rates, viz.

$$rs_t = \lambda rs_t^0 (1-\lambda)\left[\sum_{i=1}^{k} w_i rs_{t-i}\right] + \varepsilon_t \tag{8.6}$$

$$\text{such that} \quad \sum_{i=1}^{k} w_i = 1$$

Since the central bank can operationally set the short interest rate exactly, Equation (8.6) is difficult to rationalize except by reference to internal decision-making processes which preclude large and drastic changes in the actual short-term interest rates.

Returning to Equation (8.5), notice that the specification implies that the target rates are the long-run equilibrium rates implied by the VAR used by the central bank. This implies that in setting the targets, the central bank accepts that it cannot affect long-run values of the real interest rate and the real level of output (potential GDP). Of course, due to the presence of nominal rigidities, the central bank can affect output and real interest rates in the short run.

There is one additional difficulty in modelling the interest rate targeting behaviour in Japan which does not arise in the German case. That is, there is a secular decline in both the interest and inflation rates in Japan; both of these variables revert to a mean in Germany. This suggests re-writing Equation (8.5) in terms of a real interest rate target. Shifting the expected inflation term to the left-hand side yields:

$$rs_t^0 - E_t\left(\pi_{t-j}^{12}\right) \equiv rrs_t^0 \tag{8.5a}$$
$$rrs_t^0 = rrs^* + \gamma^p\left[E_t\left(\pi_{t-j}^k\right) - \pi^{*k}\right] + \gamma^{ip}\left[E_t\left(ip_t - ip_t^*\right)\right]$$

To account for the possibility that the Bank of Japan also targets other variables, such as commodity prices and the real exchange rate, we generate targets for these variables too, and enter them into the regression in a fashion analogous to the manner in which the output gap is entered.

8.4.2 Modelling Inflation Gaps

A key issue is the measurement of expectations of future inflation, and implied gaps, and at what horizon to measure them. Following Clarida and Gertler, we consider three alternatives: one-year-ahead, infinite horizon, and backward-looking.

The first one, looking forward one year, is quite reasonable. It sets the expected inflation gap as equal to the expected inflation rate over the next k period minus the equilibrium inflation rate over the next k periods,

$$E_t\left(\pi_{t-j}^k\right) = \pi^{*k} = E_t\left(\pi_t^{12}\right) - \pi^{*12}$$

In the second case, the Bank of Japan is concerned with cumulative inflation. In other words, the deviation of interest is the gap between the expected inflation in the infinite future and the equilibrium, also in the infinite future.

$$E_t\left(\pi_{t-j}^k\right) - \pi^{*k} = \lim_{k\to\infty} E_t\left(\pi_t^k\right) - \pi^{*k}$$

Since in the long run, the expected inflation must converge to the equilibrium, by substituting in the definitions for π_t^k and π_t^{*k} one obtains the result that:

$$E_t\left(\pi_{t-j}^k\right) - \pi^{*k} = -E_t\left(p_t - p_t^*\right)$$

This result means that the central bank will raise interest rates if the equilibrium price level is above the expected current price level (recall that the current price level is not observed at time t). While the reversal of signs is at first glance mysterious, the intuition is straightforward. When the trend price level (p^*) is above the current level, inflation (the first difference of log prices) is expected to be higher than trend before attaining equilibrium; the central bank therefore wishes to raise interest rates to counter this inflation burst.

The final alternative is the one-year backward-looking specification considered by Taylor; it defines the gap as:

$$E_t\left(\pi^k_{t-j}\right)=\pi^{*k}=E_t\left(\pi_{t-12}\right)-\pi^{*12}$$

where the expectations operator is still relevant because the current price level (P_t) used to calculate the inflation rate is not observed at time t.

Thus far, we have eschewed discussion of the determination of the long-run equilibrium values for inflation and output. However, it is clear that estimation of such 'targets' is of central methodological concern. In the traditional approach, the trend would be defined by the fit from a regression of the actual series on some polynomial in time.

Here we equate target levels with the permanent component of the series (either price levels or output levels). Since the variables of interest appear to be integrated of order one [I(1)], the permanent component from a Beveridge–Nelson (1981) decomposition is a natural variable to use as the target.[3]

Before proceeding further, it is useful to discuss the nature of this decomposition. Consider any nonstationary series, z; by the world decomposition theorem, the first difference of z, $w_t = z_t - zt{-}1$ can be expressed as a moving average process:

$$w_t = \mu + \varepsilon_t + \lambda_1\varepsilon_{t-1}+\ldots,$$

The εs are called innovations since they are unpredictable on the basis of past information. The expectation of z_{t+k} conditional on time t data is given by:

$$\begin{aligned}\hat{z}_t(k) &= E\left(z_{t+k},\ldots,z_{t-1},z_t\right)\\ &= z_t + \hat{w}_1(1)+\ldots+\hat{w}_t(k)\end{aligned}$$

In words, this means the best forecast of z is equal to the current z, plus expected changes between now and period k. Using the expression for w, one sees the best forecast of w at the horizon is a weighted sum of the past innovations, plus a constant. This fact, combined with the previous equation, means that at very long horizons (large k)

$$\hat{z}_t(k)\approx k\mu+\left[z_t+\left(\sum_1^{\infty}\lambda i\right)\varepsilon_t+\left(\sum_2^{\infty}\lambda_1\right)\varepsilon_{t-1}+\ldots\right]$$

$$\hat{z}_t(k)\approx k\mu+\bar{z}_t$$

Beveridge and Nelson identify the terms in the square brackets as the 'permanent' component of z. This makes sense if one views the 'permanent component [as] ... the long run forecast of the series adjusted for its mean rate of change' (Beveridge and Nelson, 1981: 156). In practice we set $k = 240$ (that is, 20 years), so that:

$$\bar{z}_t = z_t + \lim_{k \to 240} \left[\hat{w}_t(1) + \hat{w}_t(2) + \ldots + \hat{w}_t(k) - k\mu \right]$$

Typically, the permanent component is computed using univariate predictions of w. In this chapter the estimates are obtained from the vector error correction model described above.

Figure 8.6 presents nominal interest, inflation and real interest rates and their respective long-run equilibrium values. Figure 8.7a then presents the infinite horizon inflation and output gaps, while Figure 8.7b presents the same for commodity prices and the real exchange rate.

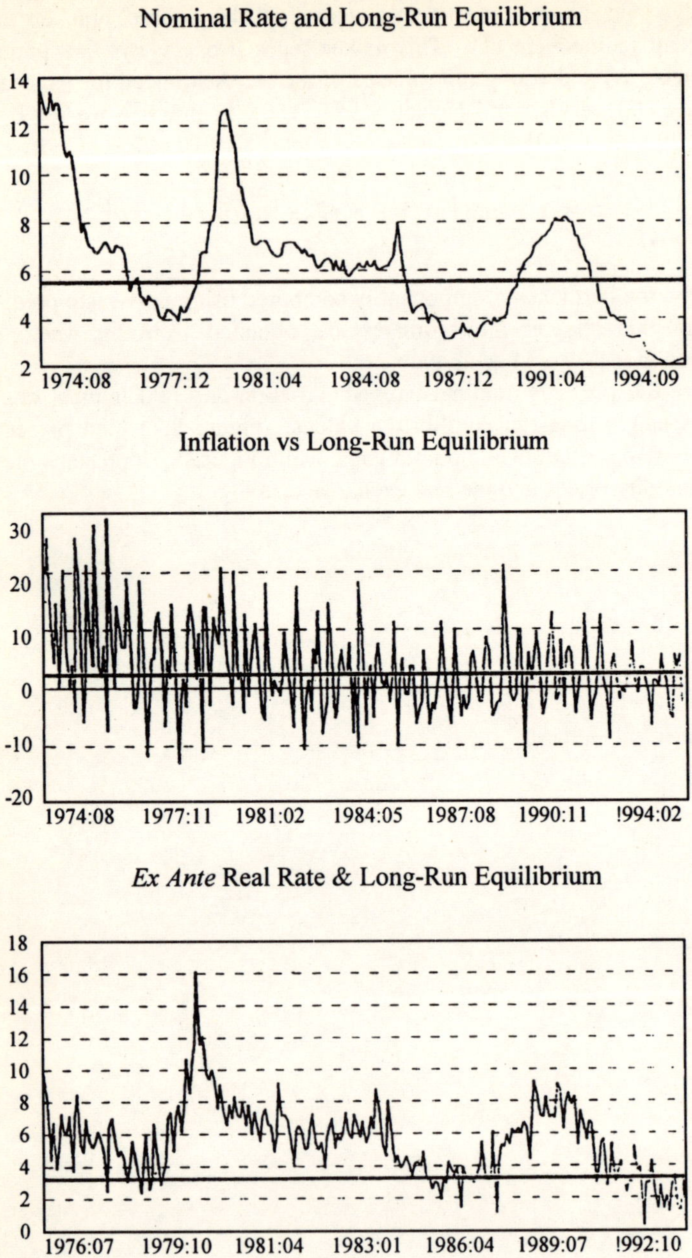

Figure 8.6 Interest rates and inflation

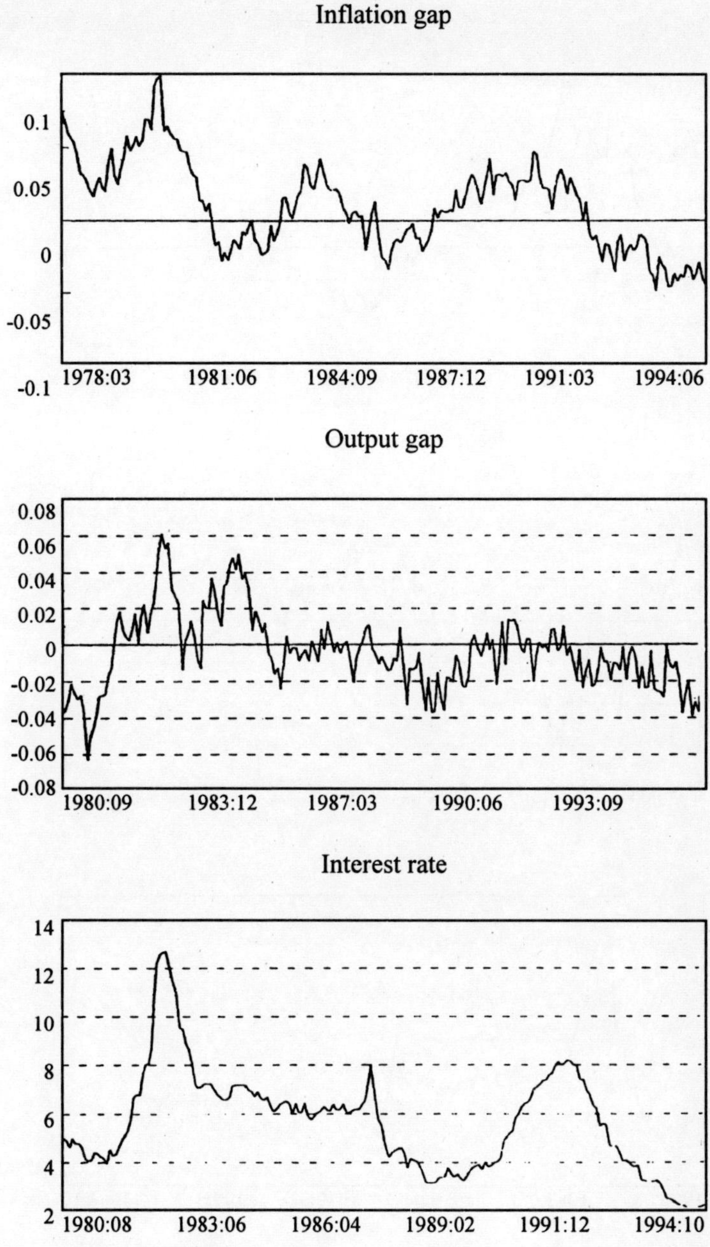

Note: Infinite Horizon case here is 20 years ahead.

Figure 8.7a Inflation gap, output gap and interest rate

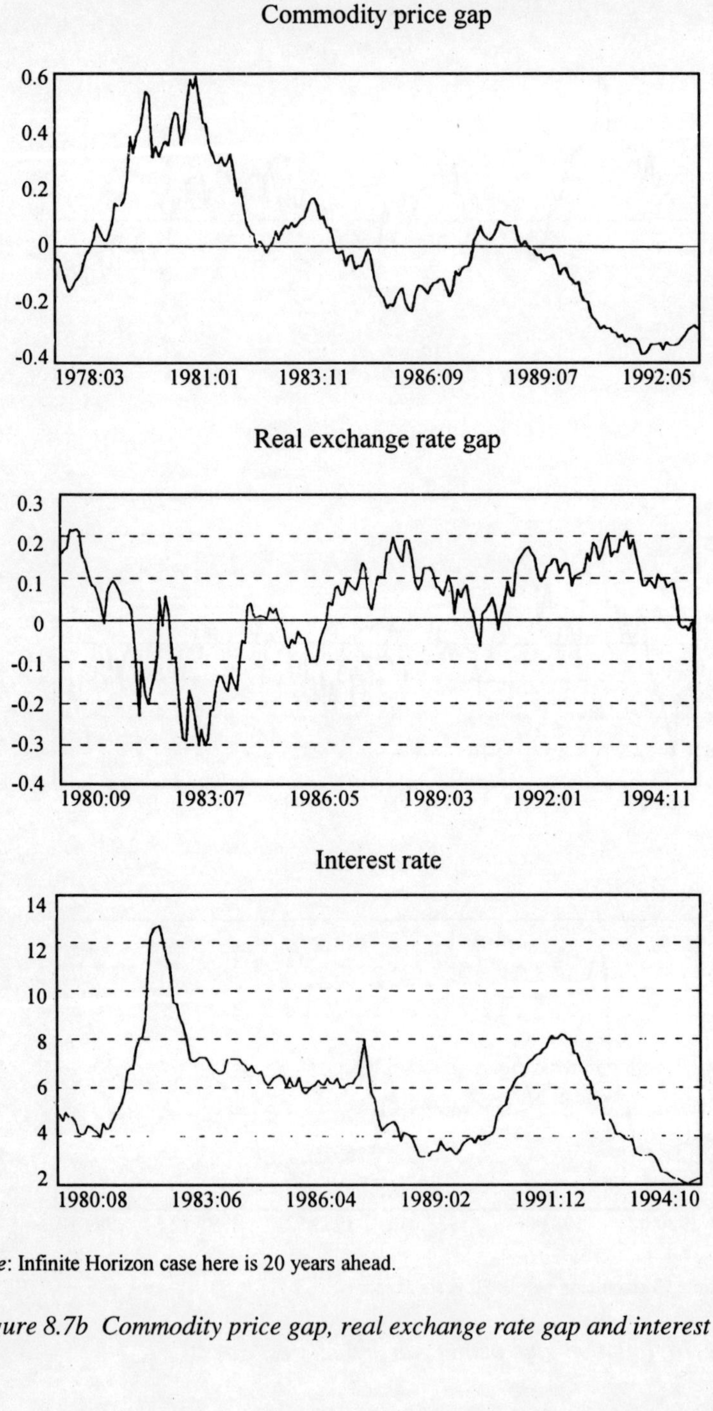

Note: Infinite Horizon case here is 20 years ahead.

Figure 8.7b Commodity price gap, real exchange rate gap and interest rate

8.4.3 Empirical Results

Inflation and output

The results of estimating the reaction function are reported in Table 8.3. For the basic specification, including only industrial production and inflation gaps, one obtains different results depending upon whether the 12-month-ahead inflation gap or the infinite horizon gap is used. If the former is used, then the point estimate indicates that the Bank of Japan *reduces* interest rates in response to a current positive output gap. This is clearly counter-intuitive, although the estimate is not statistically significant.

When the infinite horizon inflation gap is used, the coefficient signs are in accord with theory and statistically significant. A 1 per cent inflation gap induces a 0.43 percentage point increase in interest rates; a 1 per cent output gap induces a 0.79 percentage point increase. These are remarkably similar to the estimates obtained for the Bundesbank of 0.36 and 0.69, respectively. The implied equilibrium short rate is 5.42 per cent.[4]

It is of interest to compare these results to those obtained if one assumes that the *real* short-term interest rate is being targeted, as in Equation (8.5a). Then one obtains the results in Table 8.4. Once again, the 12-month-ahead forecast yields an implausible (but not statistically significant) point estimate; it implies the Bank of Japan reduces real interest rates by half a percentage point in response to a 1 per cent inflation gap. In contrast, the infinite horizon forecast produces much more reasonable estimates. It indicates that a one percentage point inflation gap yields a 0.41 percentage point increase in interest rates; a 1 per cent output gap produces a 0.85 per cent increase.[5]

Overall, the results suggest that indeed the Bank of Japan acts much like other central banks, particularly those of the US and Germany. However, it targets long-horizon inflation gaps as opposed to 12-month-ahead gaps.

Inflation, output and exchange rates

Given recent work arguing that the Bank of Japan targets the exchange rate as well as inflation and output (see Glick and Hutchison, 1994, among others), we investigated whether exchange rate gaps also entered into the Bank of Japan function. We constructed an exchange rate gap similar to the output gap. Using the 12-month-ahead forecast for inflation, one obtains the results in the top panel of Table 8.5 for the nominal short rate. They indicate that the exchange rate target does not enter significantly, in either economic or statistical terms.

Table 8.3 Bank of Japan reaction function, nominal interest rate

12-month inflation forecast
Dynamic partial adjustment equation

$$rs_t = -0.025 + 6.260(\pi^{12}_t - \pi^{*12}) - 0.9114(ip_t - ip_t^*) + 1.301\, rs_{t-1} - 0.225\, rs_{t-2} - 0.081\, rs_{t-3}$$
$$(0.091) \quad (2.541) \quad (0.704) \quad (0.075) \quad (0.122) \quad (0.079)$$

The sample is 1975:9–1994:12. Estimation is done by instrumental variables. The instruments are a constant, rs_{t-1} rs_{t-2} rs_{t-3} rs_{t-4} rs_{t-5} rs_{t-6} $(\pi^{12}_{t-1} - \pi^{*12})$, $(\pi^{12}_{t-2} - \pi^{*12})$, $(\pi^{12}_{t-3} - \pi^{*12})$, $(\pi^{12}_{t-4} - \pi^{*12})$, $(\pi^{12}_{t-5} - \pi^{*12})$, up to six lags of past industrial gaps and e_t^{com}, e_t^{ffr}, e_t^{m}, e_t^{er}. $R^2 = 0.97$, D.W. = 2.008. Standard errors in parentheses.

Implied equation for the target day-to-day rate

Not Applicable

Infinite horizon inflation forecast
Dynamic partial adjustment equation

$$rs_t = 0.488 + 3.909^*(p^*\text{-}p) + 7.085^*(ip_t - ip_t^*) + 1.103\, rs_{t-1} - 0.171\, rs_{t-2} - 0.022\, rs_{t-3}$$
$$(0.117) \quad (1.029) \quad (1.903) \quad (0.082) \quad (0.107) \quad (0.069)$$

The sample is 1975:9–1994:12. Estimation is done by instrumental variables. The instruments are a constant, rs_{t-1} rs_{t-2} rs_{t-3} rs_{t-4} rs_{t-5} rs_{t-6} up to six lags of past industrial gaps and e_t^{com}, e_t^{ffr}, e_t^{m}, e_t^{er}. $R^2 = 0.97$, D.W. = 1.91. Standard errors in parentheses.

Implied equation for the target day-to-day rate

$$rs_t^0 = 5.422 + 43.430^*(p_t^* - p_t) + 78.720^*(ip_t - ip_t^*)$$

Table 8.4 Bank of Japan reaction function, ex ante *rate*

12-month inflation forecast
Dynamic partial adjustment equation

$$rs_t = \underset{(0.707)}{2.065} - \underset{(12.287)}{16.650}(\pi^{12}_t - \pi^{*12}) + \underset{(13.102)}{42.452}(ip_t - ip_t^*) + \underset{(0.094)}{0.052}\, rs_{t-1} - \underset{(0.147)}{0.606}\, rs_{t-2} - \underset{(0.088)}{0.003}\, rs_{t-3}$$

The sample is 1975:9–1994:12. Estimation is done by instrumental variables. The instruments are a constant, rs_{t-1} rs_{t-2} rs_{t-3} rs_{t-4} rs_{t-5} rs_{t-6} $(\pi^{12}_{t-1} - \pi^{*12})$, $(\pi^{12}_{t-2} - \pi^{*12})$, $(\pi^{12}_{t-3} - \pi^{*12})$, $(\pi^{12}_{t-4} - \pi^{*12})$, $(\pi^{12}_{t-5} - \pi^{*12})$, up to six lags of past industrial gap and e_t^{com}, e_t^{ffr}, e_t^{m}, e_t^{er}. $R^2 = 0.59$, D.W. = 1.794. Standard errors in parentheses.

Implied equation for the target day-to-day rate

$$rs_t^0 = 6.090 - 49.118^* (\pi^{12}_t - \pi^{*12}) + 125.23^* (ip_t - ip_t^*)$$

Infinite horizon inflation forecast
Dynamic partial adjustment equation

$$rs_t = \underset{(0.352)}{1.868} + \underset{(3.064)}{14.564}^*(p^*\text{-}p) + \underset{(6.086)}{29.904}^*(ip_t\text{-}ip_t^*) + \underset{(0.069)}{0.266}\, rs_{t-1} + \underset{(0.074)}{0.115}\, rs_{t-2} + \underset{(0.062)}{0.267}\, rs_{t-3}$$

The sample is 1975:9–1994:12. Estimation is done by instrumental variables. The instruments are a constant, rs_{t-1} rs_{t-2} rs_{t-3} rs_{t-4} rs_{t-5} rs_{t-6} up to six lags of past industrial gap and e_t^{com}, e_t^{ffr}, e_t^{m}, e_t^{er}. $R^2 = 0.67$, D.W. = 1.90. Standard errors in parentheses.

Implied equation for the target day-to-day rate

$$rs_t^0 = 5.307 + 41.376^*(p_t^* - p_t) + 84.958^*(ip_t - ip_t^*)$$

Table 8.5 Bank of Japan reaction function, nominal interest rate

Exchange rate gap included

12-month inflation forecast
Dynamic partial adjustment equation

$$rs_t = \underset{(0.220)}{0.254} + \underset{(3.730)}{3.535}*(\pi^{12}_t - \pi^{*12}) + \underset{(5.191)}{5.722}*(ip_t - ip_t^*) - \underset{(0.512)}{0.029}(er_t - er_t^*) + \underset{(0.101)}{1.227}\, rs_{t-1}$$

$$- \underset{(0.122)}{0.202}\, rs_{t-2} - \underset{(0.078)}{0.070}\, rs_{t-3}$$

The sample is 1975:9–1994:12. Estimation is done by instrumental variables. The instruments are a constant, rs_{t-1} rs_{t-2} rs_{t-3} rs_{t-4} rs_{t-5} rs_{t-6} $(\pi^{12}_{t-1} - \pi^{*12})$, $(\pi^{12}_{t-2} - \pi^{*12})$, $(\pi^{12}_{t-3} - \pi^{*12})$, $(\pi^{12}_{t-4} - \pi^{*12})$, $(\pi^{12}_{t-5} - \pi^{*12})$, up to six lags of past industrial gap and e_t^{com}, e_t^{ffr}, e_t^{m}, e_t^{er}. $R^2 = 0.97$, D.W. = 1.91. Standard errors in parentheses.

Implied Equation for the target day-to-day rate

$$rs_t^0 = 5.644 + 78.556*(\pi^{12}_t - \pi^{*12}) + 127.14*(ip_t - ip_t^*) - 0.644*(er_t - er_t^*)$$

Infinite horizon inflation forecast
Dynamic partial adjustment equation

$$rs_t = \underset{(0.118)}{0.046} + \underset{(1.030)}{3.746}*(p^*-p) + \underset{(2.705)}{5.126}*(ip_t-ip_t^*) - \underset{(0.307)}{0.309}*(er_t - er_t^*) + \underset{(0.086)}{1.131}\, rs_{t-1}$$

$$- 0.174\, rs_{t-2} - 0.042\, rs_{t-3}$$

The sample is 1975:9–1994:12. Estimation is done by instrumental variables. The instruments are a constant, rs_{t-1} rs_{t-2} rs_{t-3} rs_{t-4} rs_{t-5} rs_{t-6} up to six lags of past industrial gap and e_t^{com}, e_t^{ffr}, e_t^{m}, e_t^{er}. $R^2 = 0.97$, D.W. = 1.95. Standard errors in parentheses.

Implied equation for the target day-to-day rate

$$rs_t^0 = 5.432 + 44.072*(p_t^* - p_t) + 60.311*(ip_t - ip_t^*) - 3.637*(er_t - er_t^*)$$

Table 8.6 Bank of Japan reaction function, real interest rate

Exchange rate gap included

12-month inflation forecast
Dynamic partial adjustment equation

$$rs_t = \underset{(0.753)}{2.406} - \underset{(14.291)}{30.677}*(\pi^{12}_t - \pi^{*12}) + \underset{(16.487)}{62.899}*(ip_t - ip_t^*) + \underset{(1.917)}{4.242}*(er_t - er_t^*) - \underset{(0.100)}{0.005}\, rs_{t-1}$$

$$+\underset{(0.153)}{0.592}\, rs_{t-2} - \underset{(0.091)}{0.008}\, rs_{t-3}$$

The sample is 1975:9–1994:12. Estimation is done by instrumental variables. The instruments are a constant, rs_{t-1} rs_{t-2} rs_{t-3} rs_{t-4} rs_{t-5} rs_{t-6} $(\pi^{12}_{t-1} - \pi^{*12})$, $(\pi^{12}_{t-2} - \pi^{*12})$, $(\pi^{12}_{t-3} - \pi^{*12})$, $(\pi^{12}_{t-4} - \pi^{*12})$, $(\pi^{12}_{t-5} - \pi^{*12})$, up to six lags of past industrial gap and e_t^{com}, e_t^{ffr}, e_t^{m}, e_t^{er}. $R^2 = 0.55$, D.W. = 1.78. Standard errors in parentheses.

Implied equation for the target day-to-day rate

$$rs_t^0 = 5.941 - 75.742*(\pi^{12}_t - \pi^{*12}) + 155.297*(ip_t - ip_t*) + 10.473*(er_t - er_t^*)$$

Infinite horizon inflation forecast
Dynamic partial adjustment equation

$$rs_t = \underset{(0.074)}{1.873} + \underset{(0.354)}{14.383}*(p^*-p) + \underset{(3.086)}{34.964}*(ip_t - ip_t^*) + \underset{(8.439)}{1.036}*(er_t - er_t^*) + \underset{(1.191)}{0.253}\, rs_{t-1}$$

$$+\underset{(0.071)}{0.120}\, rs_{t-2} + \underset{(0.062)}{0.271}\, rs_{t-3}$$

The sample is 1975:9–1994:12. Estimation is done by instrumental variables. The instruments are a constant, rs_{t-1} rs_{t-2} rs_{t-3} rs_{t-4} rs_{t-5} rs_{t-6} up to six lags of past industrial gap and e_t^{com}, e_t^{ffr}, e_t^{m}, e_t^{er}. $R^2 = 0.67$, D.W. = 1.92. Standard errors in parentheses.

Implied equation for the target day-to-day rate

$$rs_t^0 = 5.261 + 40.402*(p_t* - p_t) + 98.214*(ip_t - ip_t*) - 2.910*(er_t - er_t^*)$$

Since the 12-month-ahead results have not been very promising, we focus our attention on the infinite horizon results. They imply that an inflation gap of one percentage point induces a 0.441 increase in interest rates; an output gap induces a 0.603 increase. Holding all else constant, a 1 per cent exchange rate gap (the yen 1 per cent weaker than equilibrium, in real terms) provokes a 0.04 percentage point decrease in the short-term rate. Once again, this estimate is not statistically significant.

Considering the secular trends in interest and inflation rates, we restate the equation in terms of real interest rates. The results are reported in Table 8.6. In the 12-month inflation horizon case, the output and inflation gap coefficients are not much changed from the nominal interest rate case. However, the exchange rate gap now makes sense – a 1 per cent gap in the real exchange rate causes the Bank of Japan to raise the real short-term interest rate by 10 basis points.

If the infinite horizon is used instead of the 12-month horizon, then one finds that a similar, albeit smaller, response is obtained for the exchange rate gap. The point estimate in the estimated equation is also not statistically significant. This suggests that we have obtained mixed evidence for targeting of the real exchange rate.[6]

The evidence reported above supports the view that monetary policy in industrial countries is easily characterized. Central banks adjust very short-term interest rates in response to innovations in prices and output. But it is worth repeating that this is not a simple story that the central bank raises interest rates when inflation is 'high' or employment is above trend. On the contrary, the central bank is *assumed* not to react to the permanent component of shocks to policy goals. This is consistent with the 'bygones are bygones' view of monetary policy. It also means that secular changes in the level of inflation, for example, are a martingale with, in the case of Japan, a negative trend.

NOTES

1. We thank Hui Miao for research assistance. This research was supported by Faculty Research Funds of UCSC.
2. Cannan's (1925) introduction to a reprint of the Bullion Report notes that the restraint in money supply growth during the floating exchange rate period from 1783–1821 may have resulted from the Bank's policy of maintaining high interest rates.
3. This is a common procedure. Clarida and Gertler (1996) as well as Dominguez (1996) define the target rates as the Beveridge–Nelson permanent components of the respective variables.
4. The backward-looking gap failed to produce any meaningful results, as the estimates were of incorrect sign, and not statistically significant. This result makes sense if one believes that the Bank of Japan is looking forward, rather than backward.
5. While the implied equilibrium real interest rate is fairly high, it is important to remember that the 2 standard errors band would easily encompass a value of zero.

6. The commodity gap never enters into the regression with any statistically significant coefficients, so we eschew discussion of those results.

REFERENCES

Bernanke, B. and Blinder, A. (1992), 'The Federal Funds Rate and the Transmission of Monetary Policy', *American Economic Review*, **82**: 901–21.

Bernanke, B. and Mihov, I. (1995), 'Measuring Monetary Policy,' mimeo, Princeton University.

Beveridge, S. and Nelson, C. (1981), 'A New Approach to the Decomposition of Time Series into Permanent and Transitory Components', *Journal of Monetary Economics*, **7**: 141–74.

Blanchard, Olivier (1989), 'A Traditional Interpretation of Economic Fluctuations', *American Economic Review*, **79**: 1146–64.

Chinn, M. and Dooley, M. (1996), 'Asia-Pacific Capital Markets: Measurement of Integration and the Implications for Economic Activity', forthcoming in T. Ito and A.O. Krueger (eds), *Multilateralism versus Regional Trading Arrangements*, Chicago: Chicago University. Press for NBER.

Clarida, R. and Gertler, M. (1996), 'How the Bundesbank Conducts Monetary Policy', NBER Working Paper no.5581, May.

Dominguez, K.M.E. (1996), 'Monetary Interdependence and Coordination', Mimeo, Kennedy School of Government, Harvard University, July.

Gali, J. (1992), 'How Well Does the IS/LM Model Fit Post-War U.S. Data?' *Quarterly Journal of Economics*, **107**, 2: 709–38.

Glick, R. and Hutchison, M. (1994), 'Monetary Policy, Intervention, and Exchange Rates in Japan', in Glick and Hutchison (eds), *Exchange Rate Policy and Interdependence: Perspectives from the Pacific Basin*, Cambridge, UK: Cambridge University Press, pp. 225–57.

Hamada, K. and Hayashi, F. (1985), 'Monetary Policy in Postwar Japan', in Ando, Eguchi, Farmer, T. and Suzuki, Y. (eds) *Monetary Policy in Our Times*, Cambridge, MA: MIT Press, pp. 83–121.

Hutchison, M.J. (1988), 'Monetary Control with an Exchange Rate Objective: The Bank of Japan, 1973–86', *Journal of International Money and Finance*, **7**: 261–71.

Ito, T. (1989), 'Is the Bank of Japan a Closet Monatarist? Monetary Targeting in Japan, 1978-88', NBER Working Paper no. 2874.

Kasa, K. and Popper, H. (1995), 'Monetary Policy in Japan: A Structural VAR Analysis', Federal Reserve Bank of San Francisco, Pacific Basin Working Paper, no. PB95-12.

McCallum, B. (1993), 'Specification and Analysis of a Monetary Policy Rule for Japan', *Bank of Japan Monetary and Economic Studies*, **11**, 2: 1–46.

Pierce, J. (1984), 'Did Financial Innovation Hurt the Great Monetarist Experiment?' *American Economic Review*, **74**: 392–95.

Stuart, A. (1996), 'Simple Monetary Policy Rules', *Bank of England Quarterly Bulletin*, **36**, 3: 281–7.

Taylor, J. (1993), 'Discretion versus Policy Rules in Practice', Carnegie-Rochester Conference on Public Policy, pp. 195–214.

Walsh, C. (1993), 'What Caused the 1990-1991 Recession?', *Federal Reserve Bank of San Francisco Economic Review*, **2**: 33–48.

APPENDIX

Data Sources and Definitions

The data are of monthly frequency and cover the period 1974:8–1994:12.
Bank Credit (DC): 'Domestic Credit' (IFS line 32).
Industrial Production (IP): (IFS line 60c).
Retail Sale (RET): Retail Sale Value, Index Number in Real Terms, from OECD Main Economic Indicators.
Consumer Price Level (CP): (IFS line 64) for both US and Japan.
Real World Commodity Price (COM): World Commodity Price Level in US Dollars (IFS line 00176axd) adjusted by US Consumer Price Index (IFS line 00164x).
US Fed Funds Rate (FFR): Short-term interest rate (IFS line 60b).
Japan Short-term interest rate (*rs*): Call Money Rate (IFS line 60b) (Short-term rate between financial institutions).
Money Supply (M): Money (IFS line 34) plus Quasi-money (IFS line 35) deflated by CPI.
Exchange Rate (ER): Yen/Dollar rate (IFS line ae) at end of month.

9. Prudential Policy in Japan

Akio Kuroda[1]

9.1 INTRODUCTION

Financial institutions in Japan have recently been suffering from serious management problems comparable to those experienced during the financial crisis in the early *Showa* period (the late 1920s). Bad loans[2] have significantly restrained their lending behaviour. This constraint has contributed to continued economic stagnation in Japan.[3] The pressing need for a solution which speedily resolves this crisis should be obvious.

If we focus on bankruptcy proceedings such as those of the Tokyo Kyowa and the Anzen credit unions which led to the formation of the Tokyo Kyodo Bank or those of the financial institutions specializing in real estate (the Jusen) we end up examining specific conflicts of interest. These include conflicts between city banks and regional banks on one hand, and financial institutions for agriculture, forestry and fishery, on the other. This forces us to face the controversial issue of burden-sharing among related entities. Such discussion shifts the debate away from more fundamental and important issues concerning the Japanese financial system itself. We should rather concentrate on determining the shape and structure of a more desirable financial system and the most efficient way to attain it.

As a basis for discussing the current prudential policy in Japan, the four following basic principles are quite useful:

- First, the purpose of prudential policy is to maintain a sound and stable financial system. In order to achieve that purpose, it is very important to set up an environment in which market discipline can prevail. In Japan, however, the Ministry of Finance (hereafter referred to as 'MOF'), by employing various regulations, has restricted competition among financial institutions and thereby protected them from bankruptcy. As a result, those financial institutions which are inefficient and/or prone to excessive risk-taking continue to survive. We argue that a zero failure rate under such anti-competitive regulation is not desirable and should not be considered to be part of prudential policy.

- Second, the soundness and stability of the financial system cannot be attained by market discipline alone, due to inherent market failure. Therefore it is necessary to introduce limited regulation and supervision such as (a) a capital ratio requirement and a risk management requirement which include monitoring and on-site examination (*ex ante* measures), and (b) a deposit insurance system along with a 'lender of last resort' function provided by the central bank (*ex post* measures). It should be noted that there are clear distinctions between traditional anti-competitive regulations and those intended only to maintain a sound and stable financial system.
- Third, better information about management practices leads to more prudent behaviour by financial institutions. An informed choice by individual shareholders and depositors could force financial institutions to respond to standard market discipline. To assist this process, information as to the market value of assets and liabilities, including both on and off balance sheet items, needs to be expanded. Only then can we more accurately evaluate the net worth of financial institutions.
- Fourth, when a financial institution is in serious distress, it is necessary to force it to adopt corrective measures prior to bankruptcy proceedings. There have been numerous Japanese and overseas examples of financial institutions taking desperate gambles to avoid bankruptcy. This behaviour tends only to increase problem levels. Currently Japan lacks uniform bankruptcy laws for financial institutions. It urgently needs clear bankruptcy laws and an appropriate set of measures which can be applied expeditiously to troubled financial institutions.

9.2 FINANCIAL REGULATION AND SUPERVISION IN JAPAN

9.2.1 Regulatory and Supervisory Agencies

The Ministry of Finance

The Ministry of Finance is the dominant power with respect to financial regulation and supervision in Japan. According to the Ministry of Finance Law, MOF is responsible for the following seven areas of administration: (a) treasury, (b) currency, (c) finance, (d) foreign exchange, (e) securities transactions, (f) mint, and (g) printing. As shown in Figure 9.1, the organization of the headquarters of the MOF consists of the Minister's

Secretariat and seven bureaux such as the Budget Bureau, the Tax Bureau, the Customs and Tariffs Bureau and the International Finance Bureau. As part of its headquarters, there are also some special institutions such as the Mint Bureau, the Print Bureau, and the Institute for Fiscal and Monetary Studies. Also the National Tax Administration is an agency affiliated with the MOF.

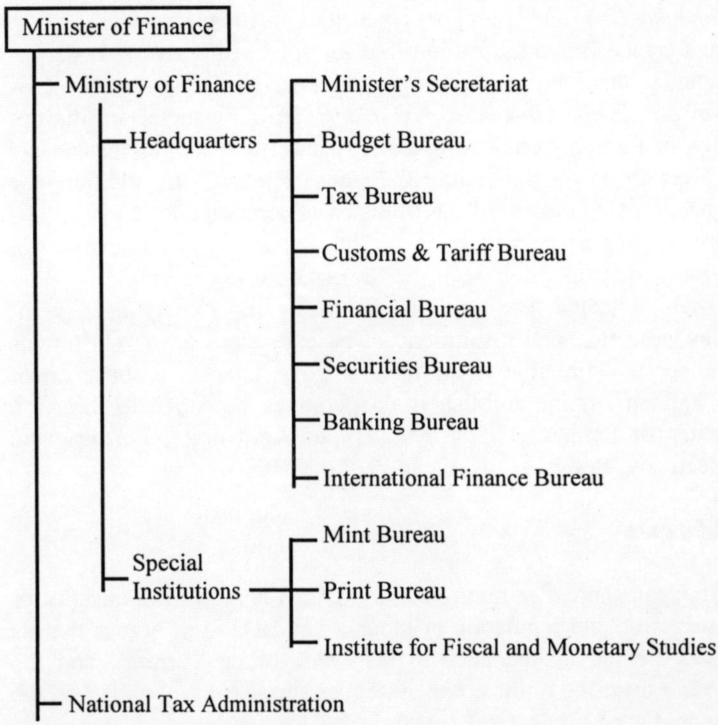

Figure 9.1 The organization of the MOF

Among those bureaux of the MOF, the Banking Bureau, the Securities Bureau and the International Finance Bureau play an important role in regulating and supervising various financial institutions. For example, the Banking Bureau is responsible for supervising most of the private financial institutions such as city banks, long-term credit banks, trust banks, regional banks, second-tier regional banks, and Shinkin banks. Its Insurance Department is responsible for supervising insurance companies. According to *Okura Zaimu Kyokai* (1993), a publication closely affiliated with the MOF, the situation can be described as follows:

> Financial institutions are under the supervision of the Banking Bureau in the sense that they have to acquire entry licenses from the Banking Bureau and are regulated by the Banking Law and other special laws. Such regulation extends over rather wide areas from as interest rate setting, to asset and liability management.

The Securities Bureau is responsible for the supervision of the stock exchanges and securities companies under the Securities and Exchange Law (*Shoken Torihiki Ho*) and monitors securities markets as well. The International Finance Bureau is responsible for supervising overseas capital movements under the Foreign Exchange and Foreign Trade Control Law (*Gaikoku-Kawase oyobi Gaikoku-Boeki Kanri Ho*). Financial institutions which engage in foreign exchange operations and international finance are under the direction of the International Finance Bureau. In addition, the Finance Inspection Department of the Minister's Secretariat conducts on-site examinations of financial institutions. The Supervisory Committee for Securities Transactions monitors securities transactions in general.

As has been indicated, the MOF is the major supervisory agency for almost all Japanese financial institutions. The exceptions are credit unions which are under the direction of prefectural governments. Labour credit associations and agricultural and fishery cooperatives are under the direction of the Ministry of Labour and the Ministry of Agriculture, Forestry and Fishery respectively, as well as the direction of the MOF.

The Bank of Japan

The Bank of Japan (hereafter referred to as 'BOJ') is partly responsible for financial supervision and regulation in Japan. The BOJ itself argues that its two objectives are the maintenance of the value of the currency and the maintenance and fostering of the credit system as stipulated in Article 1 of the Bank of Japan Law (*Nihon Ginko Ho*). The former indicates that price stability is the final target of macro monetary policy and the latter indicates that maintenance of a safe and sound financial system is the target of prudential policy.

The activities that the BOJ undertakes to maintain a safe and sound financial system are three-fold (Figure 9.2). First of all, the Credit and Market Management Department of the BOJ monitors the daily operations of financial institutions. Its Bank Supervision Department conducts on-site examinations of those institutions. When conducting on-site examinations, the BOJ staff has traditionally paid close attention to the soundness of loan assets in order to evaluate the capital level of a financial institution. More recently, the BOJ staff has also begun to pay close attention to various risks such as interest rate risks, foreign exchange risks and systemic risks. The supervision provided by the BOJ is different in purpose from the inspection undertaken by the MOF. The BOJ exercises its authority as the lender of last resort. It gives expert advice after having closely surveyed the management situation of each financial institution. On the other hand, MOF inspections are conducted in order to detect violations of the Banking Law, the Securities and Exchange Law, and so on. Despite such differences, the BOJ and the MOF strive to maintain a safe and sound financial system.

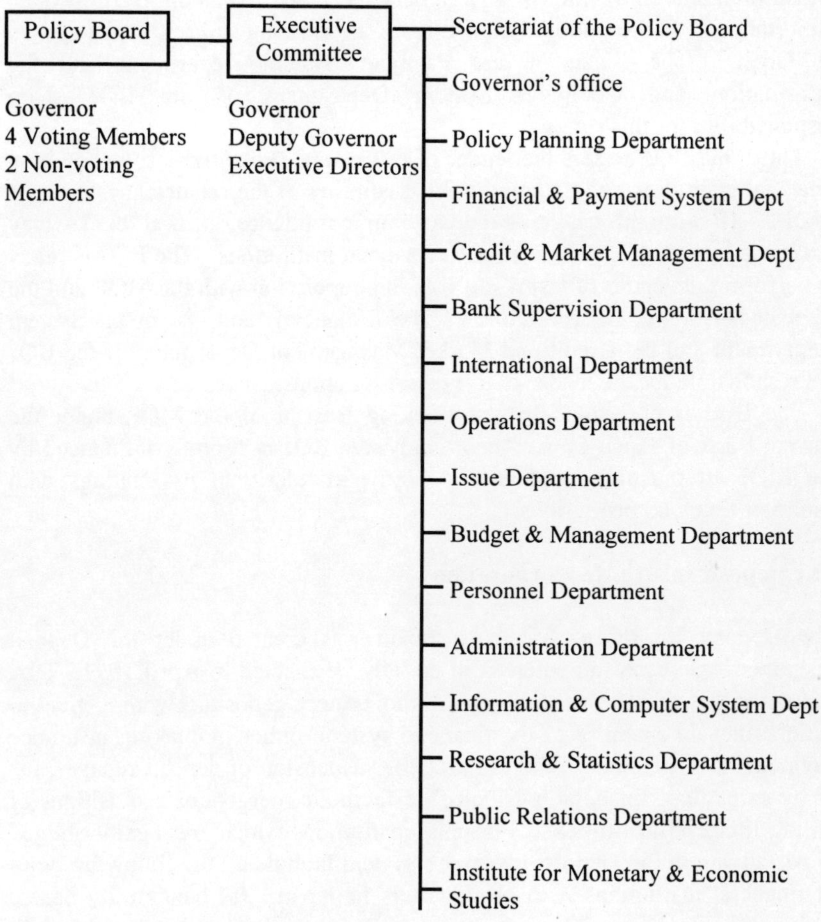

Figure 9.2 The organization of the BOJ

Second, the BOJ facilitates settlements by issuing banknotes and by transferring funds between current deposit accounts lodged with it by private financial institutions. Faced with rapid developments in computer technology and data processing, as well as financial deregulation and the progress of financial globalization, the BOJ has tried to enhance the efficiency and reliability of Japan's settlement system. Its goal is to harmonize them with international standards and practices. In particular, the BOJ has launched an on-line settlement network called BOJ-NET, which provides an electronic-based facility for operations such as current account transfers, and the registration and book entry of government securities. Thus the BOJ plays an important role in the smooth functioning of the clearing and settlement system in Japan. The Financial and Payment System Department and the Information and Computer System Department of the BOJ share responsibility for this role.

Third, the BOJ acts as the lender of last resort. Potential insolvency by a financial institution can undermine the credibility of the financial system as a whole. If it might trigger a collapse in confidence, central banks may intervene by extending credit to such financial institutions. The BOJ is ready to perform this lender of last resort role in cooperation with the MOF and the Deposit Insurance Corporation. The Financial and Payment System Department and the Credit and Market Management Department of the BOJ are responsible for the lender of last resort functions.

The BOJ is controlled by the Banking Bureau of the MOF under the current Bank of Japan Law. Accordingly, the BOJ is strongly influenced by the MOF in pursuing prudential policy, particularly in its dealings with bankrupt financial institutions.

The Deposit Insurance Corporation

The Deposit Insurance System in Japan was created under the Deposit Insurance Act (hereafter referred to as 'DIA'), enacted in April 1971. DIA stipulates that the aim of the system is to protect depositors with a view to maintaining the stability of the financial system, either by making insurance payments to depositors in the event of the suspension of deposit repayments, or by extending 'financial assistance' to facilitate mergers or acquisitions of failing financial institutions. Financial institutions which are legally obliged to participate in the Deposit Insurance System include all the following types of financial institutions with headquarters in Japan: (a) banks (city banks, regional banks, second-tier regional banks, trust banks, long-term credit banks), (b) Shinkin banks, (c) credit cooperatives, (d) labour credit associations. Government-related financial institutions and Japanese branches of foreign banks are not covered by this system.

An insurance relationship automatically exists between the Deposit Insurance Corporation and financial institutions, whenever financial institutions accept insured deposits. The following deposits and other liabilities of member institutions are insured under the system: (a) deposits, (b) instalment savings, (c) money in trusts.

The Deposit Insurance Corporation (hereafter referred to as 'DIC') was created in July 1971 under the provisions of the DIA for the purpose of operating the Deposit Insurance System. The DIC was capitalized at ¥455 million, of which the Government and the BOJ subscribed ¥150 million respectively. The remaining ¥155 million was provided by private financial institutions.

The DIC's decision-making body is the Management Committee, which consists of the Governor,[4] the Executive Director, and another six members. These members are appointed by the Governor with the approval of the Minister of Finance from among persons with expertise in financial fields. At present, the Chairman of the Federation of Bankers' Association of Japan and other representatives of the financial communities serve on this committee.

The major functions of the DIC include the collection of insurance premiums, payment of insurance claims, execution of 'financial assistance' and the management of funds. Member institutions must pay premiums to the Deposit Insurance Corporation within three months of the beginning of each business year. The premium to be paid is calculated by multiplying the premium rate[5] by the total balance of insured deposits held by a financial institution at the end of the preceding business year.

All surpluses of the DIC derived from insurance premiums and other revenues are accumulated in the Deposit Insurance Fund to be used when and if necessary. At the end of March 1995, the outstanding balance in the Deposit Insurance Fund stood at ¥876 billion. The DIC is legally authorized to borrow funds up to a designated limit (currently, ¥500 billion) from the BOJ. It is natural to regard the DIC as under the *de facto* control of both the MOF and the BOJ.

The financial system plays a greater economic role in some other industrial countries than it does in Japan. What distinguishes the Japanese system is its rather strict allocation of individual financial functions among different categories of financial institutions.

9.2.2 Traditional-Type Financial Regulations

The financial regulation and supervision in Japan has traditionally been characterized by (a) functional separation of private financial institutions, (b) interest rate regulation, and (c) regulation over international transactions, all of which serve to restrict competitive forces. However, most regulations that restricted competitive forces have been gradually abolished in the process of financial liberalization and internationalization since the late 1970s.

Functional separation of private financial institutions

Distinct allocation of financial functions can be observed in the separation between long-term finance and short-term finance, the separation between deposit banks and trust banks, and the separation between banks and securities companies.

However, regulations concerning the business areas of financial institutions have been liberalized in recent years. For example, banks have been allowed to handle many securities activities, starting with the over-the-counter sale of government bonds in April 1983. A wide range of banking institutions from city banks to credit cooperatives are now permitted to handle these bonds.

Since 1984, banks have been allowed to deal in public bonds. The opportunity for banking institutions which are permitted to deal in these bonds has been gradually increased since then. At the same time securities companies have developed, through a tie-up with Shinkin banks, a new financial instrument which links medium-term government bond funds to bank deposits. Given such financial innovation, the medium-term government bond funds became a *de facto* settlement account, even though settlements must be made through an ordinary bank deposit account. Overall, the demarcations which separated various specialized banks have gradually and effectively been reduced.

Although there still remain fundamental regulations that divide institutional categories, a further restructuring of the Japanese financial system has been seen recently. For example, the Financial System Committee of the Financial System Research Council, an advisory body to the Minister of Finance, published a report entitled 'On a New Japanese Financial System' in June 1991. In this report the Committee critically analysed the traditional Japanese financial system from viewpoints such as customer access, international standards and the maintenance of financial stability. It concluded that mutual entries among individual financial categories in the form of separate subsidiaries would be the appropriate approach for a new financial system to take. Subsequently, the Law Concerning the Reform of the Financial System (*Kinyu Seido Kaikaku Ho*) was enacted in June 1992. As of April 1993 it became possible for ordinary banks, long-term credit banks, trust banks and securities companies to set up wholly owned subsidiaries in designated financial categories. Although there are still important restrictions in terms of the type of business which banks or securities companies can engage in (for example banks are not allowed to engage in stock broking), and relatively strict firewalls exist between parents and subsidiaries, securities subsidiaries formed by city banks, long term credit banks and trust banks started operations in July 1993. Trust bank subsidiaries formed by securities companies did so in October 1993.[6]

It should be noted that additional regulations restricting competitive forces are still in place in the form of entry licence and branch admittance within the individual categories of financial institutions. For example, new entries to ordinary banking business such as city banks and regional banks have only been admitted by the MOF in a few exceptional cases.[7] Banks still need permission to open new branches. Their number and location is left to the MOF's discretion.[8] Furthermore, banks have had to report to the MOF about newly developed financial instruments before their sales. In fact the MOF has not impeded or delayed their sales. In practice market competition, in this regard, has not been restricted.[9]

Interest rate regulation

Deposit rates were first regulated in 1918. The regulation prevented competition on the basis of comparative interest rates. A strong fear existed that such competition might weaken the soundness of banks.

In December 1947, the Temporary Interest Rate Adjustment Law (*Rinji Kinri Tyosei Ho*) was promulgated and implemented. Under the Law, ceilings for deposit rates were strictly observed and were set at an artificially low level. In contrast, lending rates were more flexible. As a result, banks gained ample margins for a period of time. However, starting with the late 1980s, deposit rates were steadily liberalized. First, CDs with liberalized interest rates were introduced in 1979. Large-denomination time deposits bearing market rates and MMCs were introduced in 1985 with small MMCs having to wait until 1989. Restrictions on minimum accounts and maturities of such deposits were gradually relaxed thereafter. In June 1993, interest rates on time deposits became virtually free of any regulation. In 1994, interest rates on liquid deposits were liberalized except those on current deposits, that is, checking accounts, whose rates still remain regulated at 0 per cent.

Meanwhile, commissions for stock transactions were regulated as an exception to the Anti-Monopoly Law (*Dokusen-Kinsi Ho*) of 1948. This fixed commission system allowed securities companies important sources of revenues for long periods of time. However, starting in 1991 the liberalization of the fixed commission system for stock transactions was discussed. In 1994 the commissions for transactions which exceed ¥1 billion were liberalized.

Foreign exchange control

Rather strict control of foreign exchange during the high-growth period in the 1960s meant that domestic and foreign financial markets were segmented. However, since Japan moved to a flexible exchange rate system in 1973, there has been a gradual easing of foreign exchange restrictions in line with the international trend to liberalize cross-border capital movement.

The Foreign Exchange and Foreign Trade Control Law was fully revised in 1980 and the basic principles concerning international capital movements were changed from those of 'prohibition' to those of 'freely allowed' though regulations in case of emergency remained. In May 1984, a report by the Joint Japan–US Ad Hoc Group on Yen/Dollar Exchange Rate, Financial and Capital Market Issues (Yen/Dollar Committee) suggested a number of deregulations with respect to both the raising and investing of funds by banks and other entities in order to promote the internationalization of the yen. Included among them was the removal of limits on oversold spot foreign exchange positions of banks (that is, yen conversion limits), the liberalization of Euroyen trading, and the elimination of the 'real demand rule' for forward exchange transactions between banks and their customers. These measures expanded international financial transactions. The lifting of yen conversion limits resulted in expanding Euroyen interbank transactions and Eurodollar transactions with foreign exchange swaps, which in turn contributed significantly to increased arbitrage between domestic interbank and open markets.

As stated, financial administration in Japan was characterized by regulations which restricted competitive forces. They protected even the weakest financial institutions against bankruptcy by allowing them to attain sufficient revenue. The traditional style of Japanese financial administration during the high-growth period was often metaphorically described as a 'Convoyed Fleet of Vessels Administration' (*Goso Sendan Gyosei*, hereafter referred to as 'GSG'). However, faced with financial deregulation and internationalization in the late 1970s, such traditional-type administration was forced to change. It became increasingly difficult to maintain various regulations which restricted competitive forces. This meant that eventually some financial institutions would have to cease operations. In that sense, GSG has been gradually changing. The MOF established the Deposit Insurance System in 1971, anticipating that the traditional type of financial administration could not be maintained in the future.

The framework of financial regulation and supervision in Japan is still the same in spite of all the changes in financial circumstances. Since GSG should be replaced by a prudential policy based on market discipline, agencies responsible for financial regulation and supervision, that is, the MOF and the BOJ, must also be restructured accordingly.

9.2.3 Quest for New Regulatory Framework

We would like tentatively to propose a new framework of financial regulation and supervision in Japan (Figure 9.3).

Financial System Agency

- Planning of the financial system
- Supervision over financial services industries as a whole (risk management watcher)
- International coordination of prudential supervision

Deposit Insurance Corporation

- Pay-offs to depositors of bankrupt financial institutions
- Bankruptcy procedures (receiver of bankrupt financial institutions)
- Examination of financial institutions

Bank of Japan

- Monetary policy in order to attain price stability
- Management of the payments system
- Lender of last resort
- Monitoring and examination of financial institutions

Figure 9.3 New framework of financial regulation and supervision

First, an independent Financial System Agency (FSA) should be established by integrating the functions of the Banking Bureau, the Securities Bureau, the International Finance Bureau and the Supervisory Committee for Securities Transactions now under the control of the MOF. FSA's major functions should be: (a) planning for the financial system, (b) prudential supervision of financial institutions (for example, capital ratio and risk control), and (c) the international coordination of prudential supervision.

The necessity for establishing an FSA arises from the fact that the present MOF has been compromised by its intimate involvement with the traditional GSG type of financial guidance. Each financial bureau of the MOF has performed the role of protecting and promoting financial industries as well as the role of regulating and supervising those same industries. Consequently, financial institutions have grown to expect the MOF to protect them against severe competition. Therefore, in order to introduce a new prudential policy, the importance of market discipline must be recognized by both the MOF and financial institutions. In that sense, there should be a strict separation between the present MOF and the newly established FSA.

In addition, the current barriers between various financial businesses such as banks, securities companies, trusts and insurance companies, will be reduced in the future. As a result, overall harmonization of various financial businesses is expected to proceed gradually. The present MOF is characterized by sharp distinctions between individual bureaux with no significant integration of the administration of these bureaux. The current structure will not be able to cope with future financial environments. Therefore, it is necessary that the FSA should be solely responsible for supervising the financial service industry and for evaluating the risk positions of each member institution.

Second, the BOJ should be a central bank whose sole objective is the maintenance of price stability. For that purpose, the Bank of Japan Law should be revised to ensure central bank independence for the BOJ. Of course, the BOJ should continue to perform such functions as lender of last resort, manager of the payment system, and monitor of financial institutions which have deposit loan transactions with the BOJ. The need for MOF reform is linked to its failure adequately to deal with the Jusen problem. A proposed break-up of the MOF into two or three constituent parts would supposedly overcome any existing difficulties. This is far from certain. However, the BOJ should not be independently responsible for those functions, but should perform them with the cooperation of the FSA, which would be ultimately responsible for prudential policy.

Third, the DIC should not only make pay-offs to depositors of bankrupt financial institutions, but also manage the bankruptcy procedures for troubled financial institutions in line with the rules described in Section 9.4. The major purpose of the DIC reform is to solve the moral-hazard problems of troubled banks by forcing those institutions to adopt adequate corrective measures early on and by strictly enforcing bankruptcy procedures. In order for the DIC effectively to perform such important roles, it must be granted additional monitoring functions over financial institutions as well as acting as the receiver for bankrupt financial institutions.

Let us briefly examine recent proposals to reform the MOF and the BOJ. These gained support in the aftermath of the Jusen fiasco. Such proposals are simply destructive rather than constructive. The aim of MOF reform should be to establish a framework for financial regulation and supervision which can maintain a sound and stable financial system.

The BOJ reform proposal is simply a by-product of the suggestion for MOF reform. That is, the criticism against the MOF's dominance in the field of financial regulation and supervision has led to the parallel argument for the BOJ's independence from the MOF. It is obvious that the present Bank of Japan Law, which was enacted during World War II, should be revised to grant the BOJ complete independence to pursue monetary policy objectives. However, the independence of the BOJ is not a substitute for establishing a FSA, which is to be ultimately responsible for prudential policy. In other words, BOJ reform needs to be linked to MOF reform.

9.3 THE JAPANESE ACCOUNTING SYSTEM FOR FINANCIAL INSTITUTIONS

9.3.1 The Current Accounting System in Japan

The Japanese accounting system is based on three closely interrelated legal structures consisting of the Commercial Code (*Sho Ho*), the Securities and Exchange Law (*Shoken Torihiki Ho*), and the Income Tax Laws. The Financial Accounting Principles for Business Enterprises (*Kigyo Kaikei Gensoku*) supplements the provisions of these laws. The Business Accounting Deliberation Council (*Kigyo Kaikei Singika*i), an advisory body to the Minister of Finance, formulates accounting standards that furnish useful information for investors under the Securities and Exchange Law. The Council has also assisted in establishing accounting standards under the Commercial Code and various tax laws.

Among those laws which affect the Japanese accounting system, first, the Commercial Code assumes that the interested parties are shareholders, investors and creditors of companies. Its main statutory objectives are to calculate the profit available for distribution to shareholders and to provide sufficient information pertinent to the interest of current and future shareholders, investors and creditors. Second, the Securities and Exchange Law assumes that the interested parties are shareholders and investors. Its statutory objective is to make companies (whose shares are publicly traded) disclose information which is important for the investment decisions of shareholders and investors. Third, the Income Tax Laws assume that the interested parties are tax authorities of national and local governments as well as taxpayers. Its statutory objective is to calculate taxable income justly and correctly in accordance with a taxpayer's ability to pay. As has been indicated, the three laws have different statutory objectives, but in fact, the accounting standards based on each law are closely interrelated and tied together. These are often called the 'Triangular System' in the Japanese accounting system.

The accounting standard consistent with a prudential policy based on market discipline is very similar to that of the Securities and Exchange Law, in the sense that its major purpose is to provide accurate information about the management of financial institutions to shareholders, creditors and depositors. However, under the constraint imposed by the 'Triangular System', current accounting standards consistent with the Securities and Exchange Law do not provide sufficient information for shareholders and investors to make investment decisions. The relationship among the three accounting standards can be described as follows. According to the Income Tax Laws, taxable company income is based on the income reported in financial statements under the Commercial Code. On the other hand, the Income Tax Laws often include detailed provisions concerning the calculation of profits and losses, for example, credit loss allowances, valuation of securities, and depreciation for equipment and construction, so that the calculation of profits under the Commercial Code depends upon the Income Tax Laws to a significant extent. Moreover, the annual securities report prepared by all listed companies must conform to the accounting standards of the Commercial Code and the Income Tax Laws. It does not necessarily fulfil its original objective of providing sufficient information for investors' decision making.

Problems of historical cost accounting

Let us briefly review the problems of the current accounting system in Japan. First of all, there exists a rather serious problem of inaccurate asset valuation. In principle, asset valuation in Japan is currently based on historical cost accounting (hereafter referred to as 'HCA') as prescribed by the Commercial Code which defines historical cost as the cost of acquisition including acquisition expenses. The objective of this approach is to prevent arbitrary valuation of assets, to prohibit the appropriation of unrealized profits, and to maintain sound accounting practices. As an alternative to the HCA, the valuation by the lower of cost or market (hereafter referred to as 'LCM') may be applied to some assets such as liquid assets, listed bonds and listed shares.

The Bank Accounting Standards basically adopt the same rules with respect to the valuation of various financial assets as those applied to companies in general. As shown in Table 9.1, listed securities on trading accounts are valued by the LCM, but unlisted securities are valued by either the HCA or the LCM. Securities in investment accounts, listed government bonds and other bonds are valued by either the HCA or the LCM. Most of the financial institutions in Japan adopt the HCA for evaluating listed government bonds. Listed shares and convertible bonds are valued by the LCM, while shares of subsidiaries and unlisted securities are valued by the HCA.

Table 9.1 *Securities valuation standards of banks*

	Category	Valuation standard
Securities on trading account	Listed on Exchange	Lower of cost or market
	Others	Historical Cost, or Lower of Cost or Market
Securities on Investment Account	Listed on Exchange	
	a) Government bonds and other bonds	Historical cost, or lower of cost or market
	b) Other securities such as stock shares and CBs	Lower of cost or market
	Shares of subsidiaries	Historical cost
	All other securities	Historical cost

Accordingly, there occur significant disparities between book and market values of assets and liabilities held by financial institutions. Since profits are realized only on a settlement basis, the realized profits on their financial statements can deviate significantly from their *de facto* profits. For example, on the one hand, the profits can easily be raised through the realization of hidden profits of undervalued securities. On the other hand, they can hide valuation losses by adjusting the prices of securities via back-to-back transactions. They may sell listed securities (valued by the LCM) at a price over the market price and buy unlisted securities (valued by the HCA) at a price above the market price, thereby hiding any losses associated with securities holdings. As a result, financial statements may not reflect the true conditions of financial institutions and it is rather difficult for shareholders, creditors and investors to know the true strength of those institutions.

Another serious problem is associated with the valuation of financial derivatives. The volume of financial derivatives such as futures, swaps and options has increased dramatically in recent years because their accounting costs are lower than those of on balance sheet transactions. This reflects the rapid development of new products due to technological innovations occurring at the same time as an increase in capital adequacy requirements was agreed to in the 1988 Basle accord. It is widely recognized that market value accounting (hereafter referred to as 'MVA') is essential to grasp accurately the profits and losses arising from transactions in derivatives. However, unified standards currently exist only for off balance sheet transactions related to foreign exchange. In 1990 the New Foreign Exchange Accounting Standard (*Shin Gaitame Keiri Kijun*) was introduced and in that standard the MVA was adopted. Foreign currency denominated assets were henceforth to be valued at current foreign exchange rates. As for the other derivatives, their valuations are based on HCA, which cannot grasp the continuously changing values of derivatives.

Problems of bank disclosures

The current disclosure system of Japanese banks is based on Article 21 of the Banking Law which stipulates that documents explaining current business and financial conditions must be available at all major offices of a bank. In 1987 the Zengin Federation of Bankers' Association (*Zenkoku Ginko Kyokai*) published the uniform disclosure codes for its member banks, namely city banks, regional banks, second-tier regional banks, long-term credit banks and trust banks.

However, the disclosure of information concerning both on balance sheet and off balance sheet transactions by those member banks are quite limited in scope. They disclose information on their securities holdings by dividing them into securities for trading purpose and those for investment purpose. For each category, book values, market values and unrealized holding gains and losses are disclosed. But specified moneys in trust (*tokkin*) and fund trusts, both of which are not classified as securities under the Securities and Exchange Law, are not subject to such disclosure requirements, nor are their market values disclosed. Since market value information for private securities is not disclosed, securities which might have particularly large losses cannot be identified.

Regarding off balance sheet transactions, only the market value information on listed futures and options is disclosed. Over-the-counter transactions such as swaps are not disclosed. In May 1995, however, the Working Group on Financial Institutions Disclosure, set up by the Financial System Research Council, published a report which argues that all types of derivative transactions should be subject to disclosure requirements using either market value or fair value of all financial instruments, including derivatives, on trading accounts.

Meanwhile, the disclosure of banks' non-performing loan assets is quite limited. This is mainly because of the proviso clause in Article 21 of the Banking Law which relieves banks from disclosing information concerning 'matters which will undermine financial order, infringe upon the secrecy of depositors and other customers, hamper banking operations unduly, or incur an excessive burden of expenses for compilation'. As a result, the disclosure of Japanese banks' non-performing loans was delayed until quite recently. In 1992, in response to a request by the MOF, city banks, long-term credit banks, and trust banks began to disclose the gross value of (a) claims against bankrupt customers (bankrupt loans) and (b) claims for which interest payments are more than six months past due (problem loans). Regional banks and second-tier regional banks are also required to disclose the gross value of bankrupt loans, but they are not required to disclose the amount of any problem loans. Currently neither of these banks is required to disclose the amount of claims against customers whose interest payments are reduced or deferred (restructured loans).

The more detailed information concerning banks' non-performing loans has been collected by the MOF and the BOJ through their on-site examination and/or daily monitoring. The MOF and the BOJ in turn have utilized this information for the sole purpose of conducting their roles as financial regulators and supervisors under the framework of the GSG-type financial administration. However, this restricted information policy is not consistent with a prudential policy based on market discipline which requires the public disclosure of important information concerning bank management. The Committee for Financial System Stabilization set up under the Financial System Research Council should strongly recommend wider disclosure of a bank's non-performing loans.

9.3.2 MVA for Japanese Financial Institutions

From the viewpoint of prudential policy based on market discipline, the current system of financial accounting and of disclosure in Japan should be critically reviewed. In principle, the scope of financial assets and liabilities which are evaluated by MVA should be expanded. The major reason for expanding the application of MVA in Japanese financial institutions is to reveal their true management condition by transmitting more information concerning the market values of their assets and liabilities on a consolidated basis and by providing an accurate value of their net worth.

The expansion of MVA in Japan should be a two-step process. The first step is to increase disclosure of the market value of financial instruments. The second step is to change the accounting rules from the current HCA, with some LCM, into a MVA in principle. By increasing the disclosure of market value information, we can expect two kinds of effects. One affects shareholders, creditors and depositors when they choose among financial institutions. The other persuades managers of financial institutions to act more prudently, since they must take the feedback effects of any disclosure into account.

To whom should such disclosures be made available? The current provisions for disclosure under the Banking Law do not make this point clear. It has been widely argued that financial institutions should disclose the information to the general public, particularly depositors, so that they can make intelligent selections among financial institutions. However, it would not be an easy task for depositors in general to assess the default probability of a given financial institution even if disclosed information were increased significantly. Rather, the disclosure should be oriented to specialists, such as analysts of rating agencies and securities analysts, who could analyse disclosed information and translate such information into a signal which depositors in general could understand easily. Accordingly, information disclosure should be sufficiently thorough and detailed to be of value to those specialists as well as to professional investors.

The major purpose of changing the accounting rules from HCA to MVA is to be able to re-evaluate the net worth of financial institutions more accurately. As will be discussed in Section 9.4, we expect that the cost of solving the problem caused by a failed financial institution could be minimized by implementing bankruptcy procedures at the earliest possible time. For that purpose, it is essential to estimate the level of capital as accurately as possible by marking most of the financial assets and liabilities to market. In other words, hidden profits and losses which have characterized Japanese financial institutions should be openly assessed. It can be argued that the current amount of information disclosure is sufficient to estimate the capital level of financial institutions. Still, an objective accounting rule for calculating the level of their capital is desirable since the bankruptcy rules for financial institutions depend on this calculated capital ratio.

Finally, it should be noted that the Business Accounting Deliberation Council, whose office is managed by the Securities Bureau of the MOF, is responsible for setting the accounting rules in Japan. At the same time financial institutions are under the supervision of the Banking Bureau. This makes changing accounting rules to achieve greater prudential supervision difficult. Any change would involve successful negotiations between the Securities and Banking Bureau. Furthermore, because of the 'Triangular System', accounting rules under the Securities and Exchange Law cannot be changed independent of the various tax laws for which the Tax Bureau and the National Tax Agency are responsible. Therefore, the FSA should be solely responsible for setting accounting rules which will provide sufficient information to shareholders, creditors and depositors of financial institutions. It is expected that the accounting rules set by the FSA will be independent of the various tax laws.

9.4 BANKRUPTCY PROCEEDINGS IN JAPAN

When a financial institution is in serious distress, both regulatory supervision and bankruptcy laws should force the institution to take corrective action. Numerous examples, in Japan and overseas, demonstrate that troubled financial institutions take risky last gambles in order to avoid bankruptcies. Such gambles only increase the amount of non-performing loans and increase the cost of the financial system. At the present moment, Japan lacks a uniform set of bankruptcy proceedings that can be applied to financial institutions. The MOF has been dealing with troubled financial institutions on an *ad hoc* case-by-case basis. This has caused serious delays due to conflicts among interested parties. Therefore, the rules governing bankruptcy proceedings and prior corrective measures must be transparent and put into place as soon as possible.

In this section we explain the proceedings available under the Japanese law which relieve or otherwise deal with those banking institutions which are on the verge of bankruptcy. We intend to cover not only statutory bankruptcy, but also other available proceedings and procedures which are designed for or have the effect of relieving financially disabled banks as much as possible. Such proceedings include mergers with or acquisitions of financially distressed banks by profitable ones. Also covered are various proceedings which may be taken by a regulatory agency for or against banks in financial distress; these include the temporary suspension of their banking business and affairs or the permanent termination of their banking business licences.

9.4.1 Applicable Statutes and Bankruptcy Proceedings

When a bank is in serious financial distress and is unable to continue its business as usual, then it will, like any other corporation, naturally be subject to statutory bankruptcy proceedings under the bankruptcy law. This includes the Bankruptcy Act (*Hasan Ho*, hereafter referred to as 'BA'), the Stock Company Reorganization and Rehabilitation Act (*Kaisya Kosei Ho,* hereafter referred to as 'SCRRA'), the Arrangement Act (*Wagi Ho*) and the related provisions governing corporate reorganization and special liquidation proceedings of stock corporations included in the Commercial Code (*Sho Ho*). All of these statutory bankruptcy proceedings, if applied to a bank, have the effect of liquidating or reorganizing a bank through a set of unified and blanket legal procedures designed to adjust, in an equitable manner, the rights and interests of all parties who have valid claims against the bank. All such proceedings are under the supervision of the court.

All banks are required under Article 4.1 of the Banking Act to obtain and maintain a valid banking licence in order to engage or remain in the banking business. Dissolution and liquidation procedures are inevitably affected by the Banking Act. The Minister of Finance has the power and authority permanently to terminate their banking business licences under certain specified circumstances. In addition, banks' business and affairs may be affected by the DIA (*Yokin Hoken Ho*), which provides certain insurance coverage for the protection of depositors. In addition to the statutory bankruptcy proceedings, there are, in a much broader sense, other proceedings which are also designed for or have the effect of relieving financially unhealthy banks. Included among them is the merger of a bank which is in a financially unhealthy condition with one which is financially healthy and profitable. Such a merger is subject to the special procedural rules set forth in the Banking Act, and the Act Governing Mergers Between and Conversion of Banking Institutions (*Kinyukikan No Gappei Oyobi Tenkan Ni Kansuru Ho*), whose primary purpose is to regulate mergers between or among two or more banking institutions of different kinds. If there is a question of bankruptcy, the DIA may become operative in order to facilitate the liquidation or rehabilitation of a bank in financial distress. The DIA authorizes and empowers the Minister of Finance to act as an intermediary to promote and expedite the merger of one bank with another, or the acquisition by any other bank or banks of all or substantially all its assets and/or capital stock shares. The DIC may provide 'financial assistance' to those banks which make these suggested acquisitions.

Bankruptcy proceedings categorized

In general, the bankruptcy proceedings, which are designed for or have the effect of liquidating or rehabilitating a financially unhealthy bank, such as a bank with an extremely poor equity ratio, can be classified into the following three categories:

1. liquidation proceedings – to wind up a financially unhealthy bank and distribute its assets to its creditors and shareholders. This category includes special liquidation proceedings under the Commercial Code and bankruptcy proceedings under the BA;
2. rehabilitation proceedings – to reorganize and rehabilitate a financially unhealthy bank;
3. merger and acquisition proceedings – to let a bank in a sound financial condition acquire and assume the assets and liabilities of a financially unhealthy bank.

The DIA includes intricate provisions regulating the merger of a financially unhealthy banking institution with a financially healthy and profitable institution. Article 59 of the DIA states that any banking institution which is financially healthy and profitable and which is going to merge with any financially unhealthy banking institution, or acquires all or any part of the assets and/or capital stock shares of such a financially unhealthy banking institution may, in order to facilitate such a merger or acquisition, request the DIC to extend 'financial assistance'. The term 'financial assistance' means, by definition, the donation of cash funds, extension of loans, purchase of assets and assumption and guarantee of debts.

Technically speaking, if the DIC pays insurance claims to the depositors of a financially disabled bank pursuant to the DIA, such protection is aimed solely at maintaining the credibility of the nation's financial system as a whole. It is totally independent of any decision either to liquidate or rehabilitate a disabled bank. A 'First Class Insurance Risk situation' occurs with the suspension of payment to depositors. A 'Second Class Insurance Risk' includes the termination of a banking business licence, the adjudication of bankruptcy proceedings, or the passing of a resolution of dissolution. The DIA entitles each and every depositor to file an insurance claim with the DIC and obtain insurance proceeds out of the DIC's funds to the amount of ¥10 million per depositor.

Relationship among various bankruptcy proceedings

In Japan, bankruptcy proceedings applicable to banks are subject not only to the general rules and principles set forth in the Civil Code and the Commercial Code, but also to those set forth in three other groups of law. These are: (a) the Banking Act (in relation to the temporary suspension of the banking business or the termination of a banking business licence); (b) the bankruptcy law (which includes the provisions of the Code relating to special liquidation proceedings, BA and SCRRA); and (c) the DIA (in relation to 'financial assistance' which expedites mergers and acquisitions and which pay insurance claims).

Unfortunately, from a practical point of view, these measures are unnecessarily complicated. One cause or event which may act to trigger proceedings against a bank under one of the three groups of law does not simultaneously trigger proceedings under the others. This often creates a situation where the time to initiate proceedings under one law has elapsed, but the other groups of law are not yet effective; that is, a timing difference problem. The parties who are entitled to initiate proceedings against a bank are different from one law to another, that is, a problem involving a lack of uniformity between parties. There may also be cases where two or more proceedings under two or more different groups of laws are pending against one and the same bank, either with or without cooperation or coordination between them, that is, the problem of the cumulative nature of proceedings. How and to what extent bankruptcy proceedings, if initiated against any bank, will affect the bank's license is not altogether clear, that is, a problem involving uncertainty.

9.4.2 Cases of Financially Troubled Banks

Let us briefly review the cases of financially troubled banks in Japan and see how they were actually solved by the MOF in the past. Even under the GSG-type of financial administration, we could point out a few financial institutions that fell into distress because of reckless management as well as for other reasons. The Banking Bureau of the MOF, the supervisor of those financial institutions, tried to solve the problem by forcing them to merge with much larger and/or healthier financial institutions with which they had close relationships. The Banking Bureau would also request that their managers resign and by doing so accept the full responsibility for those failures. Accordingly, when and how those problems were solved depended solely on the discretion of the MOF. In fact, as one ex-bureaucrat of the MOF vividly stated (Sakai, 1995), cases of troubled financial institutions were perceived as offering challenging opportunities for the MOF bureaucrats to show their administrative skills and powers. Such traditional ways of dealing with bankruptcy procedures have been maintained within the MOF until quite recently. The DIC extended 'financial assistance' to a number of troubled financial institutions.

In October 1991, the Iyo bank, which has its principal office in Ehime prefecture, received approval of its application from the Minister of Finance for 'financial assistance' to facilitate its merger with the failing Toho Sogo Bank, which had its principal office in Ehime prefecture, as well. The DIC's Management Committee decided to extend 'financial assistance' to the Iyo Bank in the form of a floating interest loan of ¥8 billion for a period of five years at a rate equal to the coupon rate of ten-year government bonds minus 5 per cent. 'financial assistance' was implemented in April 1992. The Iyo Bank will save up to ¥2 billion in interest expenses by the end of the five-year period. At the same time, the Association of Second-Tier Banks implemented a loan of ¥1 billion in order to support the Iyo Bank.

In May 1992, the Sanwa Bank, which is one of the city banks and has its principal office in Osaka, received approval from the Minister of Finance for 'financial assistance' to facilitate its merger with the failing Toyo Shinkin Bank, which had its principal office in Osaka, as well. The DIC's Management Committee met in June and decided to extend 'financial assistance' (grant of ¥20 billion) to the Sanwa Bank. The grant was provided in October 1992. At the same time, the Industrial Bank of Japan and the Zenshinren Bank provided assistance of ¥55 billion and ¥20 billion respectively. Meanwhile, most of the branches of the Toyo Shinkin Bank were sold to 22 Shinkin banks in the region of Osaka.

In October 1993, the DIC implemented a 'financial assistance' program (grant of ¥26 billion) for the Iwate Bank, which has its principal office in Iwate prefecture so that it could take over the business of the Kamaishi *Shinkin Bank,* which also had its main office in Iwate prefecture. Accordingly, the failing Kamaishi Shinkin Bank was dissolved.

In November 1993, the DIC extended 'financial assistance' (grant of ¥19) to the Credit Union Osaka-Koyo which merged with the failing Osaka-Humin Credit Union. Both of those credit unions are located mainly in Osaka prefecture. At the same time, the municipal government of Osaka provided a low-interest loan of ¥10 billion for a 15-year period to the Credit Union Osaka-Koyo.

In January 1995, the Tokyo Kyodo Bank was established as a new bank taking over the failing Tokyo Kyowa and the Anzen Credit Unions. (Both of them had their principal offices in Tokyo.) Its initial capital of ¥21 495 million was contributed by the BOJ (¥20 billion), the Sumitomo Bank (¥900 million) and by the Zenshinren Bank (¥595 million) respectively. In March 1995, the Tokyo Kyodo Bank received 'financial assistance' (grant of ¥40 billion) from the DIC as well as an additional capital injection from a wide range of private financial institutions.

In March 1995, the Credit Union Kansai-Kogin, which has its principal office in Osaka, merged with the failing Credit Union Gihu Shogin, which had its principal office in Gifu prefecture, and received 'financial assistance' (grant of ¥2.5 billion) from the DIC.

In July 1995, the Kanagawa Prefecture Labour Credit Union took over the business of the failing Yuai Credit Union, which had its principal office in Kanagawa prefecture, and received 'financial assistance' (grant of ¥2.8 billion) from the DIC. The Yuai Credit Union sold its non-performing loans to the Kanagawa Prefecture Credit Union Association at their market values. At the same time, the Yokohama Bank and the prefecture government of Kanagawa implemented the assistance of ¥4.8 billion and ¥2.5 billion respectively to the newly formed association.

In August 1995, the Tokyo Metropolitan Government ordered the Cosmo Credit Union to suspend part of its business and announced a scheme for its dissolution. In March 1996, the Tokyo Kyodo Bank took over the business of the Cosmo Credit Union and received 'financial assistance' equivalent to ¥125 billion from the DIC, a fixed low-interest rate (0.5 per cent) loan of

¥220 billion from the BOJ as well as a low-interest loan of ¥223 billion from seven private financial institutions (including Sakura Bank and Sanwa Bank).

In August 1995, the MOF announced that the failing Hyogo Bank located in Hyogo prefecture would be dissolved and that a new bank named 'the Midori Bank' would be established to take over the business of the Hyogo Bank. In January 1996, the Midori Bank was established with capital of assets of ¥70 billion, collected mainly from private financial institutions. The estimated loan losses of the Hyogo Bank are about ¥790 billion. This is to be covered by its own capital, 'financial assistance' of about ¥400 billion from the DIC and from other sources.

In August 1995, the municipal government of Osaka ordered the Kizu Credit Union to suspend its business. This in turn caused a run on the Kizu Credit Union. The BOJ and the National Federation of Credit Unions made emergency loans which totalled ¥429 billion. The estimated loan losses of the Kizu Credit Union at the end of September 1995 were about ¥950 billion. Most of this is to be funded by 'financial assistance' from the DIC. It is expected that the reorganized Tokyo Kyodo Bank (to be established this summer and referred to as the Japanese RTC) would take over the business of the Kizu Credit Union as well as that of other failing credit unions.

In June 1996, the Sakura Bank, which is one of the city banks located in Tokyo, announced that the failing Taiheiyou Bank, located in Tokyo, is to be dissolved and a new bank named the Wakasio Bank is to be established in September 1996 with capital totalling ¥40 billion. The estimated loan loss of the Taiheiyou Bank is about ¥170 billion, part of which is to be covered by 'financial assistance' from the DIC as well as financial support from the Fuji Bank, the Tokai Bank, and the Sanwa Bank.

The MOF has been involved in all of these cases as the ultimate financial regulator and supervisor of Japan. It is clear that the MOF's traditional way of restoring troubled financial institutions is approaching its limit; namely it has become more and more difficult for the MOF to find a healthy financial institution which can merge with a failing institution or take over its business since an increasing number of Japanese financial institutions have recently been suffering from the burden of non-performing loans. It is also obvious that the MOF's traditional case-by-case procedure has led to a serious delay in solving the problems which characterize failing financial institutions.

The Jusen fiasco was another serious blow to the traditional case-by-case procedure of the MOF. This approach caused an enormous delay in solving the Jusen problem and consequently increased the amount of total bad loans held by those institutions specializing in real estate. The struggle between city banks and regional banks on the one hand, and financial institutions representing agriculture, forestry and fishery on the other, forced the MOF to propose a compromise plan of injecting ¥685 billion worth of public funds into these troubled institutions. This outraged the general public. The MOF has not yet reached a final solution of the Jusen problem, although a Corporation for Managing Real-Estate Financial Assets (*Jutaku Kinyu Saiken Kanri Kiko*) with more than 1000 staff is to be established under the direction of the DIC this summer.

9.4.3 Improvement of the Bankruptcy Procedures

Bankruptcy procedures in Japan are quite complicated. It is necessary and desirable that a uniform bankruptcy law dealing with financial institutions be enacted in the near future. It is very important to set up clear and objective rules for solving the problem of failing financial institutions as soon as possible in order to reduce the social cost associated with bank failures. We would like to make three suggestions which together could improve the current bankruptcy procedures for financial institutions.

First, it is necessary to set up objective rules for ordering corrective actions against those financial institutions which are in financial distress (and are likely to fall into bankruptcy) with all due speed. More precisely, the FSA, the new regulatory and supervisory agency, should accurately measure the capital level of individual financial institutions which are members of the Deposit Insurance System, by applying MVA. The FSA will classify financial institutions into groups such as 'well capitalized', 'adequately capitalized' and 'undercapitalized'. Accordingly, those financial institutions which fall into the 'undercapitalized' group will be forced to adopt the sort of prompt corrective actions which have already been introduced by the FDICIA in the United States. The FSA should watch carefully not only an institution's capital level, but also the variance of that level. In other words, the FSA should evaluate the robustness of financial institutions under the expected changes of market circumstances.

Second, it is necessary to set up objective rules for the start of bankruptcy procedures. Practically, bankruptcy procedure should be automatically applied to those financial institutions whose capital levels fall below zero (that is, negative net worth) in spite of possible corrective actions. We can find the same kind of procedures in the FDICIA, which require regulatory agencies to close financial institutions classified as 'critically undercapitalized'.

Third, the DIC should be expanded so as to become a specialized agency which is responsible for all bankruptcy procedures of financial institutions. More precisely, the major functions of the strengthened DIC should be to pay off depositors of bankrupt financial institutions, to collect loans as the receiver of those financial institutions, and to preserve their assets against creditors. Ultimately the DIC should dissolve those financial institutions or deal with them either by merger with or take-over by healthier and/or larger financial institutions. If the DIC could perform these functions, the social cost of dealing with troubled financial institutions could be minimized. Injections of public funds, for example, government expenditure, loans from the Fiscal Investment and Loans Programme, and special loans by the BOJ, should be curtailed as much as possible.

Some progress has been made in improving the speed of corrective actions as well as the effectiveness of bankruptcy proceedings. In April 1996 three finance-related laws passed the Diet. First, prompt corrective actions based mainly on capital ratios have been stipulated so that supervisory agencies can take necessary measures to improve the management of financial institutions. Second, supervisory agencies are now entitled to file a petition for the rehabilitation of troubled credit co-operatives. Third, bankruptcy proceedings for credit unions have been specified in that failed credit unions are to be taken over by the Japanese RTC, which could receive support from the DIC as well as the government.

NOTES

1. The original version of this chapter (in Japanese) was presented at the fall meeting of the Japanese Money and Banking Association (Kinyu Gakkai) in October 1995. I would like to thank Professor Toshiki Jinushi for his valuable comments. Also I would like to thank the Zengin Foundation for Studies on Economics and Finance for its financial support of this research project.
2. The MOF announced that the total amount of bad loans by Japanese banks at the end of September 1995 was ¥37 390 billion, whose contents were detailed as follows:

(Unit: ¥ billion)

	Total Bad Loans	Bankrupt or Past Due Loans	Restructured Loans
City banks	13 094	8 058	5 036
Long-term credit Banks	3 970	2 116	1 854
Trust banks	6 296	2 797	3 499
Regional banks	4 946	3 288	1 658
Second-tier Regional banks	2 789	2 208	581
Cooperatives	6 295	5 963	332
Total Banks	37 390	24 430	12 960

In the table above, the total bad loans consist of bankrupt or past due loans and restructured loans. About two-thirds of the restructured loans were those to institutions specializing in real estate (Jusen).
At the end of March 1996, the total bad loans of city banks decreased to ¥12 250 billion, while the total amount of newly defined bad loans including those to already supported firms increased to ¥14 820 billion.
3. The growth rates in Japanese real GDP were 0.3 per cent, -0.2 per cent, and 0.6 per cent in the fiscal year 1992, 1993 and 1994 respectively. The growth rate jumped to 2.3 per cent in fiscal year 1995, although it remained lower than the Government's forecast figure of 2.8 per cent.
4. The Deputy Governor of the BOJ traditionally assumed the post of Governor of the DIC since its 1971 beginning. However, Mr Matsuda, who was a former public prosecutor, was elected to be the DIC's Governor quite recently.
5. The premium rate for deposit insurance was previously 0.012 per cent. But it was raised to 0.048 per cent in March 1996 and will be raised further to 0.084 per cent during the fiscal year 1996.
6. The introduction of financial holding companies has recently been under study since the Fair Trade Committee referred to the possibility of changing the relevant clause of the Anti-Monopoly Law in December 1995.
7. Since a banking licence was granted to the Okinawa Bank in 1956, no new banks have been admitted by the MOF except the Tokyo Kyodo Bank in 1995.
8. However, the Banking Bureau of the MOF issued the 'Circular Concerning the Allocations of Branches of Financial Institutions' for fiscal year 1995, in which the quota of new branches for city banks, long-term credit banks and trust banks was abolished.
9. In September 1995 the Banking Bureau of the MOF announced that it would not require financial institutions to report newly developed financial instruments before their sales.

REFERENCES

Cargill, T.F. and Royama, S. (1988), *The Transition of Finance in Japan and the United States: A Comparative Perspective*, Palo Alto, CA: Hoover Institution Press.

Kuroda, A. (1994), 'Recent Developments in the Japanese Financial System: Prudential Supervision by the Bank of Japan', *The Bulletin of the Institute of Social Sciences*, Meiji University, **17**, 1.

Kuroda, A. and Kinoshita, T. (1993), 'Central Banking in Japan: An Overview', *Center for Japanese Economic Studies Working Paper Series*, Macquarie University 93-1, January.

Kuroda, A., Kotani, M. and Ogawa, M. (1994), 'Features and Problems of Japan's Bank Accounting System', *Bank of Japan Monetary and Economic Studies*, **12**, 1, July.

Okura Zaimu Kyokai (ed.) (1993), *Okurasyo no Kiko* (The Organization of the Ministry of Finance).

Sakai, M. (1995), *Yuichi-kun Monogatari* (The Story of Yuichi), Zaikei Syobosya, Tokyo.

Suzuki, Yoshio (ed.) (1987), *The Japanese Financial System*, London: Oxford University Press.

— (1993) 'Okurasyo no Kiko', (The Organisation of the Ministy of Finance), *Okura Zaimu Kyoka*, Tokyo.

10. Asset Prices and Consumption: The Risk Premium Puzzle in Japan

Kazumasa Iwata

10.1 INTRODUCTION

From the latter half of the 1980s through the early 1990s, equity and land prices fluctuated widely in the Japanese economy. In assessing the effects of asset price changes on consumption, a number of studies have focused on the wealth effect associated with changes in equity and land prices. These studies concluded that the impact on consumption of the sharp decline in stock and land prices in the first half of the 1990s has been rather limited. Figures 10.1(a–d) seem to confirm that consumption growth has only a limited sensitivity to changes in asset prices except for expenditure on consumers' durable goods.

These wealth effect studies often lack a sufficiently rigorous microeconomic foundation based on a consumer's intertemporal optimizing behaviour in a growing economy. In theory, a consumer's intertemporal resource allocation must recessarily be based on the relationship between the potential returns on any relevant assets and the consumer's intertemporal rate of substitution as the Keynes–Ramsey condition suggests. In standard neoclassical growth theory, it is well known that the strength of the link between the rate of consumption growth and any returns on an asset (or real capital) critically depends on the elasticity of substitution between consumption at two different moments in time. Yet the link is somewhat weakened in a world of uncertainty.

This chapter provides an empirical assessment of the relation between asset price changes and consumption based on the theory of intertemporal optimization of consumers' behaviour. Specifically we employ the consumption-based capital asset market pricing model (C-CAPM), because it is one of the few microeconomic models which can be applied to macroeconomic problems. Yet the empirical application of the C-CAPM has

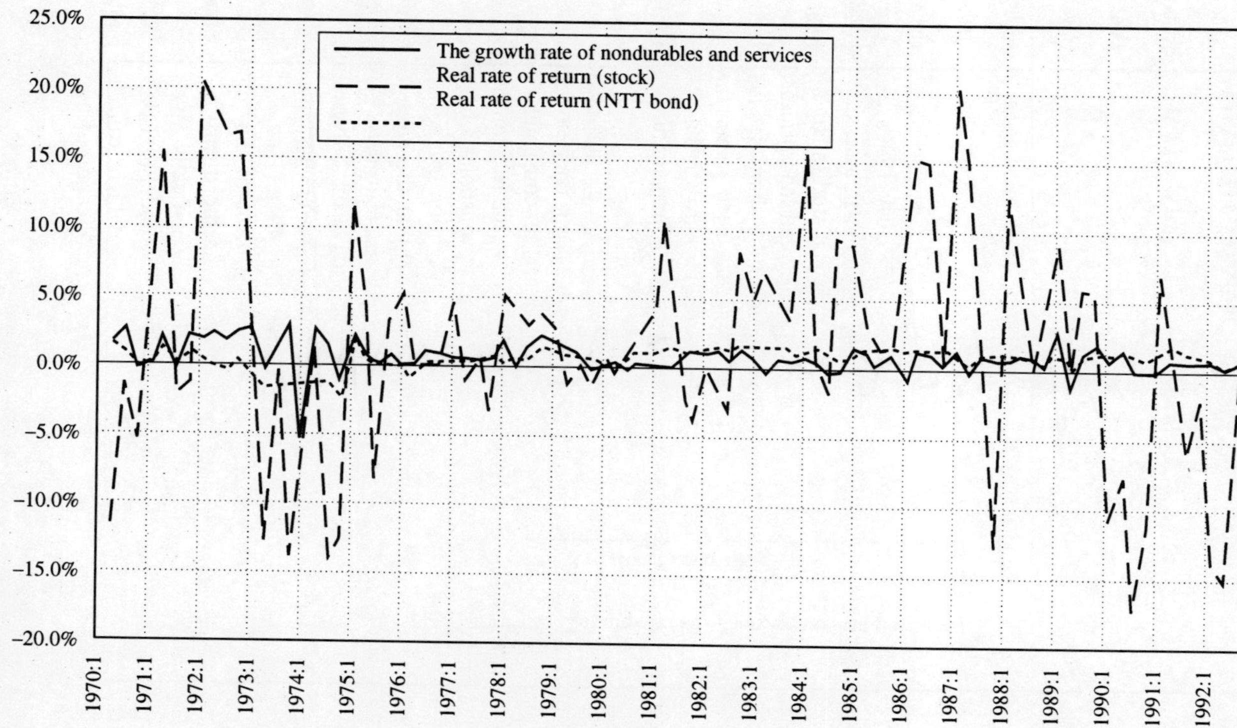

Figure 10.1(a) *The growth rate of non-durables and services and real rate of return on assets (stock, NTT bond)*

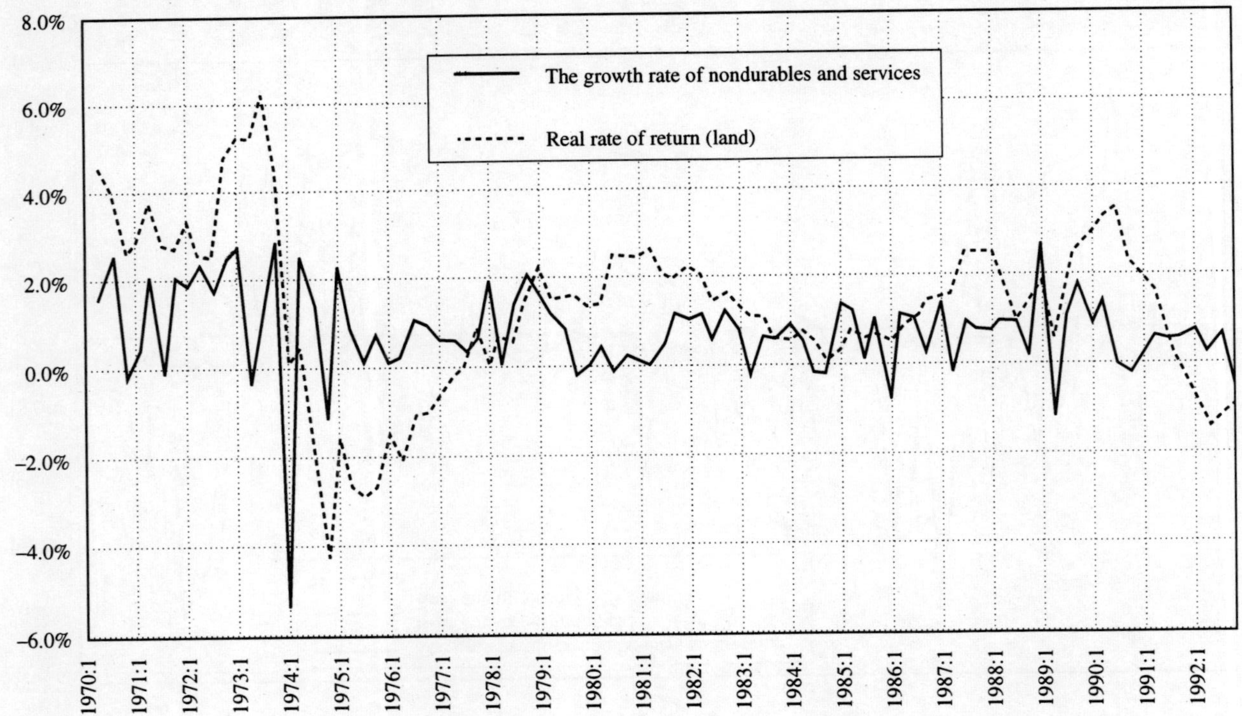

Figure 10.1(b)   The growth rate of non-durables and services and real rate of return on assets (land)

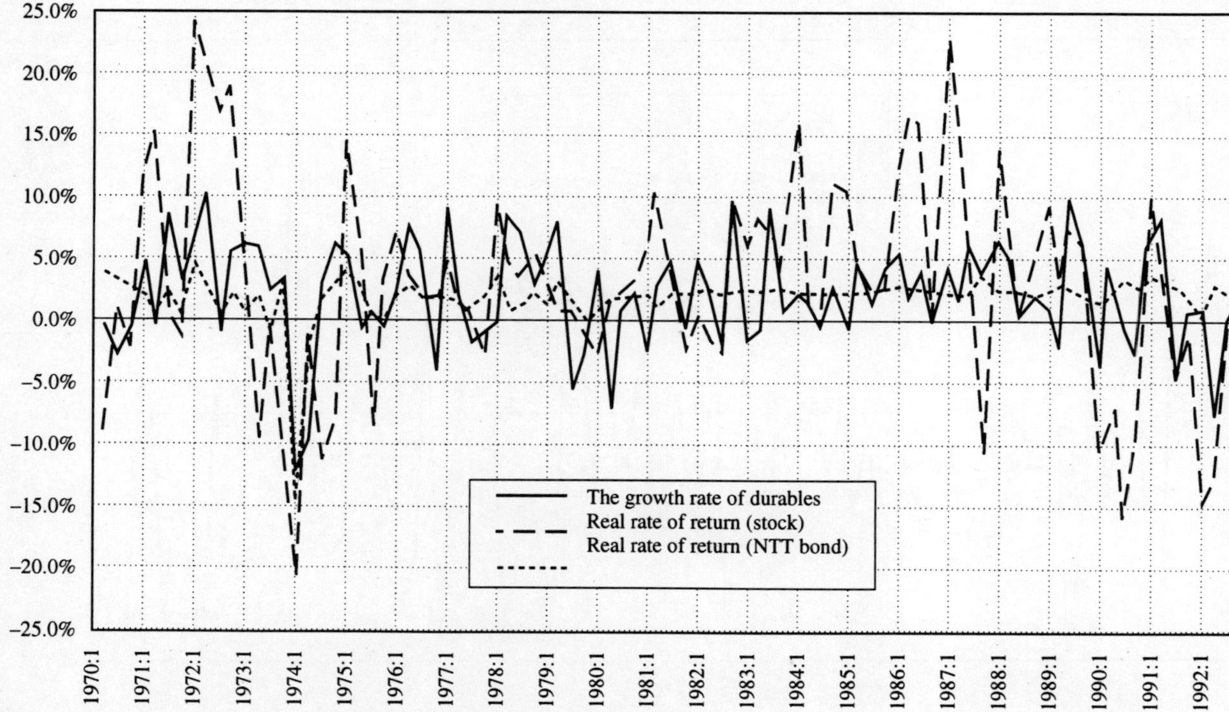

Figure 10.1(c) *The growth rate of durables and services and real rate of return on assets (stock, NTT bond)*

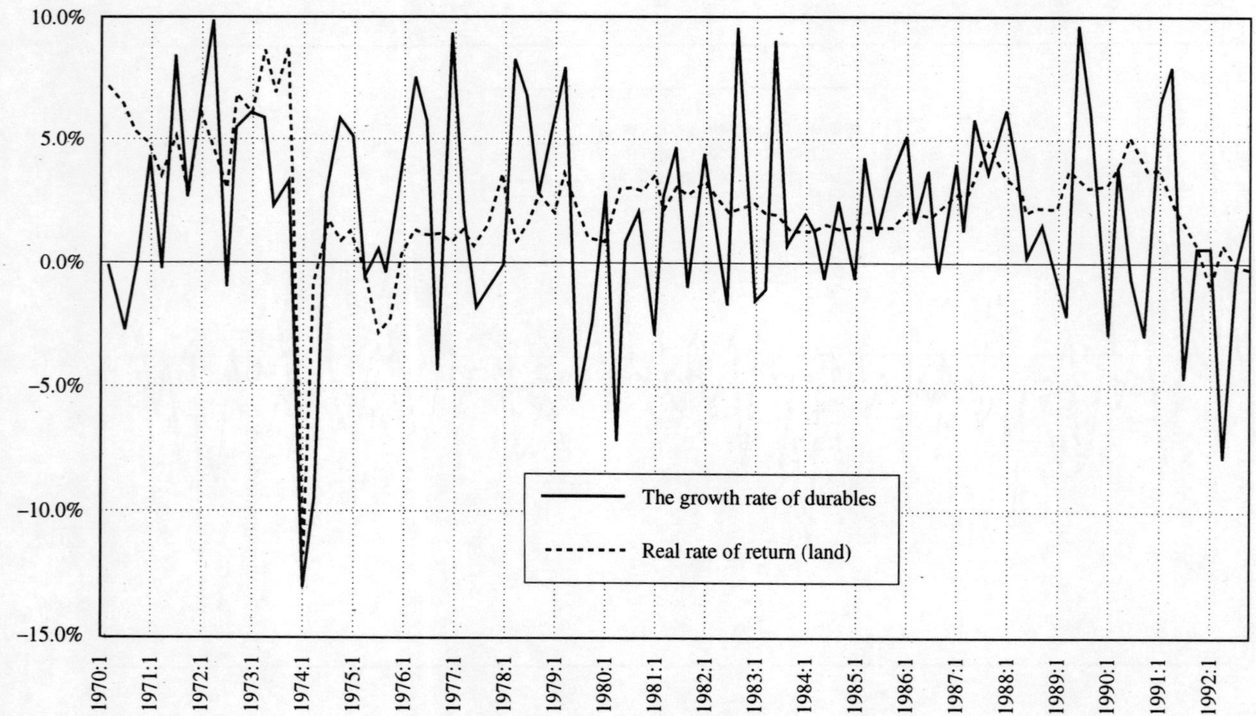

Figure 10.1(d) The growth rate of durables and services and real rate of return on assets (land)

had to confront a number of asset market puzzles. Some notable examples of this are the 'risk premium puzzle', the 'risk-free rate puzzle' and the 'stock market volatility puzzle'.

After the publication of the Mehra–Prescott (1985) article, the risk premium puzzle and its solution became a recognized field of research. This chapter reviews the risk premium puzzle and attempts to provide a solution. We can subsequently explain the interrelation between these different puzzles by using Japanese data. We employ an econometric technique (the generalized method of moments) to estimate Euler's equation for optimizing consumers' behaviour over time. This allows us to assess the link between the growth rate of consumption and the return on assets. In an attempt to provide a solution to the risk premium puzzle, we stress the time-non-separability of consumption and the intra-period substitution between the consumption of non-durable goods and the service provided by durable goods.

We specify the factors defining the upper bound of the risk premium puzzle based on the 'Jensen effect' (Section 10.2). Then we decompose the determinants of the risk premium into four factors, using a Taylor expansion of the first-order condition of optimizing behaviour by consumers (Section 10.3). We turn to the empirical estimation of the Euler equation for the Japanese economy. We employ the generalized method of moments by including the possibility of time-non-separability and intra-period substitution of consumption (Section 10.4). The final section (10.5) draws out some implications from our empirical results. These include the welfare loss suffered by consumers as the result of the postwar Japanese business cycle.

10.2 THE UPPER BOUND OF THE RISK PREMIUM

A representative (infinitely living) consumer is assumed to maximize his or her expected utility function over time, given an intertemporal budget constraint. We assume a concave von Neuman–Morgenstern expected utility function which is strictly increasing, twice differentiable and time-separable. We note that the expected utility function has the property of time-separability (additive separability) and state-separability. The former implies that the marginal rate of substitution between two moments of time is independent of consumption.

$$MAX: E_0\left[\sum_{t=0}^{\infty}\beta^{-t}U(C_t)\right] \tag{10.1}$$

$$s.t.\quad A_{t+1} = \left(1+R_{t+1}\right)\left(A_t + W_t - C_t\right)\ and\ \ \beta = 1/1+\rho \tag{10.2}$$

where:

ρ: rate of time preference
A_t: assets held at the beginning of period *t*
W_t: labour income during the period *t*
R_{t+1}: the rate of return on assets during the period *t*
C_t: consumption during the period *t*

More precisely, the utility function takes the form of a power function with the relative risk-aversion coefficient being constant.

$$U(C_t) = (C_t - 1)^{1-a} / (1-a) \tag{10.3}$$

It is well known that the relative risk-aversion coefficient (a) in the utility function is the inverse of the elasticity of intertemporal marginal substitution (1/*a*). This strict connection between the relative risk-aversion and the elasticity of intertemporal marginal substitution gives rise to a difficulty in reconciling asset market data with intertemporal asset pricing theory as discussed in the following sections.

Both future consumption and the rate of return on risky assets are assumed to be a stochastic process. The latter becomes known only at the beginning of period (*t*+1), after a decision about consumption at *t* is taken. The rate of return on a risk-free asset is assumed to be predetermined at the time a decision is made.

The first-order conditions for optimization can be obtained by applying the Bellman functional equation to our representative consumer's optimization problem. In the case of a risk-free asset, the Euler equation can be written as follows[1]:

$$\begin{aligned} &E_t\left[(1/(1+\rho)U'(C_{t+1}))/\left(U'(C_t).(1+R_{F_{t+1}})\right)\right] \\ &= E_t\left[IMRS_{t+1}\right]\cdot(1+R_{F_{1+t}}) = 1; \\ &IMRS_{t+1} = 1/(1+\rho)\ \left(U'(C_{t+1})\right)/U'(C_t) \end{aligned} \tag{10.4}$$

On the other hand the Euler equation in the case of a risky asset can be described as follows:

$$E_t\left[IMRS_{t+1}\cdot(1+R_{t+1})\right] = 1 \tag{10.4a}$$

As the right-hand side of the equation is the expected value of the product of the two stochastic variables, it can be decomposed into two terms by using a 'covariance decomposition' as shown below:

$$E_t[IMRS_{t+1}]\cdot E_t\left[1+R_{F_{t+1}}\right]+COV\left[IMRS_{t+1}\cdot\ (1+R_{F_{t+1}})\right] \quad (10.5)$$
$$=E_t\left[1/(1+r_{f_{t+1}})\right]\cdot E_t\left[1+r_{t+1}\right]+COR\left[IMRS_{t+1}\cdot\ (1+R_{t+1})\right]\cdot S_{IMRS}\cdot S_{1+R}$$

In deriving the right-hand side of Equation (10.5) we use Equation (10.4) and the definition of the correlation coefficient (*COR*). On the other hand *SIMRS* and S_{1+R} denote the standard deviations of the intertemporal marginal rate of substitution (the *IMRS*) and the return on a risky asset respectively.

It may be noted that the *IMRS* can be viewed as a stochastic discount factor which determines asset prices, as implied by Equations (10.4) and (10.4a). In this case, the *IMRS* is called the 'pricing kernel'. A stochastic discount factor is employed by Hansen and Jagannathan (1991) to judge to what extent the asset market data are anomalous from the vantage point of intertemporal asset pricing theory.

If the riskless rate includes the 'Jensen effect' for the risk averter as follows:

$$E_t\left[1/(1+R_{F_{t+1}})\right]\cdot E_t\left[(1+R_{F_{t+1}})\right]\geq 1 \quad (10.6)$$

then we can show that the modified right-hand side of Equation (10.5) is less than one.

$$1\geq E_t\left[1+R_{t+1}\right]/E_t\left[1+R_{F_{t+1}}\right]+COR\left[IMRS_{t+1},(1+R_{t+1})\right]\cdot S_{IMRS}\cdot S_{1+R} \quad (10.7)$$

Alternatively it is easy to demonstrate the 'Jensen effect' by using a covariance decomposition.

$$1=E_t\left[1/(1+R_{F_{t+1}})\cdot(1+R_{F_{t+1}})\right] \quad (10.6a)$$
$$=E_t\left[1/(1+R_{F_{t+1}})\right]\cdot E_t\left[1+R_{F_{t+1}}\right]+COV\left[1/(1+R_{F_{t+1}}),(1+R_{F_{t+1}})\right]$$

It is clear that the second term of the right-hand side is negative, implying that the Jensen inequality holds true.

As a result, the upper bound of the risk premium on a risky asset is limited by the covariance (with negative sign) between the intertemporal marginal rate of substitution (*IMRS*) and the return on a risky asset. Further, if we take into account the fact that the coefficient of correlation takes a value equal to or less than one, then we get the following inequality:

$$E_t[1+R_{t+1}]/E_t[1+R_{F_{t+1}}]-1 \leq -COV[IMRS_{t+1},(1+R_{t+1})]$$

$$= -COR[IMRS_{t+1},(1+R_{t+1})] \cdot S_{IMRS} \cdot S_{1+R} \leq S_{IMRS} \cdot S_{1+R}$$

Thus, risk premium

$$= E_t[1+R_{t+1}]-(1+R_{F_{t+1}}) \leq (1+R_{F_{t+1}}) \cdot S_{IMRS} \cdot S_{1+R}$$

$$= [(1+R_{F_{t+1}})/(1+\rho)] . S[(C_{t+1}/C_t)^{-a}] \cdot S_{1+R} \tag{10.8}$$

From the inequality above, we can see that the upper bound of the risk premium (defined as the difference between the returns on a risky and a risk-free asset) is determined by the following five factors or parameters as:

1. the standard deviation of the return on a risky asset
2. the standard deviation of per capita consumption growth rate
3. the rate of return on a risk-free asset
4. the rate of time preference
5. the coefficient of relative risk-aversion.

Mehra–Prescott (1985) argued that the value of the risk premium derived from calibrating a general equilibrium model in the US economy is less than 1 per cent, assuming that the relative risk-aversion coefficient ranges between 0 and 2. They argue that the tolerable limit of the coefficient is 10, given the actual values of the four remaining parameters derived from data covering the period from 1889 to 1978 in the United States.

As shown in Table 10.1, the actual value of the risk premium during the relevant period was 6.2 per cent. The theoretical value of the risk premium cannot account for the actual value ('the risk premium puzzle'), given a reasonable range for the degree of relative risk-aversion. The main reason for a low upper bound value is that the consumption growth rate is not sufficiently volatile.[2]

Table 10.1 Basic data on consumption and excess return in Japan and the United States

	Japan	US
Equity: mean	0.1305	0.0599 (0.0698)
STD	0.1947	0.1293 (0.1653)
Bond: mean	0.0316	0.0299 (0.08)
STD	0.0303	0.0214
Excess Return: mean	0.0989	0.03 (0.0618)
STD	0.1976	0.1235
Land: mean	1.1059	
STD	0.1139	
Excess Return: mean	0.0743	
STD	0.1036	
Per Capita Consumption Growth: mean	1.0513	1.0236 (1.0183)
STD	0.0310	0.0178 (0.0357)

Notes:

Figures in parentheses are derived from Mehra–Prescott (1889–1978). They use the TB rate as return on bond, while I use the 10-year Treasury Note for data covering 1956 to 1994. The return on equity is defined as the sum of capital gain/loss and dividend payment divided by equity price. The return on land for Japan is defined as the sum of change in valuation and rent in the National Account Data divided by land value.

The risk premium on equity is 9.9 per cent while that on land is 7.4 per cent in Japan during the period from 1956 to 1994. Table 10.2 shows that the relative risk-aversion coefficient must rise to a value between 60 and 80 in order to fill the gap between the actual and the theoretical upper risk premium bound for equity. With respect to land, the relative risk-aversion coefficient must increase to more than 80 for both the postwar US and Japanese economy. In the case of the US the required relative risk-aversion is smaller (between 16 and 20). Yet this may be partly due to using the rate of a long-term government bond instead of a treasury bill. If we adopt the treasury bill rate, the risk premium on holding equity rises to 4.3 per cent. This implies that the relative risk-aversion coefficient must lie between 20 and 40.[3]

If we admit a larger value for the relative risk-aversion coefficient, it leads to another puzzle. The actual risk-free rate is too low. This is shown more explicitly in the next section which concerns the determinants of returns on risk-free and risky assets. Intuitively speaking, the risk-free rate must rise substantially if the investor is strongly risk-averse. Given a strong tendency to borrow, an extremely risk-averse investor must noticeably reduce his or her growth of consumption. This strong desire to borrow must be compensated by a negative rate of time preference ('the risk-free rate puzzle').

Table 10.2 The upper bound of risk premium and the relative risk-aversion in Japan the the US (1956–94) (under the assumption that the rate of time preference is equal to the return on bond)

RRA	Upper Bound: Japan		Upper Bound: US
	Equity	Land	Equity
a=0.5	0.0028	0.0015	0.0011
a=1	0.0060	0.0034	0.0023
a=2	0.0106	0.0056	0.0043
a=4	0.0193	0.0101	0.0084
a=8	0.0324	0.0170	0.0156
a=12	0.0414	0.0217	0.0192
a=16	0.0477	0.0250	0.0273
a=20	0.0523	0.0275	0.0326
a=40	0.0676	0.0354	0.0527
a=60	0.0865	0.0453	0.0731
a=80	0.1156	0.0606	0.0994

Note: The upper bound of risk premium is calculated based on Equation (10.8) in the text.

Although a negative rate of time preference is not inconsistent with the existence of an equilibrium in a growing economy in so far as the consumption growth rate is larger than the returns on risky assets (Kocherlakotas, 1990), it seems odd for individuals to save given a significantly negative rate of time preference. In this case the precautionary motive for saving must be very strong.

Another stock market puzzle is created by the excessive volatility (the 'stock market volatility puzzle'). Yet we should notice that a smaller volatility of returns on risky assets lowers the upper bound of the risk premium as Equation (10.8) suggests. It is really difficult to reconcile the 'stock market volatility puzzle' with the risk premium puzzle. It is more of an 'either/or' relationship.

10.3 THE DETERMINANTS OF THE RISK PREMIUM

In a continuous time model, the Euler equation can be rewritten as follows:

$$MAX: E_0 \int_0^{\infty} e^{-\rho s} U(C_{t+s}) ds \tag{10.9}$$

Now the Euler equation is expressed as below:

$$E_t\left[U'\left[C_{t+s}e^{-\rho s} / U'(C_t)\right]\right](1 + R_{t,t+s}) = 1 \tag{10.10}$$

Applying a Taylor expansion to Equation (10.10) in the vicinity of C_t and R_t, we can obtain an Euler equation in the case of a risky asset, recalling the fact that the instantaneous rate of return is equal to R_t:

$$E_t\Big[1 + U''(C_t)dC_t / U'(C_t) + (1/2)U''(C_t)\,(dC_t)^2 / U_t + R_t$$
$$+ U''(C_t)dC_tR_t / U'(C_t)\Big] = 1 + \rho \tag{10.11}$$

Alternatively, we can obtain Equation (10.11) by assuming that both consumption in the future and the returns on a risky asset are in a stochastic diffusion process. Then we can apply Itoh's lemma to the product of the marginal utility and the returns on an asset ($U'(C_t{+}S)(1{+}R_t{+}S)$). Finally we can derive the same result (10.11) by dividing this stochastic partial differential equation by $U'(C_t{+}S)(1{+}R_t)$.

Since a risk-free asset's rate of return is not stochastic, an Euler equation can be approximated by applying a Taylor expansion:

$$E_t\left[1 + U''(C_t)dc_t / U'(C_t) + (1/2)U''(C_t)(dC_t)^2 / U'(C_t) + R_{F_t}\right] = 1 + \rho \tag{10.11a}$$

Both Equations (10.11 and 10.11a) can be rewritten in a more standard form which specifies the determinants of the expected rate of return on risky assets by using the definition of relative risk-aversion $(a = C_tU''(C_t) / U'(C_t))$.

$$E_t[R_t] = aE_t[g] - (1/2)a(1 + a)VAR(g) + aCOV(R_t, g) + \rho;$$

$$a = C_t U''(C_t) / U'(C_t), \ \ g = dC_t / C_t \tag{10.12}$$

Higher consumption growth and the rate of time preference coupled with larger values for the coefficient of correlation brings about a higher rate of return on risky assets. High volatility in the rate of consumption growth is associated with lower returns on risky assets.

In the case of a risk-free asset, the covariance term is eliminated from Equation (10.13). We can see clearly that a larger coefficient for relative risk-aversion must be compensated for by having a lower rate of time preference and a large variance in the rate of consumption growth. Yet actual consumption volatility is small due to a smoothing motivation by consumers. In order to explain the relatively low level for the risk-free rate, the time preference rate must be negative.

Table 10.3 provides the implied time preference rate which explains the level of the risk-free rate given a larger coefficient of relative risk-aversion. If we assume that the relative risk-aversion coefficient is 10, then the time preference rate must be substantially negative (–42.9 per cent in Japan and –18.9 per cent in the US).

If there are two risky assets in the economy, we can take the difference of the two expected rates of return. The difference is described as below:

$$E_t\left[R_{i_t} - R_{j_t}\right] = aCOV(R_{i_t} - R_{j_t}, g) \tag{10.13}$$

In the case where one of the assets is a risk-free asset, the difference is equal to the risk premium:[4]

$$\begin{aligned} E\left[R_t - R_{F_t}\right] &= aCOV(R_t - R_{F_t}, g) \qquad (10.14) \\ &= aCOR(R_t - R_{F_t}, g) \,.\, S_g \ S_{R-R_F} \end{aligned}$$

We can now observe that the risk premium is determined by the following four factors:

1. the standard deviation of excess return on the risky asset
2. the standard deviation of the consumption growth rate
3. the coefficient of correlation between excess return on the risky asset and the consumption growth rate
4. the relative risk-aversion coefficient.

Table 10.3 Negative rate of time preference and the coefficient of relative risk-aversion

Country	Return on bond	Consumption growth: mean	STD	Relative risk-aversion	Implied rate of time preference
Japan	0.0316	0.0513	0.00096	a=0.5	0.0061
				a=1	−0.0019
				a=2	−0.0068
				a=10	−0.4286
US	0.0299	0.0236	0.0178	a=0.5	0.0182
				a=1	0.0066
				a=2	−0.0162
				a=10	−0.1885

Note: The implied rate of time preference is calculated based on Equation (10.12) in the text, thereby excluding the term of the covariance between the return on bond and the consumption growth rate.

Compared with the determinants of the upper bound of the risk premium in (10.2), the rate of time preference is dropped from the determinants of the risk premium, because it is a common determinant for both the returns on a risk-free and a risky asset.

A lower correlation between excess returns and the consumption growth rate, combined with a smaller standard deviation in consumption growth, requires larger values for the standard deviation in excess returns as well as a larger coefficient of relative risk-aversion.

Table 10.4 shows the theoretical value of relative risk-aversion, given the actual coefficient of correlation between excess return and the consumption growth rate. In Japan the theoretical value of relative risk-aversion is 63.4 (equity) and 34.2 (land). Both of them lie within the upper bound calculated in Table 10.2. Yet in the case of the US the theoretical value exceeds the upper bound. This may imply that the rate of time preference is much higher than the (real) risk-free rate (3 per cent).

Table 10.4 Theoretical value of the relative risk-aversion coefficient

Country	Excess return	Coefficient of correlation	Consumption growth: STD	Excess return: STD	Covariance : (*dC/C*, *ER*)	RRA
Japan: equity	0.0989	0.254	0.0310	0.1976	0.00156	63.4
Japan: land	0.0743	0.676	0.0310	0.1036	0.00217	34.2
US: equity	0.03	0.250	0.0178	0.1235	0.00055	54.5

Note: The theoretical value of the RRA is calculated based on Equation (10.14) in the text.

10.4 ECONOMETRIC ESTIMATION OF THE EULER EQUATION

After discussing the asset market puzzles, we now turn to the empirical estimation of the Euler equation. Given the information set (I_t) available at time t, the necessary first-order condition for optimizing behaviour of a representative consumer with rational expectations can be written as below:

$$E_t\left[IMRS_t \, . \left(1 + R_{t+1}\right) - 1 \mid I_t\right] = 0 \tag{10.15}$$

If we use instrumental variables $\left(z_t\right)$, then we obtain

$$E_t\left[\left(IMRS_t \, . \left(1 + R_{t+1} - 1\right) \mid z_t\right)\right] = 0 \tag{10.16}$$

At equilibrium, the left-hand side of Equation (10.16) is orthogonal to all the elements (or the instrumental variables used as a proxy) of the information set. The generalized method of moments (GMM) utilizes the orthogonality conditions (the moments conditions) in estimating a non-linear rational expectations model. If the number of moment conditions (= number of instrumental variables multiplied by the number of equations) exceeds the number of parameters to be estimated (that is, it implies overidentification), we can apply the chi-square adequacy test to the overidentification. The GMM estimator minimizes the quadratic form of the sample means of the orthogonality conditions. In other words, we can test the goodness of fit of the moments conditions by using 'Hansen's J test' (Hansen and Singleton, 1982).

The estimator obtained has several desirable properties such as consistency and approximate normality.

It is important to note that the generalized method of moments requires that the stochastic Euler equation should be a function of stationary variables including the instrumental variables. We confirm that the variables used in the estimation (except for return on land, which is omitted from the estimation) pass the statistical test (the augmented Dicker–Fuller test) given a null hypothesis of non-stationarity.

Using quarterly data for per capita consumption adjusted for the imputed rent of durable goods, the return on bonds (the yields of a Telephone & Telegram bond) as a proxy for risk-free assets, and using equity (the total return on equity calculated by the Japanese Securities Research Institute) as our risky asset, we estimate our Euler equation by employing the generalized moments method. The estimation period covers 1971:2 to 1992:2. We adopt a constant, the rate of consumption growth, and the returns on bonds and equity with a one- or two-period lag as instrumental variables.

For a one-period lag we have eight (4 x 2) moment conditions to estimate two parameters (the rate of time preference and the relative risk-aversion coefficient). Thus we apply a chi-square adequacy test with six degrees of freedom. For two-period lags we carry out the test with twelve degrees of freedom.

The estimated results are presented in Table 10.5 (panel 1). The coefficient relating to rate of time preference is statistically significant and its size is within a reasonable range. Yet the sign of the relative risk-aversion coefficient reverses for the case of a two-period lag. The goodness of fit is poor in terms of p-value (probability value of the chi-square adequacy test). The p-value shows the probability for variables with a chi-square distribution to exceed the minimized sample values of criteria functions under the condition that the null hypothesis (no correlation between the instrument variables and the error terms) holds true.

The poor results can be attributed to a number of assumptions which underlie the model. Time-separability as well as state-separability are implicitly assumed in the von Neuman–Morgenstern expected utility function as described in Equation (10.1). Yet consumption may be neither time-separable nor state-separable. In addition, there may be a possibility for intra-period substitution between non-durable and service consumption and the consumption of service flows from durable goods. This is important, because we observe that a large portion of the capital gains derived from selling risky assets during the bubble period was spent on luxury goods such as cars and other high-quality durables. If we neglect the substitutability between durable goods and non-durable goods, it may understate the impact of asset price changes on total consumption.

We now take up the case of time-non-separability but also include the possibility of intra-period substitution. First, the time-non-separability of consumption arises from durability and persisting consumption habits. It is an empirical question as to whether durability or habit formation dominates consumption.

Table 10.5 GMM estimation results: one-good model (non-durables and services plus service flow from durable goods)(1971:–1992:2, number of observations = 85)

Instrument variables	β	A	b	χ^2	DF	*p*-value
Panel 1: time-separable model						
First set	0.999	0.997		24.13	6	0.0005
(lag 1)	(0.003)	(0.368)				
Second set	0.980	–1.700		19.40	12	0.079
(lags 1 and 2)	(0.003)	(0.335)				
Panel 2: time-non-separable model						
First set	0.992	0.015	–0.861	14.59	5	0.012
(lag 1)	(0.004)	(0.600)	(2.44)			
Second set	0.980	–1.523	–0.180	15.43	11	0.164
(lags 1 and 2)	(0.005)	(0.604)	(0.097)			

Note: Standard errors are in parentheses. *p*-value is the probability that a χ^2 variant exceeds the minimized sample value of the GMM criterion function.

The function that Ferson and Constantinides (1990) employ helps detect the dominance of either durability or habit. Taking into account durability and the habitual nature of consumption, we derive a utility function as shown below:

$$E_t \sum_{t=0}^{\infty} \beta^t \left(a_0 \sum_{s=0}^{\infty} b_s C_{t-s} \right)^{1-a} \bigg/ (1-a); \tag{10.17}$$

$$where\ b_0 = 1,\ b_s = a_s - h \sum_{i=0}^{s} e_i a_{i-s};\ \ e_s \geq 0,\ \sum_{s=1}^{\infty} e_s = 1$$

The value of a_s denotes durability, while the values of h and e_s indicate the degree of habit persistence. If the estimated value of b is negative, then the persistence of habit dominates.

The first-order optimization condition can be written as below:

$$E_t\left[\sum_{\tau=1}^{\infty}\beta^{\tau}\left(C_{t+\tau}/C_t\right)^{-a}\left(b_{\tau-1}R_{t+1}-b_{\tau}\right)-1\right]=0 \tag{10.18}$$

If we assume a one-period lag $(b_s = 0, s \geq 2)$, the Euler equation is as follows:

$$E_t\Big[\beta\left(C_{t+1}bC_t / C_t + bC_{t-1}\right)^{-a}\left(R_{t+1}-b\right)$$

$$+\,\beta^2\left(C_{t+2}+bC_{t+1} / C_t + bC_{t-1}\right)^{-a}bR_{t+1}-1\Big]=0; \tag{10.18a}$$

$$b=\left(a_1/a_0\right)-he_1$$

We include the possibility of intra-period substitution between non-durable and service consumption and the consumption of service flows produced by durable goods after including the possibility of time-non-separability in consumption. With respect to the possibility of intra-period substitution we utilise a Cobb–Douglas type production function with constant elasticity of substitution.

Then the objective function and the Euler equation can be described as below:

$$MAX\colon E_0\left[\beta^t\left(U\left(S_t+bS_{t-1}\right)^{1-a}-1\right)/\left(1-a\right)\right] \tag{10.19}$$

$$s.t.\;\; S_t = N_t^{\alpha}.D_t^{1-\alpha}$$

The Euler equation can be written as below:

$$E_t\left[\beta\left[\left(S_{t+1}+bs_t/S_t+bS_{t-1}\right)^{-a}\left(N_{t+1}/N_t\right)^{\alpha-1}\left(D_{t+1}/D_t\right)^{1-\alpha}R_{t+1}-b\right]\right]$$

$$\beta^2\left(S_{t+2}+bS_{t+1} / S_t + bS_{t-1}\right)^{-a}\left(N_{t+1} / N_t\right)^{\alpha-1}\left(D_{t+1} / D_t\right)^{1-\alpha}bR_{t+1}-1\Big]=0 \tag{10.20}$$

The estimated result of Equation (10.20) by using the generalized method of moments is presented in Table 10.6 (panel 2). Now we have a positive coefficient for relative risk-aversion. Compared with the estimates calculated in the absence of either durability or habit persistence, the p-value improves significantly. Moreover, the significantly negative value of b indicates that habit persistence dominates durability.

Table 10.6 GMM estimation results: two-goods model (1971:–1992: 2, number of observations = 85)

Instrument variables	β	A	b	χ^2	DF	p-value
Panel 1: time-separable model						
First set	0.995	0.655		26.58	8	0.0008
(lag 1)	(0.002)	(0.198)				
Second set	0.993	0.404		28.47	16	0.028
(lags 1 and 2)	(0.001)	(0.156)				
Panel 2: time-non-separable model						
First set	0.998	0.011	–0.208	14.54	7	0.042
(lag 1)	(0.003)	(0.319)	(0.165)			
Second set	0.993	0.473	–0.324	19.69	15	0.184
(lags 1 and 2)	(0.001)	(0.130)	(0.106)			

Note: Standard errors are in parentheses. p-value is the probability that a χ^2 variant exceeds the minimized sample value of the GMM criterion function.

The Euler equation (10.20) in the steady state can be transformed into the following:

$$E_t\left[\beta(1+g_s)^{-a}\left[1+\beta b(1+g_s)^{-a}\right](1+R_{t+1})\right]=1+b\beta\,;$$

$$g_s=(S_{t+1}+bS_t)/(S_t+bS_{t-1})=(S_{t+2}+bS_{t+1})/(S_{t+1}+bS_t) \quad (10.21)$$

It is easy to see that a larger volatility for the consumption growth rate due to habit persistence works to raise the upper bound of the risk premium. This also reconciles the asset market data with the theoretical value of the coefficient of relative risk-aversion.

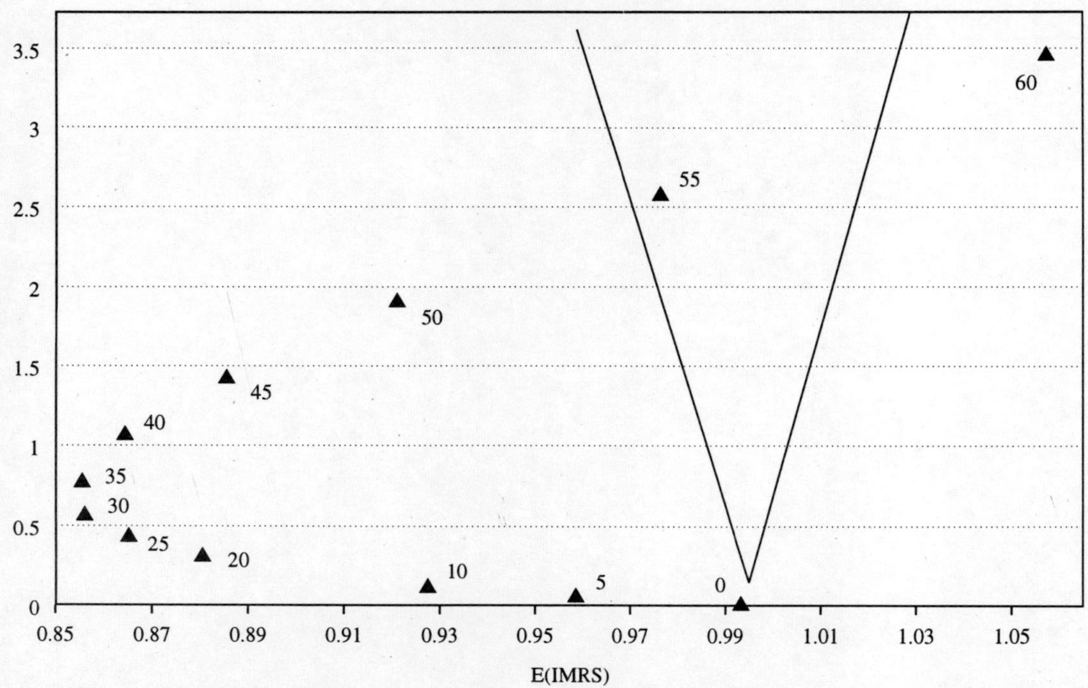

Figure 10.2 Hansen–Jagannathan bound and computer IMRS (time separable model, A=0 to 60 in steop 5)

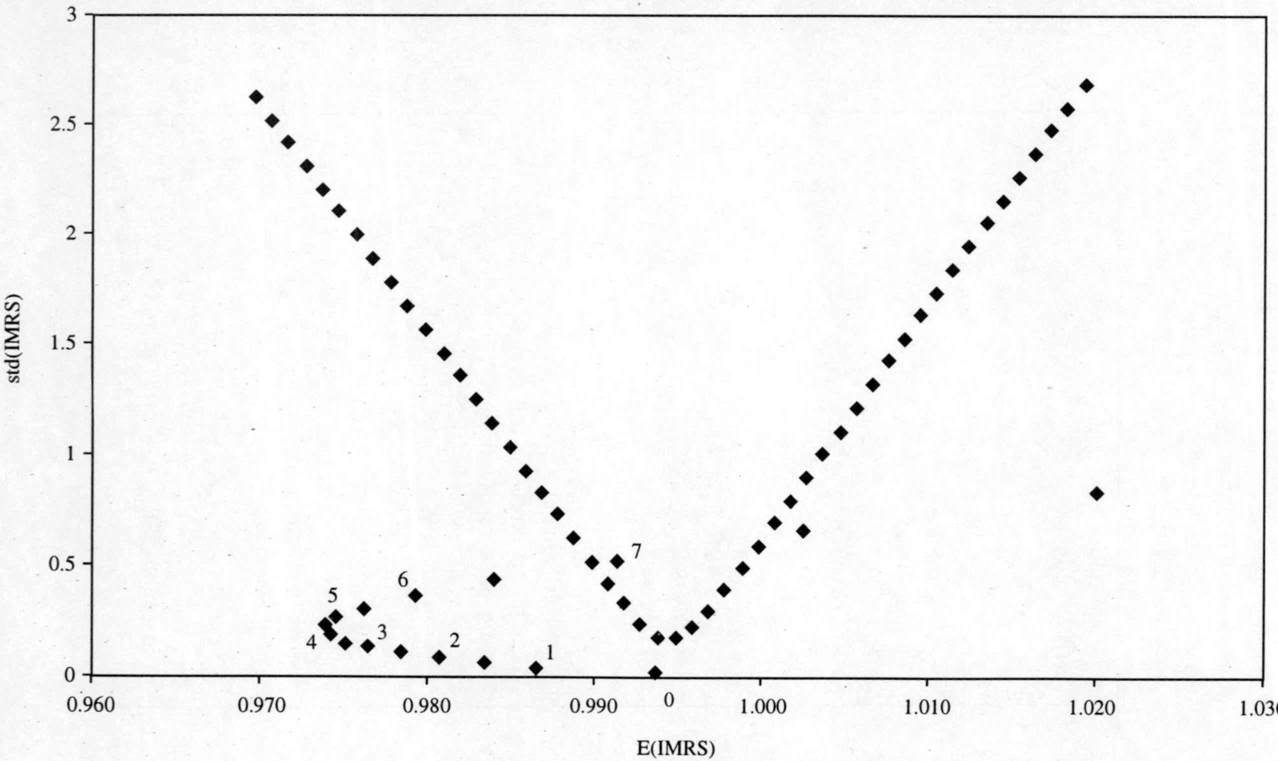

Figure 10.3 Hansen–Jagannathan bound and computer IMRS (2-goods model with habit persistence (b=0.342),step of A=0.5)

10.5 CONCLUSION: SOLUTION OF THE RISK PREMIUM PUZZLE

The results obtained have important implications for solving the risk premium puzzle. The mean–standard deviation frontier for the intertemporal marginal rate of substitution can be constructed indirectly by using actual data giving the returns provided by the asset market. The cup-shaped frontier shown in Figure 10.2 is derived as the minimum standard deviation of discount factors which satisifies the Euler equation (10.4). It is interesting to note that the IMRS frontier is the dual of the usual mean–standard deviation frontier for asset payoffs.

On the other hand, we can calculate directly the mean–standard deviation of the intertemporal marginal rate of substitution generated by the power utility function for a given degree of relative risk-aversion. We use quarterly data on consumption and adopt a subjective discount factor of 0.993 as obtained in Table 10.6.

On the IMRS–RRA line the increasing relative risk-aversion (a) initially magnifies the volatility and reduces the mean of the IMRS. Yet after a certain value of the relative risk-aversion coefficient, both the volatility and the mean of the IMRS start to increase.

We see that the IMRS–RRA line intersects with the discount factors (the IMRS) frontier only where the relative risk-aversion coefficient is close to 55. This expresses the risk premium puzzle using a non-parametric method.

If we take into account habit persistence as measured by the GMM with two goods (with the habit formation value of b being equal to –0.324), the volatility of the IMRS increases substantially. As a result, the IMRS–RRA line based on the power utility function intersects with the IMRS frontier at a much lower value for a relative risk-aversion coefficient close to 7 (Figure 10.3). Now the relative risk-aversion coefficient is in a tolerable range.

Another implication is the relationship between the business cycle and a consumer's utility. Lucas (1987) argued that postwar cyclical fluctuations resulted in only a minor welfare loss for consumers. He assumes that consumption follows a stochastic process with trend. He compares a consumption path without volatility (the consumption path I) to a higher consumption path which compensates for volatility (the consumption path II) as follows:

$$C_t = \left(1+\lambda/a\right)\left(1+g\right)^t\left(-1/2\right)e^{-(1/2)\sigma^2} z_t \; ; \tag{10.22}$$

$$log\, z_t - N\left(0,\sigma^2\right); \quad E_t\left[e^{-(1/2)\sigma^2} z_t\right] = 1$$

- consumption path I: $\lambda = 0, g > 0, \sigma^2 = 0$ (10.23)
- consumption path II: $\lambda > 0, g > 0, \sigma^2 > 0$ (10.24)

By comparing the two paths, the additional consumption growth rate needed to compensate for any volatility is directly derived as below:

$$\lambda = (1/2)\sigma^2 a \tag{10.25}$$

Given the small deviation of consumption from its underlying trend (as approximated by the standard deviation of the growth rate in Table 10.1), the estimated loss in the US is only 0.3 per cent of consumption even when the relative risk-aversion coefficient is as high as 20. Lucas (1987) judged that any economic instability after World War II had to be a minor problem. (Actually he used the values obtained by Mehra–Prescott (1985) and argued that the welfare cost for each consumer in 1983 was 0.1 per cent of consumption and thus only $8.50.).

However, welfare loss is much larger if we take into account the fact that consumption, if adjusted for habit persistence, shows greater volatility. In Japan, the variance from trend-adjusted consumption is twice as large as in the United States (as indicated in Table 10.2). In addition, the standard deviation of consumption adjusted for habit persistence is also three times larger than consumption without such an adjustment. This implies that economic instability is in the order of 1 per cent – 3 per cent of consumption, instead of 0.3 per cent. This is not a negligible welfare loss. For instance, Lucas (1987) calculates that a 10 per cent inflation rate costs 0.5 per cent. He further estimates that tax reform leading toward an efficient taxation system would involve a welfare gain of 1 per cent.[5]

We conclude that monetary authorities should also pay attention to movements in asset prices, especially those of risky assets. Traditionally, monetary authorities have concentrated on short-term rates (possibly long-term rates as well). Yet the impact on consumption of any change in the returns on risky assets, given our estimation, can be significant.

NOTES

1. We can easily derive the Euler equation in the case of mixed portfolio of risky and riskfree asset.
2. Prof .Kawai noted from Table 1 that the standard deviation of excess returns on equity and land is so large that the size of risk premium becomes meaningless. The question why the excess volatility of excess returns appears is not answered in this chapter.
3. The calculation of the upper bound bears on the mean-standard deviation frontier generated by the power utility function in Section V.

4. The derivation is initially made by Mankiw and Zeldes (1990).
5. Obsterfeld (1994) provides the estimate of larger welfare loss arising from postwar business cycle by assuming that the consumption follows the martingale process: in the martingale process, where a unit root exists, innovations in growth have cumulative effects on the level of consumption.

REFERENCES

Constantinides, G.M. (1990) 'Habit Formation: A Resolution of the Equity Premium Puzzle', *Journal of Political Economy*, **98**, 3: 519–44.

Ferson, W. and Constantinides, G.M. (1990), 'Habit Persistence and Durability in Aggregate Consumption; Empirical Tests', *Journal of Financial Economics*, **29**.

Hansen, L.P. and Singleton, K.J. (1982), 'Generalized Instrumental Variables Estimations of Nonlinear Rational Expectation Models', *Econometrica*, **50**, 4.

Hansen, L.P. and Jagannathan, M. (1991), 'Implications of Security Market Data for Models of Dynamic Economies', *Journal of Political Economy*, **99**, 2.

Iwata, K. (1991), 'Land Premium Puzzle and Taxation System', *Quarterly Journal of Housing, Land and Economy*, **3** (in Japanese).

Iwata, K. (1994), 'Risk Premium and Consumption', *Quarterly Journal of Housing, Land and Economy*, **3** (in Japanese).

Iwata, K. and Shimotu, K. (1996), 'Asset Prices and Consumption: Durability, Habit and Plural Goods', *Quarterly Journal of Housing, Land and Economy*, **1** (in Japanese).

Kocherlakotas, N.R. (1990), 'On the "Discount Factor" in Growing Economies', *Journal of Monetary Economics*, **25**.

Lucas, R.E. (1978), 'As set Prices in an Exchange Economy', *Econometrica*, **46**, 6: 1429–45.

Lucas, R.E. (1987), *Models of Business Cycle*, Oxford: Basil Blackwell.

Mankiw, N.G. and Zeldes, S.P. (1991), 'The Consumption of Stockholder and Non-stockholders', *Journal of Financial Economics*, **29**, 1: 97–112.

Mehra, R. and Prescott, E.C. (1985), 'The Equity Premium: A Puzzle', *Journal of Monetary Economics*, **15**, 145–61.

Obstfeld, M. (1994) 'Evaluating Risky Consumption Paths: The Role of Intertemporal Substitutability', *European Economic Review*, **38**, 7: 36–54.

Index